The Evergreen Collection

The Evergreen Collection

EXCEPTIONAL STORIES FROM ACROSS WASHINGTON STATE

Edited by Larry Clark and Adriana Janovich

WSU PRESS

Washington State University Press
Pullman, Washington

Washington State University Press
PO Box 645910
Pullman, Washington 99164-5910
Phone: 800-354-7360
Email: wsupress@wsu.edu
Website: wsupress.wsu.edu

Library of Congress Cataloging-in-Publication Data

Names: Clark, Larry, 1970- editor. | Janovich, Adriana, 1975- editor.
Title: The Evergreen Collection : exceptional stories from across
  Washington State / edited by Larry Clark and Adriana Janovich.
Description: Pullman : WSU Press, 2023. | Includes index.
Identifiers: LCCN 2023037178 | ISBN 9780874224238 (paperback)
Subjects: LCSH: Washington (State)--History, Local--Anecdotes. | Washington
  (State)--Social life and customs--Anecdotes. | Washington
  (State)--Biography--Anecdotes. | BISAC: LITERARY COLLECTIONS / American
  / General | LITERARY COLLECTIONS / Interviews
Classification: LCC F891.6 .E94 2023 | DDC 979.7--dc23/eng/20230818
LC record available at https://lccn.loc.gov/2023037178

Cover design by TG Design

The Washington State University Pullman campus is located on the homelands of the Niimíipuu (Nez Perce) Tribe and the Palus people. We acknowledge their presence here since time immemorial and recognize their continuing connection to the land, to the water, and to their ancestors. WSU Press is committed to publishing works that foster a deeper understanding of the Pacific Northwest and the contributions of its Native peoples.

Dedicated to all those who love
Washington state, its endless
stories, and its beauty

Contents

A morning view of Mount St. Helens
Photo Denis and Kim Hang

A Milky Way panorama
as seen from near Waterville
Photo Josh Tarr

Introduction

It must be either age or appetite, with their irksome intimations of mortality, that drives one to seek meaning amongst the levels of landscape, to imagine, with deep satisfaction, one's place when landscape, culture, history, food, all blend into one. But perhaps that is simply the definition, the emotion, of home.

— Tim Steury, *Washington State Magazine*

This is a state of wonder.

Washingtonians, people who have lived here before, and visitors to the state—repeat and first-time alike—experience a sense of awe at the overwhelming beauty of the ocean, mountains, forests, prairies, and rivers across Washington.

This anthology gathers a broad swath of stories reflecting the state of Washington—not only of the land, but also of the people, history, unique features, and delicious bounty of fields and orchards. For more than 20 years, *Washington State Magazine* has shared these stories with alumni and friends of Washington State University.

However, what you read in this collection is not only about the university. The stories of WSU are the stories of Washington state. The university extends into every corner of the state through research, Extension outreach, and alumni, and these articles reflect a wide expanse of the Evergreen State.

Just as the majestic Columbia River winds its way through the state, the stories you'll find in these pages will carry you on a journey from Willapa Bay on the coast to Steptoe Butte towering over the Palouse on the eastern edge of the state. No matter where you go, whether riding a ferry or driving a rural highway, there's a rich history of people and events that have transformed this place.

Founding editor of the magazine Tim Steury recognized that the soul of the state lies beyond its picturesque beauty.

"If there were a scientific way to measure the grandeur and diversity of landscape within a given area, Washington has the stuff to rival any region in the world. But diversity and grandeur are only a part of that landscape's appeal," he wrote. Indeed, shifts in geology—volcanoes erupting, floods scouring, wildfires scarring—along with the work of humans in transforming the land are chapters in the full tale of Washington state. Ancient and recent cataclysms, massive redirection of water into irrigation, migrations of people, and the construction of signature buildings and even nuclear reactors; all are woven into the tapestry of this place we call Washington.

Steury and the other contributors to *Washington State Magazine* bring these stories to life. Some of the chapters span the entire state; others concentrate on the rain-soaked coast, shady forests, sharp-edged mountains, powerful rivers, bountiful fields of crops, basalt-lined scablands, and unique cities.

While you're on this journey, you will meet people who call this state home and enlighten us with their history, perspectives, and talents.

No one has longer history or perspective than the Native people who came to this region thousands of years ago. Their stories in this collection, like the rediscovered village of Ozette on the Olympic Peninsula or the life of Chief Kamiakin on the central plateau, tell but a fraction of the long history of Indigenous people in this part of the world.

Many other people you'll meet in this collection will fascinate and amuse you. Here you'll be introduced to gardeners, architects, winemakers, orchardists, biologists, poets, cheesemakers, mountaineers—even a man who gave away mountains.

Speaking of cheese, no survey of Washington state is complete without food. Cougar Gold's signature sharp cheddar flavor—in a can, no less—may have originated in a WSU lab during World War II, but you can find fans all over the state and the country.

So many foods hail from Washington, and whether they're made, grown, or caught, they tantalize our senses. Rainier cherries, with their gold and pink hue like a buttercup, offer a culinary and visual delight. We have trout, salmon, onions, potatoes, so much local food to savor.

Of course, Washington's signature fruit, the apple, makes an appearance in the form of Cosmic Crisp® and Sunrise Magic. They are rising stars and newcomers to the fruit universe, but we also meet an apple detective who's identifying forgotten heirloom apples all over the Pacific Northwest.

And here you'll find wine. Washington's transformation over the last 75 years into a wine powerhouse was not an accident. The state has the terroir, the enthusiastic vintners and talented wine blenders, and growing prestige of an internationally recognized winemaking region, all making for a compelling yarn.

While we celebrate culinary pleasures and amazing places, we don't shy away from some of the tough problems in the state. Waterways threatened by invasive weeds and pollution, radioactive waste at Hanford, cities with growing pains, native animals' shrinking habitat, farmers facing water shortages, and other issues are thoroughly explored from multiple angles.

My fellow editor of this anthology, Adriana Janovich, grew up in Seattle while I spent most of my childhood on the opposite side of the state, among the forests and mountains near the Pend Oreille River. Still, we share a love for the variety and magnitude of our home state. Both of us have lived in several regions of Washington and have experienced the powerful pull to tell its tales.

The other contributors to this collection were also drawn to the mystery and magnificence of the Evergreen State. Through their narratives, readers of these Washington stories will be captivated by the people, the culture, the history, and the mountains and rivers and prairies without end.

— Larry Clark, Editor, *Washington State Magazine*

Diablo Lake
Photo Zach Mazur

Across the State

Ship at the mouth of the Columbia River
as seen from the north jetty
Photo Matthew Olson

A Place at the Table

Tim Steury

Something very interesting is going on in the state of Washington and across the country.

Maybe you've noticed the steady increase in the number of farmers markets. Or a new diversity in the produce section at the supermarkets. Not just new exotic fruits and vegetables transported by ship from some tropical corporate farm, tasting nothing like they do when consumed in their native countries. But new varieties produced locally, maybe by your neighbor, better tasting and fresher. Or maybe you've tasted a raspberry dessert wine—made from Skagit Valley raspberries—with the purest raspberry taste you can imagine. Or maybe you had a great loaf of artisanal bread made from Washington wheat.

But wait, you say, isn't all of Washington's wheat exported for Asian cookies? Yes, something's going on here.

In a sense wine led the way. The phenomenal success of the Washington wine industry has prompted people to admit that maybe our food could be better. Why eat California cauliflower when Washington cauliflower tastes better? Why succumb to produce with all the life and taste shipped out of it?

And just as Washington vintners refuse to produce a generic jug wine, other Washington farmers are realizing maybe the state's growing conditions and diverse infrastructure are simply too good to devote to indeterminate commodities that just get lost in a homogeneous global distribution system.

So what's going on? For one thing, said Washington State University sustainable agriculture specialist David Granatstein, farmers are trying to take back their fair share of the food dollar. In his office in Wenatchee, Granatstein pulls up a chart created by University of Maine agricultural economist Stewart Smith. Smith analyzed the share of the consumer food dollar that went to the American farmer from 1910 to 1990. In 1910, the farmer got 40 percent. By 1990, that share had dropped to less than 10 percent. Today a decent chunk of that dollar is going to the input sector, the seed and fertilizer dealers, and other farm suppliers. But the lion's share is going to the marketers—the brokers, distributors, and supermarkets. "Here's the driver," said Granatstein, pointing to the big blue area on the chart that represents the marketers' share of the food dollar. "You can invest all you want in increasing efficiency," he said, referring to the prevailing economic mindset of industrial agriculture, as well as the main thrust of the agricultural university of the last few decades. "It's a pittance. There's nothing there," he said of the pennies left the farmer under the conventional means of production. "It's chasing crumbs."

"*Here's* the action." His finger rests in the middle of the big blue realm of marketing.

Staying in the Game

So now that we understand where the money is, what do we do? Americans spend $145 billion a year on food. How much does the American farmer get? Well, figure less than 10 percent. A lot less, actually, for much of our food supply now comes from other countries. And getting any more of that dollar away from the marketers is not going to be easy. So why not market it themselves? Good point. That's exactly what some of the most diligent are doing. But doing so is not exactly straightforward.

Consider this: Washington is the third-largest raspberry growing region in the world. But when 1967 WSU alumna Jeanne Youngquist of Mount Vernon goes into a local grocery during raspberry season, the raspberries she finds for sale are not from local farms, but from Canada.

Those Canadian raspberries—or New Zealand apples and lamb, Argentine beef, or Chinese strawberries—are both symbol and symptom of the global food system that confronts the American farmer.

No one is arguing that there's anything wrong with fresh pineapple year-round. Or being able to buy French cheese at the local grocery. Variety and availability make this a wonderful time for the gourmand. But there is an enormously complex assortment of problems associated with a system that can give you great French cheese on the one hand and, on the other, insipid produce shipped halfway around the world rather than across the county.

Despite the intricacies of the system, however, the upshot is simple. The food you eat is more likely to be grown thousands of miles away than by your neighbor. Chances are, you buy it for less than what your neighbor could grow it for. What suffers, however, is freshness, taste—and your community's economy.

In fact, the current state of American agriculture has led economist Steven Blank of the University of California to declare "the end of agriculture in the American portfolio" in his recent book of that title. Obviously, Blank's pronouncement has resulted in mixed reactions.

"It made me so damn mad when I heard him speak," said Mike Youngquist, a 1966 WSU alum. "But he's right in a lot of ways."

Blank argued that the extreme efficiency of industrial agricultural production, particularly as practiced by other countries, has led to a situation where Americans ought to be putting their financial efforts into more lucrative enterprises than growing food. Of course, Blank tended to disregard such unmeasurable things as taste and community stability.

Besides, most American farmers are a long way from rolling over and playing dead. The most innovative of them, the most dogged and cantankerous, think they've figured out some ways to survive, no matter what some ag economist from California said.

Blank followed a fairly conventional line of thought that the only way to compete globally is to become more "efficient." Although this trend has its roots in the mechanization of agriculture in the first third of the 20th century, it gained its battle cry with Nixon administration secretary of agriculture Earl Butz's admonition to "get big or get out."

Farmers took him seriously, content to fight the indignities of one of the lowest profit margins of any industry with economy of scale, massive debt, and federal subsidies.

And some of those who got truly big did truly well. Really big operations, nurtured with the political influence, subsidies, and so forth that accompany our free market, just got bigger and bigger, doing better and better. Meanwhile, the little guys—the ones without the buying power and economy of scale of the big guys—started dropping like flies.

So all of this kind of thinking, plus steady industrialization, specialization—and the "G" word, globalization—joined with a curious conviction that Americans deserve to spend a smaller portion of their income on food than anybody else, led Blank to his dismal conclusion.

"No, it's the other way," said WSU rural sociologist Ray Jussaume. You don't compete through technological efficiency. Jussaume has long studied Japanese and American agricultural markets and currently is analyzing how food systems in Washington's Grant, Chelan, Skagit, and King counties are changing.

Jussaume conceded that most American farmers cannot compete directly. Labor and other costs are simply too high.

"So you have to compete indirectly—with quality and variety," he said.

Quality and variety. What a great idea! World class. On your plate.

Doing it Better

"It's reclaiming taste," Granatstein said. "And place. Where'd that food come from?"

And face. Who are the people behind it?

"From the consumer side, it's reclaiming things that were lost as we've gone mass market and industrial."

So consumers reclaim lost virtues, and farmers reclaim a chunk of the food dollar. What a deal!

But hold on. We're not there yet. Unfortunately, there is no shining path toward our ideal conclusion. However, across the state, a number of alumni farmers have discovered their individual paths, if not to prosperity, then at least toward survival.

Shukichi Inaba emigrated from Japan in 1907 to clear sagebrush and dig the first canals near Harrah. When he lost his land under the Alien Exclusion Act, he switched from the conventional hay and potatoes to vegetables, because that was the only way he could make any money sharecropping. Today, Inaba Produce Farms grows 20 different crops from April to October on 1,200 acres, with a crew of nearly 200 at peak season. Managed by Shukichi's grandson, Lon Inaba, who graduated from WSU in 1979 with a degree in agricultural engineering, the farm sells its produce throughout the western U.S. and some onions in Japan. Brother Wayne is the farm's accountant and salesman, and Norm, who graduated from WSU in 1981 with an economics degree, handles the payroll.

Nobody's getting rich at Inaba Produce Farms. But its very existence in a cut-throat market is testimony to Inaba's innovation and persistence. They hang on to some of the marketing dollar by doing their own wholesaling. Wayne is the farm's salesman. "We'd rather have 100 little guys to sell to than one big guy," Lon said. "One big guy can control it, especially if you're trying to get a premium."

That premium is another part of Inaba's strategy. "We have our name on that box, and that level of quality is always going to be a little bit better than somebody else's. We just try to do what the consumer wants."

Inaba has tried more direct marketing. "We tried farmers markets," he said. "But they didn't really fit our operation."

So they went back to concentrating on moving the highest quality produce. They grow about 20 different crops, including asparagus, onions, sweet corn, peppers, and tomatoes. The key to their high quality is good farming techniques. Although they have about 200 acres in certified organic production, Inaba is reluctant to talk about it. Organic production really isn't all that different from the way they've always farmed, he insists.

We drive past a field in its first year of transition to organic. "Compost works for our program," Inaba said. "Cover-cropping works into our program. Crop rotation works into our program.

"We just try to do things that work," he said.

"We don't do anything fancy. We try not to do anything to get ourselves too much in debt. We don't change very much. We don't do something unless we think it's going to fit long-term."

Once the Inabas make a decision to move into a new crop, they know they're going to stick with it. Vegetables might be annuals, Inaba said. But they still require a lot of capital for start-up.

Another thing that has helped the Inabas is the Food Alliance, based in Portland, Oregon. The Food Alliance came about as a cooperative development of WSU, Oregon State University, and the Kellogg Foundation in 1994. Granatstein was instrumental in forming the alliance, which uses market forces to effect change. Certification by the Food Alliance means that the farmer has met certain standards in working toward environmental and social responsibility. The certification process considers such varied factors as level of chemical use, tillage practices, and social responsibility, then rewards certified farmers with a label that indicates to consumers the alliance's approval. Food Alliance approval of Inaba Produce reflects not only the farm's sustainable agricultural practices, but also its treatment of workers.

Across the Cascades, the Youngquists are celebrating the fruition of a Food Alliance certification connection. Food Alliance approval has allowed them a greater market share and brand loyalty for their Cascade Snow brand cauliflower and IQF Raspberries.

Mike and Jean's Berry Farm was selected in part for their social impact. The Youngquists developed a daycare and preschool for farmworkers' children, and have worked hard to improve farmworker housing.

Still, they have no illusions that labeling is going to solve American agriculture's problems. "Everybody wants the cheapest product," Mike said. Farmers are also subject to the whims of the market and the actions of buyers. Because of a major consolidation shift in purchasing and the related confusion by one of the large grocery chains they supply, the Youngquists lost over $200,000 in sales to that customer last year in cauliflower.

They are looking more to the potential for specialty niches. They supply raspberries to a couple of wineries, Bonny Doon in Santa Cruz, California, and Pasek Cellars in Mount Vernon, for dessert wine. Last year, they shipped three semitruck-loads of raspberries to Santa Cruz. Winemaker Randall Graham has requested that they expand production of a specific WSU-developed raspberry variety, Morrison, to five times the present output in the next three years.

Anne Schwartz, who graduated from WSU in 1978 with a degree in animal science, long ago set out on a much different path, squeezing her entire production onto 22 acres. Tucked into the forest up the Skagit River, her Blue Heron Farm produces organic raspberries, blueberries, and vegetables. About nine of those acres are in nursery crops, including hardy bamboo.

Organic production has provided a small portion of American farmers with a lucrative niche. But successful organic production requires a high level of agronomic skills and is very labor intensive.

After increasing 25 percent a year for 10 years, organic represents about 3 percent of American food sales, so it's not an economic blockbuster. Still, the growth and consumer acceptance are impressive, and organic production has provided Schwartz a reasonable livelihood.

However, organic's very popularity is increasingly putting organic producers, like other small farmers, on the defensive. Corporate producers are moving into the growing market. That's good for the environment, not so good for a small farmer with production capacity maybe one millionth that of General Mills. Some growers are giving up their certification, focusing more on place or other attributes to market their goods.

The middle is disappearing, said Schwartz, somewhat matter-of-factly. "Though it isn't going to go without a fight. The smart ones will figure something out. More will figure something out that is more direct, local, and diversified."

Breaking Out of the Trap

For wheat farmers in eastern Washington, foreign competition, surplus production, and the resulting perpetually depressed prices take that already paltry share of the food dollar down to a miniscule two cents or less. Ideal growing conditions, high-producing varieties developed by WSU breeders, and federal commodity subsidies have helped wheat growers stay alive in a brutal Asian market. But it's a helluva way to make a living.

Karl Kupers, who graduated from WSU in 1971 with a pharmacy degree, got tired of it. He's tried a lot of different things since he decided he didn't like working inside as a pharmacist and returned to Harrington in 1973 to help his dad farm the land he started sharecropping in 1946. For a while, they followed the conventional wheat/fallow rotation that nearly everyone in the dryland wheat region of Washington does. But finally, said Kupers, he got to the point where he had to break out of that trap.

First thing, he gradually shifted his 5,500 acres from a wheat/fallow rotation to direct seeding. Direct seeding means just that. You plant a crop without tilling. The resulting improvement of soil tilth over the years provides a healthier environment for more diverse crops. Kupers's whole system is certified by the Food Alliance.

The capability of his healthy soil allows him to grow niche crops, sunflowers, safflower, edible soybeans, restoration plants. And now, he really thinks he's on to something. One day he realized, "We're not wheat producers, we're flour producers."

So rather than shipping his wheat off to Asia along with the other 130 million bushels from eastern Washington, he started milling his own flour and selling to Grand Central Bakery in Portland and, just recently, Bon Apetit Caterers. None of this is easy. Look over Karl Kupers's bookshelf in his office, and you find an extraordinarily eclectic mix: *Complexity, Weeds of the West, The Corporate Coach.* Kupers has to be an expert on everything from soil microbiology to marketing. In Rockport, the demands on Schwartz are no less. She not only handles production, but sales, accounting, and mechanical upkeep. And she has been widely in demand throughout North America as a speaker. The Younquists and Inaba face all these challenges and many others unique to their businesses. Produce and berry markets change daily.

And even if such creativity and innovation could be magically transferred to the marketing disadvantaged, some farmers are going to be left behind.

"The only way we're going to survive is through value-added," Mike Youngquist said. "And if our consumers demand it."

"No, the only way we're going to survive," Jeanne Youngquist said, "is if we bring the processing and production industry that we've lost to other countries back. We must encourage production agriculture to be innovative and find a way to help the government and consumers to figure out why it's so important to have a U.S.-based agricultural system."

Unfortunately, the trend in the "other" Washington is toward more globalization. Corporate farms and their shareholders are happy wherever the conditions are most favorable.

Still, there's hope.

"You fight imports by locking up contracts," said WSU ag economist Tom Schotzko. "There are lots of opportunities out there."

But those opportunities are different. You can't farm like your dad did and expect to make it in the current economy. And farmers can't do it all themselves. They need help in meeting those opportunities.

Washington State Agricultural College started helping state farmers match their abilities to opportunity in 1889. Since then, much has changed. But as a land-grant institution, WSU continues to support farmers as much as possible. Units such as Small Farms Program and the Center for Sustaining Agriculture, both with offices in Puyallup, provide support, market research, and advice. Research stations at Vancouver, Puyallup, Mount Vernon, Wenatchee, and Prosser continue to perform the production research and extension support they were formed to provide.

But there are limits.

Twenty thousand farmers in Washington raise the top five crops—tree fruit, wheat, dairy, beef, and potatoes—said outgoing College of Agriculture dean Jim Zuiches. The other 20,000 raise the other hundred or so crops. "We serve the big ones pretty well," he said. "But it spreads us thin in everything else." There is also the reality of funding, or lack thereof.

Although Washington is second only to California in crop diversity and fifth in the nation in production, it ranked 44th in 2000 in the nation in research dollars from the state, the Youngquists point out. California, by the way, is number one in both research funding and production.

And there are distractions provided by the funding that does exist. "There's pressure to do big grants and research," Jussaume said. "But is that what farmers need?" Much of that research tends to serve corporate interests rather than address specific problems of Washington farmers.

Given the volatile mix of global competition and economic pressures, it's a brave new world for Washington farmers. However you interpret it, the ultimate result could indeed mean the end of agriculture in America. Or it could be a bright new, very different, agrarian era.

Meanwhile, this is one of those rare things you can actually do something about. And it's pleasurable. Next time you go shopping, buy Inaba asparagus, Cascade Snow cauliflower, bread made from Shepherd's Grain flour or Washington grass-fed beef. Or stop by the Twisp Farmers Market and check out Schwartz's carrots. Eat well, and we all, farmer and consumer alike, will be a lot happier.

A Feast of Good Things

Hannelore Sudermann

Fall was a fortunate season at the Tonnemaker farm in Royal City. A warm October provided brothers Kurt and Kole a few extra weeks of squash, tomatoes, and peppers to load into their trucks and deliver to farmers markets and restaurants around the state.

This family farm has changed since the current generation took charge of it. It was established by extension agent Orland Tonnemaker, a 1922 graduate of what's now Washington State University, and his wife, Pearl. In 1962, they planted orchards of cherries, pears, and apples. Like many of the farms around them, they sold their fruit to area warehouses.

During cherry harvest in 1981, Orland died, and his grandson Kole Tonnemaker, a University of Idaho graduate, stepped in to help. After a few years, Kole decided to diversify so the farm wouldn't be solely dependent on the fluctuating commodity fruit market. By the late 1980s, he was planting produce for retail sale, and the Tonnemakers started trucking their produce to farmers markets around Washington. In 1992, Kurt Tonnemaker, who studied business at WSU, took on the marketing and distribution, while Kole focused on the orchards and fields.

Their timing was just right. "Then there was a lot of demand, a real upsurge of people wanting to connect with their food," said Kurt, a 1984 WSU graduate. They started with two farmers markets. Today in the high season, they deliver to 18 a week. While Kole stays on the farm, Kurt is based out of Bellevue where he is closer to the majority of the retail customers.

A few years ago, the brothers noticed chefs wandering into their market stalls looking for fresh and interesting produce to incorporate into their menus. They realized they could be much more efficient delivering directly to these Puget Sound-area restaurants. Today, their customer list reads like a best restaurants article: among them Poppy, Emmer and Rye, the Dahlia Lounge, and Spring Hill (now Ma'ono), which is co-owned by WSU alumna Marjorie Chang Fuller.

"Restaurant people are really concerned about where our food is coming from," Kurt said. The chefs eagerly read the Tonnemakers' fresh sheets to see which of the more than 400 varieties of apples, peaches, pears, and other fruits and vegetables, including melons, eggplant, heirloom tomatoes, squash, cucumbers, and dozens and dozens of pepper varieties, are coming in that week. It seems that there's more demand for this type of produce than local farms to meet it, Kurt said. "Restaurants I've never even heard of are asking for our stuff."

The Tonnemakers' farm adaptation of direct selling, experimenting with new varieties and new crops, and transitioning to organic has helped the bottom line. "Our farm has survived while many around us have closed," Kurt said.

The Discovery of Abundance

In 1906, Seattle had a vegetarian café. Food historian Jacqueline Williams found this tasty detail in an advertisement in a small, blue-covered cookbook published that year. She shows me as we sit in her living room in one of the city's older hillside neighborhoods.

In the 1990s, Williams wrote *The Way We Ate*, a history of the Northwest pioneers told through their food. If anyone has some perspective on early Washington cuisine, it would be this author and vintage cookbook collector.

From the time her book was published, Williams has continued to add cookbooks to her collection, most of which were published before 1940. Beyond the recipes, they're pretty useful, she said, as she pulls out others. She shows me they are laced with advertisements—diaper services, restaurant fliers, advice for new brides. "You can learn a lot about what's going on in the Northwest by them."

Until last year, the oldest Washington cookbook she had ever seen was *A Feast of Good Things*, the title of many a church-published cookbook around the country. This one was published in 1895 in Spokane by the Ladies of the First Presbyterian Church and for decades was thought to have the distinction of being the oldest cookbook in the state. But one day recently, while Williams was looking through the collection at the Museum of History and Industry, she found a small collection of pages that she determined was the earliest cookbook in Washington, *What the Plymouth Brethren Eat and How the Sisters Serve It*. It is dated 1889 and from the Plymouth Congregational Church in Seattle. "I was so excited," said Williams, who brought it to the archivist's attention. "They didn't even know they had it."

Frankly, much of that cookbook and the others that followed featured traditional cooking that Washington's early settlers brought with them from the East Coast and Europe. These settlers were not at all bedazzled by delicate chanterelle mushrooms, charmed by briny clams, or particularly fond of fiddlehead ferns. "There was really no Northwest cuisine like we see today," Williams said. According to the early cookbooks, as well as the letters, newspapers, and diaries that Williams studied, the settlers liked the wild game, the shellfish (particularly oysters until local stocks were nearly wiped out), and the abundant berries.

For years the food selection was meager. Williams found recipes for cakes made without eggs and coffee from bran and molasses. But as settlements developed all across the state, wheat, potatoes, and apples quickly factored into the early diets. Most of the time, though, the settlers bemoaned the lack of good staples. What you ate very much depended on where you lived, Williams said. Those in larger cities had readier access to basics like salt, flour, and sugar. Even those a few miles out along the Puget Sound relied on ships to bring in goods and had to be inventive with what was available.

The first wave of settlers were White, middle-class, and mostly Protestant. The later waves brought new ethnic groups and new cuisines. Chinese workers arriving in the 1850s brought not only their style of cooking, but also many of their vegetable crops. Settlers from rural Japanese communities came in the 1890s. Italians and Jews traveled from the East Coast. While they brought new cuisines, Williams said there wasn't much sharing across cultures early on. There was adaptation, though. Gefilte fish, for example, a Jewish fish ball traditionally made with pike or other whitefish, was given a Northwest spin. "Out here it was made with salmon," Williams said.

As each new wave of immigrants turned to farming, their crops found a way into the cities through the groceries and markets. It's at places like Pike Place Market and the Olympia Farmers Market that a real Northwest approach was formed, said Mark Musick, a farmer and social activist who co-founded Washington Tilth in the 1970s. The nonprofit agriculture alliance helped put in place organic farming standards for the state. Musick recently donated Tilth's first 22 years of documents and photographs to WSU's archives.

Our food may not be as easily defined as the deep-fried South or the corn-fed Midwest. But it is a food legacy rich with cultures and characters, said Musick, who today works as a food policy consultant.

Musick's first exposure to agriculture was harvesting strawberries alongside migrant workers near Puyallup. He started college at WSU in 1965 intent on studying communication, but by 1967 knew he wasn't ready to complete his degree. So he dropped out. Ultimately, he finished his degree at another school, worked as a community organizer, and joined Pragtree Farm, an organic collective near Arlington. He later worked for Larry's Markets, one of the first Washington groceries to seek out and feature local produce, and was for a time farmer liaison for Pike Place Market.

Historian Jeffrey Sanders, an assistant professor at WSU, writes about Tilth, Musick, and the Pike Place Market in his book *Seattle and the Roots of Urban Sustainability*. He starts the market section with artist Mark Tobey and his sketches depicting the market "as a fecund blend of nature, commerce, and urban democracy."

His canvases captured a built environment teeming with organic energy. In a 1942 painting titled *E Pluribus Unum*, the frame is packed with a sea of human faces, signs, and piles of fruits and vegetables—all the weltering diversity he saw at the market in the early 1940s.

The market was at the heart of our state's food culture, Musick said. It has been an entry point for each new generation of immigrants to bring their cuisine into Washington. Vendors like Pasqualina Verdi, an Italian woman who moved to Washington after World War II and who farmed near the Duwamish River in South Seattle, have pushed us in new culinary directions.

"She was the empress of the Pike Place Market in the 1950s," Musick said. "And there was a real cultural churning there." From her stall at the market, Verdi introduced fresh basil to the Northwest palate. Thirty years later, she pushed us into arugula. It's likely that another Italian immigrant, Seattleite Angelo Pellegrini, was the first in the country to publish a pesto recipe—in a 1946 issue of *Sunset* magazine. In his 1948 book *The Unprejudiced Palate*, Pellegrini wrote about a simple life of eating straight from the garden and with care for the ingredients. His approach is classically Northwest, Musick said.

Pellegrini wrote: The hearty discriminating eater "knows, too, that simplicity and variety, both in ingredients and in their preparation, are the abiding principles…"

Following and alongside the Italians at the market were the Japanese farmers, the Filipinos, the Hmong, and the Mexicans, Musick said. Each group delivered new food and new approaches. The Hmong, for example, got us eating pea vines. Now, thanks to Central and South American influence, peppers and peanuts are claiming their places at the markets.

In the 1970s, chefs and restaurants, particularly Bruce Naftaly of Rosellini's Other Place, made a point of visiting the market to incorporate local seafood and produce into the menu. He traveled out to Pragtree Farm to collaborate on developing seasonal salads for the restaurant. They used not one lettuce, or one salad, but dozens of different greens, herbs, even native plants.

Naftaly, now owner and chef at Le Gourmand, was the first in the city to produce farm-to-table cuisine, Musick said. The restaurants were the vanguard. And then business leaders like Larry McKinney of Larry's Markets moved this food into the grocery stores. "This was before Whole Foods," Musick noted.

From the markets to the restaurants to the grocery stores, now to an explosion of farmers markets around the state, farm subscriptions, and food cooperatives, it all flows into our culinary scene.

So is there a Washington cuisine? It's more that there are Northwest ingredients and a really eclectic range of cultural influences and multitude of styles, Musick said. "This is not San Francisco. This is not New York." We have a whole different culture and economy. But our one constant theme is that we like to venture into new territory and embrace variety. When you think of the many fruits and vegetables, the cheeses, the seafood, the grains, mushrooms, the meats, and thousands of fresh and delicious things available to us, the mind boggles. And we haven't even yet mentioned the wine.

"We don't know how lucky we are," Musick said.

Well, maybe Jamie Callison does. As executive chef for the WSU School of Hospitality Business Management, he eagerly scours our campus and the surrounding farmlands for ingredients—which he uses to teach his students the techniques of cooking. One morning this fall, Callison's gang is preparing for the Feast of the Arts dinner. A few are setting up tables in the Todd Hall dining room, while Callison stashes apples he had just collected from the Tukey Orchard into the cooler. He is waiting for the next night's line-caught salmon to arrive from the airport. Produce, apples, beef, art—all components of the event, all from around the Pullman campus—were on his mind. "We're showcasing the whole university on one table," he said. "We use whatever we possibly can from what the students are involved in on campus."

The tenderloin came from the Ensminger Beef Center, the fall vegetables, tomatoes, and beets from the organic farm, and the huckleberry ice cream from Ferdinand's. "My philosophy is to keep it simple," Callison said. "We're really about showcasing good food and to show its connection with wine." The pairing provides a valuable tool for Callison: using bridge ingredients to link a featured food with a wine. The first course, a wild Alaska king salmon will be dressed with a *beurre blanc* to cut the acid in the featured wine, a Barnard Griffin Viognier.

His goal is to have that bite of food finished with a sip of the wine. It rounds out the taste experience, completing the sauce, he said. "If you hit that perfect pairing once in a five-course dinner, then you have success."

Callison works with 27 student employees for these fall season meals. Of them, maybe four or five are thinking of going into the culinary field. But all of them will benefit from taking part. Whether they go into hotel or restaurant management, or some other part of the hospitality industry, "an understanding of food and wine in this day and age is becoming essential," Callison said.

In Callison's view, the Washington style is really good local, simple products, he said. That's the advice he gives his students: "Make sure you buy high-quality product, and try to source locally."

From Farm to Table
We're having dinner in a sleek blond wood booth in West Seattle's Spring Hill restaurant. It's a Tuesday night, but the place has quickly filled up. Servers are carrying peculiarly-shaped plates across the concrete floor from the open kitchen to the tables around us.

Co-owner Marjorie Chang Fuller, who earned degrees from WSU in 1989 and 1990, slips in across from me. By day she's an architect who works for a construction company, but at night and most of the rest of the time, she's a restaurateur.

She's had a hand in the space's hip, contemporary feel. And while her husband, chef Mark Fuller, runs the kitchen, she works with the front of the house.

Both grew up in Washington, he in Seattle, and she out on the coast in Montesano, she explained. They met in Portland, where she had her first job out of college with Hoffman Construction and he was the chef at Lucy's Table, a well-loved Pearl District fixture known for featuring fresh, local products.

They moved to Seattle when Mark took a job with chef Tom Douglas as a line chef at Etta's, at the Pike Place Market. He eventually became the executive chef at the Dahlia Lounge before breaking away in 2008 to open Spring Hill.

Here the menu is built on a foundation of fresh seafood and produce from around Washington, Marjorie explained. "We do it because it's the right thing to do." Mark sources sea salt from his family in Hawaii, and uses local eggs, shellfish, greens. "We don't look solely for organic," she explained. "We want to feature local food. I think we're very fortunate in the Northwest. We have a lot to use."

My dining companion, Zach Lyons, president of the Seattle Chefs Collaborative, arrives and hugs Marjorie before trading places with her in our booth. "Oh, sure, we know each other," he said. "Seattle, and Washington in general, operates as a community." As he picks up the menu, it becomes clear that ordering will be a negotiation. Will I share plates? If he gets the oysters, will I get the soup? Which entrées sound most intriguing?

As the first plates arrive, our table goes quiet. I look up to realize Zach has just bitten into a crispy fried Washington oyster that he dipped into a harissa mayonnaise. The silence ensues. Then…a smile.

What about the mayonnaise flavored with the hot chili sauce? I ask. That was good, too. But this is a prime example of Washington cooking, he said. "The harissa is…hmm…trendy. It's featured in restaurants everywhere in the country," Lyons said. "But here in Washington, the oyster is the star." That's one thing our chefs do very well, he explained. They try new things, but do it to elevate the incredible ingredients we already have.

This is something Lyons preaches regularly. Now a freelance writer, co-author of the Washington State Farmers Market Manual (published in cooperation with WSU), coordinator of Taste of Washington State University, and former executive director of the Washington State Farmers Market Association, he has deep ties with the state's food scene and its small-scale farmers, the kind like the Tonnemakers who sell directly to restaurants like this.

We're not in this lively West Seattle joint just to share a meal. Our mission is to try to define Washington cuisine. And somewhere here, between the butter lettuce and the popcorn ice cream, we hope to discuss not just what it was. Or is. But what it's becoming.

Maybe we're not as noisy about our food as other parts of the country, Lyons said. Northwest chefs are not celebrities. They're not self-promoters, he said. It's a subtler and friendlier scene than in many other cities. When it comes to ideas, inventions, it's a free-for-all. "They're all stealing from each other all the time," he said. "And nobody cares."

The notion of sharing manifests itself in many ways. The trend now is toward small plates—like the ones we're sharing this evening. It's why we can both try the oysters, the potato leek soup with turkey leg confit, the butter lettuce with radishes, the bavet steak with purple and orange cauliflower, and the roasted hen-of-the-woods mushrooms served with grits enriched with Beecher's cheese, owned by Kurt Dammeier, a 1982 WSU alum.

It makes sense in a place like Washington, where there is such a variety of good things to taste. "It works on so many levels," Lyons said. "It's far more interesting for the customer and the chef."

It's also time for us to realize we have incredible local food every season, not just in the summer and fall, Lyons said. "There's a vigorous, year-round food pattern happening." Even in the leanest months of February and March, we have parsnips, rutabagas, sunchokes, potatoes, and Brussels sprouts.

The driving force is not the customer. It's not even the chef anymore. "Now it's the farmer," Lyons said. He points to the orange cauliflower next to the steak. "That's cheddar cauliflower. The farmer decided to grow that, that's why we're trying it here," he said. "People are taking risks, trying new things."

Chefs read cookbooks and magazines for ideas. In the winter, the farmers are poring over their seed catalogs with the same intensity, he said. "The whole region has this culture, and the farmers are driving it."

Tender

"Taste, taste, taste, taste, taste," chef Tamara Murphy advised 1978 WSU graduate Jody Ericson Dorow as they were testing recipes for *Tender*, a book project connecting Washington eaters with their food that they worked on with Nancy Gellos, a 1976 WSU alum, and Marlen Boivin.

"I always thought you had to wait until the end of the recipe when all the ingredients were in before you could taste," Dorow said. Besides learning to taste as she goes, and that olive oil went well with certain things, and that pairing basil with fresh cherries could be quite interesting, she discovered that we all have a bit of the intuitive cook inside us.

Dorow and Gellos were classmates and sorority sisters at WSU. After college, Dorow went into corporate marketing, and Gellos pursued a career in graphic design. A few years ago, Gellos convinced Dorow to join her working for a Seattle-based custom book publisher. They got a taste for completing projects together and co-created ShinShinChez, their own publishing company.

For their first project, they wanted to create something that connected farmers, farmers markets, chefs, home cooks, and eaters. They found Murphy, a Seattle chef whose approach of using local and seasonal ingredients and of maintaining connections with the farm and the farmer resonated with them.

"We were looking for somebody who could help put together all these things and show how simply one could eat," Gellos said. "She was walking the talk."

They crafted a book that would both document the local food community and capture the cuisine in a simple, straightforward way. The result of their collaboration is a beautiful, colorful mix of text and photographs of farms and markets and food. It contains 100 recipes featuring some of Washington's finest produce—like Swiss chard with garlicky chickpeas, cinnamon rice pudding with caramelized apples, and cherry salad with basil and mint.

"I don't call it a cookbook," Dorow said. "It's a beautiful book with recipes."

Faces of Small Farmers

Adriana Janovich

Pablo Silva started working in the fields as soon as he arrived in the United States. He was 14, picking strawberries in California. Agriculture, he said, is in his blood.

Silva was born in the village of Santa Cruz Yucucani in Guerrero, Mexico, and spent a lot of time growing up at his grandmother's house outside of town. She raised animals and grew corn and beans and, he said, in Spanish through a translator, "I always helped her."

When his father in California called for his son to join him, they worked together in the strawberry fields for a couple years before moving to the Skagit Valley. Silva picked strawberries in western Washington for about 15 years before making a transition most pickers never achieve: from farmworker to farm owner and operator.

While Latino people make up 83 percent of all farmworkers, according to the U.S. Department of Labor, they account for just 3 percent of farm owners. Language and other barriers keep many from making the move. Washington State University Food Systems' Immigrants in Agriculture Program helps farmers like Silva write business and whole-farm plans, apply for grants and loans, explore value-added products, connect with markets and buyers, and more.

The Immigrants in Agriculture Program, jointly housed out of WSU Skagit County Extension and the School of the Environment, is just one way that WSU Food Systems helps Washington agriculture, particularly first-time and small farmers. Those farmers can take classes, tour farms, attend specialized farming conferences, and meet with and learn from successful farmers. The program also offers online farm finder tools that make it easier for consumers to connect with local food producers.

"The small farmers of Washington state are really the backbone of the local food community," said Nicole Witham, statewide coordinator of Food Systems, a program of WSU Extension within the College of Agricultural, Human, and Natural Resource Sciences.

"If we don't foster and support them and lift them up, they don't thrive. They don't become mid-sized farmers," she said. "We need a pipeline for new and beginning farmers. They are the farmers we're going to be relying on to provide us food within our local community."

We'll rely on them more than ever in the future. With the world population expected to reach 9 billion by 2050, the United Nations Food and Agriculture Organization estimates that, to feed everyone, sustainable food production will have to increase by 70 percent. However, there is an across-the-board decline in the numbers of farms, farmers, and farmland, as well as an aging group of farmers, in the United States.

Although American farmers are historically White, male, and older, the faces of small farmers in Washington state are becoming more diverse. They include more women and people of color—particularly Latino—as well as young, military-veteran, and first-time farmers. Among their biggest challenges: coming up with capital and locating land.

Despite the hurdles, a new crop of Washington's small farmers are finding their way to farming from varying backgrounds and employing different entry points into agriculture.

They are farmworkers like Silva; Melony Edwards, a young Black woman who started in food service; and Jim Long, a first-time farmer after 30 years in the United States Air Force.

Pablo Silva
Silva Family Farms, Burlington and Oak Harbor

"Owning a business was completely new to me," Silva said. "I had never owned a business before. I had always worked for someone else in agriculture. In a way, that's easier. You work and, yes, it's really hard work. But at the end of the day you can go home and you don't have to think about the business."

Now as an owner and operator, "you go home and you have to think about it—from planting all the way to sales."

Silva is no stranger to long hours. As a longtime farmworker, he would often leave for work around 4 in the morning and return around 10 p.m. or midnight, depending on harvest and additional duties. "I couldn't see my kids," he said. "I would leave while they were sleeping, and I would come home when they were sleeping."

Most days, it's still like that, leaving around 5:30 in the morning before his children wake up. But now he works during the day for a smaller organic berry farm with stable hours and returns home from his own agricultural enterprise at night.

Silva and his wife, Maura, established Silva Family Farms in small steps with support from the Food Systems Immigrants in Agriculture Program. "In Mexico, I just finished third grade," Silva said. "We lived so far from town. It was hard to get there, and the teacher was not there every day."

He took English as a second language classes at Skagit Valley College, a tractor-driving class through WSU Skagit County Extension, and Cultivating Success, which offers an overview of production and marketing options for modern small farms. "I learned how to start a farm business, write a business plan, and think about your goal and your mission," Silva said. "I also learned how to create your own policies and how to comply with government regulations."

In 2016, his employer, Bow Hill Blueberries, rented a quarter of an acre of certified organic land to Silva so he could cultivate his own berries on his off hours. The following year, Silva expanded, renting an acre for organic strawberries at Viva Farms, a nonprofit farm business incubator and training program in King and Skagit Counties. Its mission is to empower aspiring and limited-resource farmers by providing bilingual training in holistic, organic farming practices as well as access to land, infrastructure, equipment, marketing, and capital. Since its founding in 2009, Viva Farms has trained more than 900 small farmers in sustainable organic farming.

Today, Silva cultivates three and a half acres of organic strawberries and raspberries at the farm incubator. He also grows organic blueberries, raspberries, and blackberries on four acres at his own farm in Gig Harbor, which offers U-pick on weekends. "It's a lot," he said. "My wife helps me a lot. That's why I can do it. Otherwise I won't make it."

Silva met his wife picking berries. They were working at the same farm in Skagit Valley and discovered they came from the same village in Mexico. They've been married 15 years and have five children ranging in age from 3 to 15. The oldest, Pablo Jr., helps his parents on their farm.

The Silvas bought a blueberry farm in 2019 from friends on Whidbey Island, more than doubling their operation. With the training he pursued through Viva and WSU, "we were able to advance and expand quite a bit," said Silva, who didn't quit his day job once he became a business owner. He continues to work as a field manager at Bow Hill, where he's worked for nearly ten years. In fact, Bow Hill sells his blueberries. Silva's berries can also be found at the Bayview Farmers Market in Langley, through the Puget Sound Food Hub, Food Co-op in Port Townsend, Skagit Valley Food Co-op, Chimacum Corner Farm Stand, and more.

"We hope to continue to build our business," Silva said. "No one in our family before us has ever been a business owner. We want to show our kids they can start their own business. It's not necessary that they have to go be farmers. But we want to show them how to start a business and teach them about that."

And he encourages others who are thinking about starting a business to "go for it and start and try. With the support that's available from places like WSU you can really move forward. So go for it."

Melony Edwards
Ebony by Nature, Whidbey Island

Melony Edwards found her way to farming through food service. But she likes to joke her name might've had something to do with it, too. "Melon with a 'y,'" she notes, adding the pull of the land was probably inside of her all along. She just didn't know it.

"I recently learned that my ancestors, after they were emancipated from slavery, became sharecroppers in Tupelo, Mississippi," Edwards explained. "I learned my paternal great-grandmother followed her siblings to Detroit for a better life."

Some six million Black people left the rural South for the urban West, Midwest, and Northeast to look for jobs, often as industrial laborers. The Great Migration lasted from 1916 to 1970. Now, Edwards said, "I want to acknowledge my ancestors and their struggle and the land."

Since going through WSU's Cultivating Success program, Edwards has become not only a farmer but an advocate and activist, sharing her story to encourage other aspiring farmers, particularly young people of color and especially women. It's part of her mission of changing the narrative around people of color joining the farming community, specifically in rural areas.

"I'm young and Black, and I'm a woman. There's not a lot of farmers like me in Washington, especially in rural farming," Edwards said. "You see it in the urban landscape. Seattle has a lot of urban farms run by people of color, but not in rural farming."

Her LinkedIn and Instagram accounts describe her as a "Melanated Woman Farmer." On social media, she uses the hashtags #PNWMelanatedFarmer, #ReClaimingFarmingOnMyOwnTerms, and #TheUnbearableWhitenessOfFarmingPNW.

In Washington state, there are fewer than 200 Black-only or mixed-race Black farmers. Not quite 70 are women. And about 40 are new or beginning farmers, with fewer than ten years of experience. "There's definitely a growing network," Edwards said. "We're starting to get more visibility."

Blacks historically played a significant role in American agriculture, enslaved for centuries, followed by sharecropping and tenant farming. Racist violence against Black farm owners in the South and decades-long, well-documented discrimination against Black farmers by the USDA—which excluded Black people from farm loans and assistance— contributed to their decline. In fact, the number of Black farmers fell so drastically that, in 1982, the U.S. Civil Rights Commission predicted there would be none left by 2000.

In the Pacific Northwest, systematic disenfranchisement of Black farmers predates statehood. Exclusion laws prevented Black people from settling in what was formerly known as Oregon Country and, later, the Oregon Territory, including present-day Washington.

"Today's current lack of land ownership for African American farmers in the PNW is a direct result of those laws," Edwards wrote in *Sound Consumer*, a publication of the Seattle area's PCC Community Markets. "The majority of Black farmers in the PNW are leasing land with the hopes of owning it one day. But the limiting factors, such as increasing cost of land and lack of land-purchasing knowledge within the Black community, add steep barriers to an already disadvantaged field. …With land ownership we could reclaim our ancestral skills and re-associate farming with power versus slavery."

A century ago, there were nearly a million Black farmers in America. Today, there's not quite 48,700, making up 1.4 percent of all farmers. Most of them—88 percent—live in the South and Mid-Atlantic.

Edwards, originally from Ohio, moved to Washington state with her family as a teen. She majored in hospitality in college and also studied culinary arts at Portland's now-closed Le Cordon Bleu. Her career in food service raised questions. "I really wanted to know where my food came from," she said. "It led me on this journey of discovery."

Edwards began volunteering on a farm, and "it was awesome," she said. "I fed chicken and pigs, and I scooped a lot of cow poop." That experience led her to Cultivating Success. The classes, she said, "really got me thinking about what I wanted to do."

Afterward, she pursued an entry-level rural farm internship, which proved difficult to find. She landed phone interviews only to be later told she was either "over-qualified" because of her work experience and salary history or "under-qualified" because of her lack of farm experience. "They would also say I wouldn't fit in because I was too old. I was just going into my 30s at the time. I applied for internships for two years, and I got denied for two years. I was ready to give up."

Then she interviewed at Willowood Farm of Ebey's Prairie in Island County, where the population is about 85 percent White, and got the job. She was excited, but nervous. "It's really scary to move out to a rural White community where you don't know if you're going to be accepted or not," said Edwards, who was hired as an intern in March 2016 and was slated to stay through October.

At meet-ups for interns from regional farms, she noticed she was the only person of color. "I remember when I first moved to the farm, I actually kept my bags packed for a period of time because I was afraid I would get chased off the property," she said. "I felt like I was putting myself in a very vulnerable situation."

Now she feels "empowerful." She's traveled to Washington, D.C., twice with the National Young Farmers Coalition to lobby for funding for young farmers, including beginning farmer training, outreach to socially disadvantaged farmers, and mental health services for farmers. She was recently appointed to serve on the coalition's board of directors. She's also shared her story and perspective in essays and on panels, including, in 2018, the inaugural Seattle Food Tank Summit and the Tilth Alliance Conference, where she gave a talk titled "The Unbearable Whiteness of Farming in the PNW." Today, she's working on building a network of Pacific Northwest Black farmers. She's also working with the Organic Seed Alliance to help build a network of Black seed growers.

She's participating in the 2020 Heirloom Collard Green Variety Trial, hosted by Seed Savers Exchange and Southern Exposure Seed Exchange, and growing some 20 different varieties of heritage collard greens, including a few that were almost forgotten.

Edwards recently started her own enterprise: Ebony by Nature, a fiber arts farm selling plants for home dye gardens and naturally dyed fiber as well as seeds. She also continues stewarding the land at Willowood, where she ended up staying through winter 2016 and getting hired back for subsequent seasons eventually as both farm and harvest manager.

Now she's pondering her next steps, working with local land trusts, incubator farms, and farmer-to-farmer land-linking programs to help her find her own land—and remaining optimistic.

"I want to farm," said Edwards, whose goal is to raise sheep and expand her seed-growing business. "And I'm determined to reclaim farming in my own way."

Jim and Connie Long
Fresh Cut Farms, Deer Park

When Jim Long was preparing to retire from a 30-year career with the United States Air Force, he and his wife, Connie, considered a transition to farming. They had cultivated a small garden when they lived in South Dakota and were interested in scaling up. "We saw that we could make an income and not have to punch a clock," said Jim, who grew up in Mead and was stationed around the country and overseas.

He and his wife had been planning to move to Montana in retirement until they stumbled upon property outside of Spokane that seemed a perfect fit. "It was the old house that really drew us in," Jim said, noting, "There were only two other owners besides us."

The original homestead stretched some 250-plus acres. The Longs bought three 10-acre parcels, including a pre-1900 farmhouse and 1947 rancher, in July 2015. Most of the acreage, Jim noted, was overgrown. "Saplings were coming up in the fields," he said.

Sheep provided "quick entry" into farming, so the property—zoned for agriculture—could "start showing some kind of revenue," said Jim, who spent his first 10 years in the military "turning a wrench" and his last 20 years in management.

Of Washington state's nearly 63,300 farmers, just over 8,100 served in America's military. Seventy percent of them farm fewer than 50 acres. Eighty-two percent are 55 and older. And 92 percent are men. But new farmers, with fewer than 10 years of farming experience, like Jim, make up less than a third of all farmers with military service in Washington state.

The Longs founded Fresh Cut Farms in 2016, planting berries, starting a garden, and taking the name from the road where they live: Cross Cut. "We're Fresh Cut on Cross Cut," said Jim, who retired with the rank of chief master sergeant in April 2019.

In 2017, just one year into their farming operation, he was stationed overseas for a 12-month assignment, leaving Connie to manage their new venture on her own. Before he left they sold off the cows and goats to help lighten her load. She brought berries to the farmers market for the first time that year.

When Jim returned, the couple sold berries and other produce at two farmers markets instead of one. They also planted 120 cherry, apple, peach, nectarine, and apricot trees on about a half-acre. They're hoping to increase their orchard to an acre and a half during the next several years.

The Longs also hope to expand their garden, which now stretches about a third of an acre, to an acre and a quarter, but not much more. "We're both hands-on," said Connie, who worked in management for a hospitality company before retiring a couple of years before her husband. But, "that's enough for the two of us," Jim said. "We can't do much more than that."

Last winter, with the help of a USDA grant, they installed two high-tunnel greenhouses to expand their offerings. "We want to make it like a grocery store experience, so we have variety and you can get all your vegetables at one stop," Jim said, noting, "We won't sell anything we don't grow ourselves."

While their farm isn't certified organic, the Longs use organic practices. Among their crops: kale, kohlrabi, Bibb and other lettuces, spinach, peppers, raspberries, strawberries, squash, tomatoes, potatoes, corn, cabbage, and more.

Now they're regulars at three farmers markets: Clayton on Sundays, Fairwood on Tuesdays, and Emerson-Garfield on Fridays. Twice a week, they also offer online ordering with pick-up on Thursdays and Saturdays.

Their plan is to grow slowly—and that's something they learned through WSU. They went through Cultivating Success as well as five or six other classes through Extension and Spokane Neighborhood Partners. Lessons learned include, Connie said, "Don't try to tackle everything at one time. Start small, then move on to the next step. Master that and keep going."

The classes "gave us ideas and contacts," Connie said. "They laid the foundation."

Long-term plans include turning two small grain silos into campsites, and maybe adding U-pick opportunities. The Longs are also thinking about adding flowers and Christmas trees. And, when the historical farmhouse is renovated, "We want to get into agritourism," Jim said. "We'd like to be self-sustaining, like the farms of old. We would like to grow and take care of ourselves."

Changing Ag

The US Department of Agriculture's latest Census of Agriculture shows an across-the-board decline in the numbers of farms, farmers, and farmland, with serious implications for food production, the environment, and the next generation of farmers.

Small farms make up 90 percent of farms nationwide but account for just over half of America's farmland. It's a similar landscape in Washington state, where there are nearly 35,800 farms—down from just over 40,100 farms 20 years ago. Of those, about 33,000 are considered small farms.

American farmers average 58 years of age—more than a third are 65 and older, and more than another third are between the ages of 55 and 64.

Of this country's 3.4 million farmers, 70 percent are potentially slated to retire within the next 20 years.

Most—95 percent—are White. And most—64 percent—are men.

Master Gardeners

Hannelore Sudermann

On Saturday mornings, the Issaquah farmers market is abuzz. People line up outside the city's historic Pickering barn to buy big red wands of rhubarb, strawberries from Puyallup, and armloads of flowers. Music flows through—reggae, elementary school choirs, jazz.

Amidst the din and bright colors from the multitude of vendors and visitors, keen experts with nothing to sell at all set up their table. They wait while people bring things to them—baggies full of leaves, vials holding insects, and dozens and dozens of questions. These are Master Gardeners, trained by Washington State University and empowered by their communities to advise, serve, and instruct their friends and neighbors on gardening and the environment.

At the same time, just a few miles away in Redmond, a similar table is set up at the farmers market on Leary Way. And still others in the Magnolia neighborhood of Seattle, at the Village Green market on Vashon Island, in Edmonds, in Port Orchard, and south in Puyallup.

These Saturday morning experts are not just at the farmers markets, they have tables at the Fred Meyer in Shoreline, outside a historic mansion in Ferndale, at the Lowe's in Tacoma, and at the County Fairgrounds in Spokane. They are part of one of the longest-running, most successful programs ever to come out of Washington State University. Master Gardener programs not only train and certify thousands of volunteers state-wide, but they have branched all across the country into communities as far off as New York, Puerto Rico, and Guam.

For all that Master Gardeners are and do, once they were just a good idea.

In the early 1970s, Washington State University extension agents Dave Gibby and Bill Scheer were new hires with joint appointments for both Pierce and King Counties. They divided their time between the Seattle offices on Queen Anne and the offices in Tacoma. While Scheer's focus was commercial agriculture, Gibby was assigned urban horticulture—a weighty duty given the population base of more than 1.5 million.

"I had two days in one county, three days in the other," Gibby said. "Each time I got to the other office, I would have hundreds of call-back slips." And when Gibby wasn't available, people would turn to Scheer with their questions. "We tried to be of service to people," Scheer said. "But we were overwhelmed with the demand."

Why is my grass dying? When should I plant fruit trees? What's eating my peonies? There was a large public demand for horticulture information, and the university knew it. The solution was Gibby. "They called me the 'sacrificial lamb,'" he said.

Gibby grew up in Utah, in a large family that had a commercial nursery and greenhouse. Scheer was born in the Dutch East Indies, and after WWII went to school in the Netherlands, where horticulture was a major field of study, and so it became his. The pair are credited with concocting and honing one of the best public outreach ideas ever to come from Washington State University.

Gibby tried to address the gardening questions on television, on the radio, and in the newspapers. He would write up tip sheets and leave them next to the cash registers of nurseries. "All it did was make the problem worse," Gibby said. Thanks to his outreach, those gardeners thirsty for information now knew where to find him. "Fifty to eighty calls a day became up to 500 calls a day," he said.

Gibby would sit at his desk and cull through the piles of the messages, answering those who had called more than once, those whose names he recognized, and those who were prominent in the community. The rest he threw away. "I just couldn't get to everyone."

He started attending garden club meetings, hoping to preemptively address questions specific to the season. There between the pruning course and the refreshments, he found a patch of life-long gardeners who were already experts. In many cases, these were the people to whom everyone in a certain neighborhood would gravitate for help. He saw a solution. "I thought, 'What's the problem with having volunteers help out?' " he said.

So he went back to the extension office with the idea, turning to Scheer. They talked about the German system where a mastery of a certain field brought you recognition. Those who brewed beer were *Braumeisters*, those who were expert foresters were *Waldmeisters*, Scheer said. Why not create a program to train garden experts? They took the German notion of "Gartenmeister" and "We Americanized it," Scheer said. "Master Gardeners. We knew people would be proud to have the title."

Both men believed in the idea. But they had to sell it to their colleagues at the research stations.

"To my surprise, I received a hailstorm of criticism," Gibby said. Though it was more than 30 years ago, he can still count off all the reasons his fellow extension agents and supervisors said it wouldn't work: 1. Volunteers could not meet WSU's standards. 2. They had to be licensed to provide advice on pesticides. 3. The public wanted the information when it wanted it—gardeners wouldn't come to a planned clinic. And finally, "they said people would not volunteer," he said.

But Gibby had worked with volunteers before. He had no doubt he could find gardeners willing to give their time to the public.

He proposed holding a single clinic, something at a public venue where WSU faculty experts on plants, disease, insects, and soil could be available to answer questions. "I had an ace up my sleeve," he said. Of all the least garden-like places, he chose the Tacoma Mall. The mall administrators were thrilled to make room for the event and agreed to post fliers advertising it. Then he went to the *Tacoma News Tribune* and pitched a feature about it. Finally, he plugged the event on a local television program. And that first evening when the WSU experts set up their card table at the mall, "We got mobbed."

That wasn't enough, though. Gibby walked into the Seattle offices of *Sunset* magazine and approached writer Steve Lorton with an idea of plugging the volunteer program in the popular regional gardening magazine. Lorton was impressed with both the man and the idea. "He was tall, handsome, articulate," Lorton said. "Sort of Jimmy Stewart out of a '30s movie."

"He said, can you do this for me?" Lorton loved the idea. "It was just like lighting a stick of dynamite for me." Beyond the idea of building an army of volunteer gardening experts, the magazine journalist liked the challenge of flying down to *Sunset* headquarters in Menlo Park and convincing his editor to print something immediately.

It wasn't a hard sell. "Proc's (Proctor Mellquist) eyes twinkled, and he said 'Let's do a spread,'" Lorton said. A two-page spread on short notice? It was unheard of. But the story fit with the flavor of the magazine. "In those days we were kind of a publication of community action," Lorton said.

They needed art to run with the story, "so we made up this little sign that said 'Master Gardeners wanted' and hung it up over a card table at an Ernst (garden store)." Then they went out and collected pictures of some sick and hideous looking plants. "Then we wrote the story."

On page 188 in the September 1972 issue of *Sunset* ran the piece titled "Wanted: home gardeners to become Master Gardeners." The story said that WSU's extension service was seeking experienced gardeners to be volunteer garden experts. Those who volunteered would get 55 hours of free training on subjects such as garden techniques, the care and proper use of garden equipment, and the use of pesticides. The story ended with modest hopes that "as the system develops, representatives will be placed in an increasing number of locations through the Puget Sound area and eventually in all the populated areas of the state."

Even to Gibby's surprise, more than 300 people volunteered. He narrowed it down to 75 candidates in King County and 75 in Pierce. "It was a total mixed bag—retirees, a few professionals," he said. "I looked for a passion for gardening, good communication skills, and some gardening expertise."

In January of 1973, they started the classes, teaching in places like Northgate and the Kent library. Sharon Collman, who had a background in entomology, was among the first trainees. Gibby and Scheer taught most of the classes. It was challenging and interesting, she said, but she had no idea she was at the beginning of something big. Collman was also charged with setting up the first plant clinics where, once trained, the Master Gardeners could meet with the public and answer questions. "In the first season, we served 5,000 people," Gibby said.

"Of course it worked," Lorton said. With a maritime climate that could host all kinds of different plants, the Pacific Northwest is a gardener's paradise. "Gardening wasn't huge back then," he said, "but there were a lot more gardeners here than in any place in the country."

It may have been difficult to get support for the idea in the first place, but it said something that two extension agents in Washington, in the Puget Sound region, were able to get it started, Scheer said. Anywhere else, and it might not have happened at all.

Gibby left WSU in 1974 for a private industry job that was "too good to pass up," he said. Collman, who had been working as a temporary extension agent, was hired to replace him and took over the coordination of the Master Gardener training. Scheer and other faculty continued to help with teaching, and soon Spokane County was starting up its own Master Gardener program.

The notion quickly spread across the state and then the country. According to a recent survey from the U.S. Department of Agriculture, the United States has nearly 95,000 active Master Gardener volunteers. In the past year they donated more than five million hours in their communities. They gave nearly 700,000 pounds of produce to local food banks and spent close to 300,000 hours teaching gardening to children and young adults.

In Washington, 36 of 39 counties host more than 4,000 active Master Gardener volunteers. The bulk of them are in the higher density communities around Puget Sound.

"There really is no typical Master Gardener," said Elaine Anderson, the Master Gardener coordinator for King County, which has over 700 Master Gardener volunteers, the highest number in state. "Other than they all love gardening and all have a real interest in volunteering in their communities," they come from all walks of life. Doctors, dentists, truck drivers. "This year we even had our first 16-year-old in training," she said. She is the youngest Master Gardener ever to be trained in Washington.

It almost didn't happen, said Anderson, who screens the applicants each year to select the best candidates for the training. When Anya Puceta, a Seattle high school junior, called about joining, Anderson repeated what she had been told, that no one under 18 could participate. Puceta, 16, already had some experience gardening at the organic pea patch at her high school and was even assisting in instructing her classmates. "I wanted more information to support what I was doing," she said. One of her mother's friends is a Master Gardener, as is a neighbor. Puceta thought she could squeeze time for the 60 hours of training over 12 weeks between school and studying for her SATs.

When she was turned away because of her age, she was discouraged. "But I'm not one to give up very quickly," she said. "Just ask my mom. It drives her crazy. " She e-mailed and asked for specific reasons why she couldn't participate. "I learned about liability," she said. Then, with her parents' promise to sign a waiver, she called Anderson back.

Anderson, impressed with Puceta's persistence, took the issue to Tonie Fitzgerald, WSU's statewide Master Gardener program leader, who double-checked the policies and encouraged the teen's application.

"She was great," Anderson said. "It was a delight to have somebody that young in the classes." Though many of the volunteers were retirees, two AmeriCorps students in their 20s joined the King County class as well.

"I don't come from a family of gardeners," Puceta said. "At home we have a mid-sized, untended lawn. We just let it be." But she has lately introduced a vegetable patch. "Let's see," she said looking into the yard. "We have nasturtiums and kale and fava beans, rhubarb, chives, and parsley."

Now that the 2009 class of Master Gardeners has finished training, Puceta and her classmates are required to perform at least 50 hours of volunteer time within a year. She is hoping to help at plant clinics as well as offer presentations on organic gardening to people in urban neighborhoods who may not already have access to it. She also wants to work at one of the several demonstration gardens in King County, perhaps the fragrance garden at the Seattle Lighthouse for the Blind, she said.

Plant clinics were the first focus for the Master Gardeners, but in the 1980s demonstration gardens began sprouting around the Puget Sound. Anderson points out the Bellevue garden, which was started in 1984, as one of the community's great assets. "They built themselves up from a blackberry patch," she said. Today, in addition to a regular diagnostic plant clinic, the garden holds a compost center, a children's garden, and gardens designed for shade, drought, and native plantings. "Now they're a kind of a model," she said.

As is the newer xeriscape demonstration garden at the Riverfront Park in Wenatchee, Fitzgerald said. Besides offering a beautiful scene, the Master Gardeners selected plants like lavender and sedum that are especially drought tolerant. With the support of the county public utilities district, they are showing eastern Washington homeowners how to cut down on their water use.

Beyond the clinics and the gardens, much more is going on with the program. There's more awareness of environmental impact, Fitzgerald said. In the 1970s, Master Gardeners' focus was outreach. "Now it's not so much changing the environment just to look pretty," she said. "Now it's a much more proactive program. We're working with municipalities and parks," as well as water conservation districts, historical societies, public schools, and nonprofit groups.

Master Gardeners are teaching their communities to identify and fight invasive plants and insects, limit unnecessary fertilizer and pesticide applications, hold surface water on their properties so it doesn't pour into local streams and scour them of fish habitat, and even to landscape in a way that keeps homes warm in winter and cool in summer, said Collman, who now works as an extension agent in Snohomish County. "The issues we're facing as a society, that's where we're putting our programming."

WSU is lucky to have this army of dedicated volunteers, said Dan Bernardo, dean of the WSU College of Agricultural, Human, and Natural Resource Sciences. "They really multiply our impact on urban and environmental horticulture," he said. To arm them with solid science-based training, and then to send them out to educate others, it's really a noble goal, he said. "It's a nice marriage of our sciences and the needs of the communities around Washington state."

While Master Gardener training in Washington is now county specific, the university is working to unify the core training program to provide the same access to the experts for everyone, whether they're in the populated Puget Sound region or far off in Grays Harbor or Adams counties, Bernardo said. Now horticulture information is widely available—in the media, on the internet, he said. Still, the Master Gardeners program is a model for its connections to the university and all its resources.

Also, thanks to their training, the volunteers are the experts' ears and eyes, watching for infestations of disease, insects, and invasive plant species, helping natural resource agents and scientists cope with the changing environment.

Can they do all this in the 50 hours they're required to volunteer to stay certified? Probably not, say the coordinators. But that's of no consequence, since most of them go far beyond their required time. Of course they're committed, Fitzgerald said. Gardening, for many of them, isn't just a hobby, it's a passion. "We are so lucky to have these people who want to learn and contribute to their communities, and they do it in the name of Washington State University Extension," she said.

Now Master Gardener programs operate out of land grant universities in more than 40 states. In Mississippi they're leading volunteers in projects to rebuild the public landscapes decimated by hurricanes Rita and Katrina. In Wisconsin they're helping gardeners identify and protect local pollinators. And in Nebraska, they're helping the Pawnee tribe revive its traditional corn variety, and through the corn, its agricultural traditions.

Though they never imagined the Master Gardeners program would be an international model or that it would reach so far into society, Gibby and Scheer knew it was a good idea from the beginning. "I felt if we primed the pump, it really would spread," Gibby said. "I'm proud of what we started."

Something Old, Something New— A History of Hospitality

Hannelore Sudermann

Every wedding needs something old.

Why couldn't it be one of the grandest old hotels in the Pacific Northwest? Dana Schroader wondered.

It's mid-afternoon and about 250 guests are due to arrive at the Fairmont Olympic in a few hours for an elegant evening wedding. Schroader, dressed discreetly in a black skirt and jacket, slips through the two-story lobby of the 1924 Seattle landmark toward the Spanish Ballroom, stopping at the base of the stairs to straighten a welcome table. She steps up to the foyer, which is dotted with tables for a cocktail hour, and pushes open the gilded doors to the ballroom, where a florist is dressing tables with cream cloths and towering floral arrangements rich with hydrangeas and roses.

"Oh, this is a pretty wedding," said Schroader, surveying the room and opening her list and seating chart to run a quick check. She sweeps past the cake table to pick up the bride and groom topper, takes another look around the room, and heads down a long, cool hallway to the kitchen, where a pastry chef is assembling and frosting the cake.

There are a lot of moving pieces in a wedding this size. While Schroader, a 2007 Washington State University graduate, stops to check in on the prep for the *à la minute* meal service, the bride dresses in a room upstairs with her bridesmaids. A photographer is posing the groom and the men of the wedding party on an upper landing of the lobby. The bride's father in his tuxedo strolls through the reception site. A worker delivers the wine and champagne. And out-of-town guests check into their rooms.

Schroader's job as the hotel's catering sales manager, or more simply, wedding coordinator, touches on many components of the field of hospitality, including the lodging of the family and guests, planning and coordinating the cocktails and meals, and running the event itself with its waiters, bartenders, and musicians. And she gets to do it in the heart of a city that she loves in a spectacular setting. The job is not what she imagined when she was working after classes at Pullman's Holiday Inn Express and Fireside Grill to gain experience and pay for college. "It's better," she said.

Washington state has a $16.4 billion travel and tourism industry, according to the Washington Tourism Alliance, making it the fourth largest industry in the state. The leisure and hospitality sector alone, which includes restaurants, hotels, and motels, employs about 330,000 Washington workers.

Like Schroader, many of the Washington State University students who graduate with a hospitality business management degree go straight from Pullman to a management job in the industry, said Nancy Swanger, director of WSU's School of Hospitality Business Management. One reason for that is the rigorous business training they get in Pullman, and now at WSU Vancouver as well. About 25 percent of their curriculum is in core business subjects including finance, business law, economic statistics, and accounting.

The program requires 1,000 hours of industry or internship experience before a student can graduate. "It allows them to have practical experience to compare to the theoretical things they have learned in class," Swanger said. "And recruiters want experience."

But that's just a part of it. As the concept of hospitality grows and changes, the school is adapting, too. It must, to prepare its students for an ever-changing industry.

Back in 1932, when Washington State College introduced its hospitality program, no one had yet imagined an airport hotel, a drive-through restaurant, a convention center, or the boom of international travel. According to old program paperwork, the hospitality degree was founded simply for the purpose of "training men in hotel operations and women in dietetics."

Georgina Petheram Tucker, now 102, was a student in Pullman when the Washington State College introduced a limited curriculum in hotel management. "Possibly no single action involving curricular expansion ever brought [WSC President] Holland more praise from the College's constituency than did this one, as compliments continued to reach him from year to year," according to the book *E.O. Holland and the State College of Washington*. The Spokane-born girl found more than a major. She found a role shaping a young industry.

Tucker's degree led her to housekeeping and dining services work in Spokane, Boise, San Francisco, and Los Angeles and a 42-year career with Westin Hotels. Her jobs in housekeeping and later as Westin's corporate food director included menu creation, staff training, and developing food service plans. As she grew in her career, her focus grew from simply cleaning rooms and coordinating schedules to managing issues of health and safety, staff diversity, and working with unions. "She really professionalized housekeeping in hotels," Swanger said.

"She is such an amazing person," Swanger said. The toilet paper end folded into a triangle is her most amusing legacy. "It's called the Tucker point."

After retiring, Tucker, a 1933 alumna, worked as an industry consultant and wrote *The Science of Housekeeping* and *The Professional Housekeeper*, which for years were used for training industry-wide.

As the years passed, the Washington State program grew. A page tucked in with the hospitality program's archival materials from the 1940s shows how the school recruited new students. "Our graduates have the advantage of stepping out of college into a new and uncrowded field…rapid advancements are assured on securing a position, for the men now actively engaged in the work have nothing but the school of hard knocks as a teacher."

In 1942, the program was temporarily halted because of war. It started up again in 1946, but recast as a training program for hotel, motel, and restaurant managers and relocated from Home Economics to the newly-formed School of Business and Economics. Early coursework included personnel administration and institutional purchasing, and was later enhanced to include the law of innkeeping and tourism.

Jerry Burtenshaw, who enrolled at WSU in 1952 and graduated in 1956, said it wasn't all numbers and textbooks. He'll never forget the interactive class in how to break down a pig carcass. It made sense back then, he said, because it was valuable to know the process for anyone wanting to go into restaurant management. And he did, since his family operated the Alpine Cafeteria in Bellingham.

"The program was only 20 years old," he said. "It was still in the embryo stages." But the country was seeing a boom in the industry. Chains like Hilton and Sheraton were fast expanding, and Holiday Inn had started up in 1952. The demands of a mushrooming industry and the influx of Korean War veterans studying hospitality on the G.I. Bill "really gave it a big push," Burtenshaw said.

The program took advantage of the campus resources, putting students to work in the dining halls. "We'd go in early each morning and help set up the food," Burtenshaw said. They were also involved in creating plans for what would become the Rotunda Dining Center.

Burtenshaw's training served him when his family expanded their local Alpine Cafeteria into a major industrial catering business with outlets in Everett, Seattle, and Tacoma, as well as concessions contracts at places like Husky Stadium, the Kingdome, the Tacoma Dome, and Joe Albi Stadium in Spokane. As more people dined out and sought food at entertainment venues, the business grew. And as the nation's hospitality industry evolved with expanding restaurant chains, hotels, and motels, the program adapted again.

In the 1970s, Brian McGinnis found his way into the hospitality program and discovered that he enjoyed the coursework, which included an internship requirement. To fill it, he took a summer post as *maître d'* at the Rosario Resort in the San Juan Islands, tying together his training and his love of beautiful places.

After graduation in 1977, McGinnis went to Hawai'i for a vacation and stayed for a job at Westin Hotel's resort in Waikiki. He became front office manager, was transferred, and started to climb the corporate ladder. "People think of hospitality as just minimum wage and tip jobs," he said. "But where else can you start out as a bellman or dishwasher and move up to general manager? There are many rags to riches stories within hospitality."

Eventually, McGinnis went to work for Westin's development group and had a role on a number of projects including the Westin Tokyo. In 1997, after 11 years in development, he left the company and stepped into one of the most interesting resort projects to take place in Washington in the last 20 years: the Alderbrook Resort.

The old Hood Canal vacation site was up for sale. The facility had been established in 1913 as a collection of camp tents outfitted with potbelly stoves and accessible only by water. Over the years, it changed hands, a highway came in, buildings went up, and with each new owner, it engaged a new generation of guests.

A family with a home nearby asked McGinnis to help them make an offer. It didn't suit the Alderbrook's owners, who instead sold the property for more money to another buyer. McGinnis went on to other projects, but was brought back in in 2001 when the new owner, who hadn't made the place profitable, was looking to sell. This time Jeff Raikes, a former Microsoft executive, and his wife Tricia, a 1978 WSU alumna, were interested in restoring the property. With McGinnis coordinating the negotiations, the deal succeeded.

Buying the property was only the first step, said McGinnis, pointing to an aerial photograph of the site. The overhaul involved moving a half-mile of the highway back into the hillside. Then it required taking down some buildings, restoring others, and building new elements to harmonize the architecture of the entire place—which included 21 small cabins from the 1940s. "It had been operated as a funky old inn," McGinnis said. "It was in rough shape."

Once the sale was complete, "I got in the car with my construction manager and my designer and said we're going on a road trip," McGinnis said. "We went to the Salish, Semiahmoo, Skamania, and the Salishan, all the S's." He wanted his team to see each Northwest resort and pick the brains of the owners and operators to "understand what we should be doing here to make it successful."

The Alderbrook project included new kitchens, meeting rooms, a spa, a bar, waterfront dining, a ballroom, and repairs to the marina. At the same time it protected the saltwater shoreline as well as the freshwater streams that run through the site. It enhanced the Northwest vibe with elements like peeled wood posts in the lobby, pine floors, fireplaces, works from artists of the Skokomish tribe, and inviting furniture.

The whole idea was to create the feel of an old family beach house—only in the hands of a new tech-friendly generation, McGinnis said. That in itself was a good notion, since a number of long-established Northwest families have their beach retreats nearby.

Alderbrook reopened in June 2004 as a full-service upscale hotel and resort. Not everyone can own a house on the beach, McGinnis said. But with Alderbrook they can have that experience.

Washington has been fortunate when it comes to investors willing to rescue and restore historic hospitality landmarks. In Spokane, thanks to a couple willing to venture into the hotel business, the 1914 Kirtland Cutter gem known as The Davenport was saved from the wrecking ball. The downtown grand hotel had been shuttered since shortly after Matthew Jensen attended his senior prom there.

Jensen, who credits his time as one of the first Cougars to study at Institut Hôtelier "César Ritz" in Le Bouveret, Switzerland, with his understanding of luxury hotels, is today the Davenport's director of marketing.

Jensen's career route back to Spokane started with a job as a resort and management trainee at the Hyatt Hotel and Spa in Monterey, California. He soon transferred to the Grand Hyatt in San Francisco. He next took a job with Kimpton Hotel Group, which has boutique hotels in cities around the country. He became Kimpton's director of sales at the San Francisco Hotel Monaco, moved to Seattle to open another Hotel Monaco, and then became the regional manager overseeing the Monaco, the Alexis, and the Hotel Vintage Plaza in Portland.

To succeed in hospitality, you have to be ready to respond and adapt, even if it means moving from hotel to hotel, said Jensen, a 1988 WSU alum. "It's a 24-hour-a-day business. And the only thing you can absolutely count on is change."

One day a friend in the business encouraged him to look into Spokane's Davenport Hotel, which had been closed for 15 years but was in the midst of a $30 million restoration. He moved back to his hometown and took the post of director of marketing for the hotel. In just five months, he put together a sales team and a marketing plan to launch the reopening. Eleven years later, the Davenport owners have added a tower to the hotel and picked up the boutique Hotel Lusso across the street to form The Davenport Collection. They are planning still more projects. It's quite a success for an old grand hotel that was nearly demolished, Jensen said.

As the hotel has modernized, so have the operations. The Davenport's guests are more savvy and traveled than ever, Jensen said. They have high expectations and many take the extra time to research hotels before making their choice. And the hotel has had to keep apace, Jensen said. "There are so many ways now to show people what you're like."

Back in the 1980s, when Jensen was at WSU, the school ran a Seattle Center for Hotel and Restaurant Administration based at Seattle University. Students could spend the last two years of their degrees working in hotels and restaurants in the highly-populated Puget Sound region. The program ended in 1998 after funding was reduced.

It was a real loss, Burtenshaw said. But he and other alumni have created other ways to connect industry leaders with the students in Pullman. In 1981, Burtenshaw and his wife Angelina started a lecture series in honor of their son Brett, who died a few months before his freshman year as a hospitality major at WSU. Each year, the program brings in speakers from around the industry like the co-founder of Panda restaurants, 1984 alum Joe Fugere of Seattle's Tutta Bella, Napa Valley vintner and 1978 alum Stan Boyd, the chairman of McCormick & Schmick's seafood restaurant management group, and most recently the president of the Holland America cruise line. The diversity of speakers shows that there are so many directions to go in the hospitality industry, said director Swanger.

Food alone offers so many opportunities. Under the guidance of faculty and alumni advisors, the culinary program has been enhanced to reflect the growing focus on food in the travel and hospitality industry. The school now has a commercial kitchen, and is using local produce and expertise in training students in the essentials of cuisine. The school also recently added a degree in wine business management. Given that there are now nearly 700 wineries in the state, it's time, Swanger said.

As hospitality is growing in new and unexpected directions, the school is working to respond. Cruise lines are bringing a new wave of tourists into our region, and they're spending extra days in our hotels and exploring our cities and landmarks. And the state now has more than 30 casinos, many of them with accompanying hotels, restaurants, and entertainment stages. Those are more opportunities for exploration and training, Swanger said.

The school is already diving into the new senior-living operations around the state. Much more than senior apartments and cafeterias, they offer restaurant-style dining, housekeeping and linen services, outings for shopping or cultural events, even a concierge. The people who plan, coordinate, and manage these places use the same skills WSU's hospitality students learn on campus, Swanger said. In 2011, WSU offered its first course in senior living management, tapping into several industry experts from around the state to help teach the course.

More recently, alumni like McGinnis, who now leads the board of advisors for the hospitality program, encouraged Swanger to push the curriculum to include hotel development. A class debuted last spring bringing hospitality students together with students in architecture and construction management to learn first-hand from developers and designers the process of siting and building a new property. They learned about siting projects from representatives of Marriott, land use and design planning from architects Degen & Degen, budget from hotel developer and 1964 WSU alum Larry Culver, and revenue projections from the company that manages the Salish Lodge.

Hospitality students today are still grounded in those original subjects of management and food service, but they're also learning how to build hotels, run senior living campuses, address changing consumer behaviors, and work in an international setting.

"I think that business foundation helps us right away," said 2005 WSU alumna Sarah Carter, who works with Schroader at the Fairmont Olympic. When Carter came to the hotel in 2007, her job was in conference services running events like small corporate board meetings and large conferences. She has recently moved over to sales, where she plans meetings and hotel stays for corporate clients, advisory boards, sports teams, and government delegations.

Since they are trained in so many areas of the business, graduates like Carter can adapt quickly, moving from one area of the business to another, Swanger said. Carter said her time abroad through the program at César Ritz was probably the best part of her degree.

"You really learn how to work with other cultures and overcome language barriers," she said. "Our industry is definitely global." Carter also credits the industry classes, the help in knowing what to put on her resume, how to dress for her job, how to interview, and how to adapt. "The professionalism they taught us, that really gave us an edge.".

Washington's Wine Crush

Hannelore Sudermann

Seattle

It's hard to say when it all started. Maybe it was back in 1874, when Washington's first winery opened in Wenatchee. But then Prohibition forced that winery and its neighbors to close their doors.

Maybe it was in the late 1930s, when wine in the state rebounded, peaking at 42 wineries in 1937. That lasted until a succession of disastrous freezes wiped out the grape crops.

Maybe it was in the 1960s, when Washington State University researchers convinced fruit farmers in the Yakima Valley they could successfully grow wine grapes.

But for our story, perhaps the best place to start is 30 years ago when Washingtonians were learning to drink and appreciate wine. It was August 1975, in a white brick house on Queen Anne Hill. A small group gathered for an impartial judging of Northwest wines. There were five experts: Stan Reed, a food writer from the *Post Intelligencer*, wine writer Leon Adams, German grape breeder Helmut Becker, *Seattle Times* wine writer Tom Stockley, and Chas Nagel, the food scientist and bacteriologist who made the first wines to be tested at Washington State University.

"Chas was a good judge," said Glenn White, one of the founding members of the Northwest Enological Society and host to the private tasting. "He can identify every chemical in a wine." He taught many others, including some of today's winemakers, to do the same.

The judging started in the afternoon around the walnut dining room table. White, future winemaker Mike Wallace, and just a few others looked on. The living room offered a spectacular view over the Seattle Center to downtown and Elliott Bay. But the judges were focused on the glasses in front of them.

"There were some pretty bad wines in that group," said Nagel, noting that more than a couple samples had sulfide problems, which meant a rotten egg taste. But others were good. Nagel, excited by what he was tasting, tried talking with Becker. But the German expert diverted him, lest the discussion mar the judging. "Near the end, he started showing me glasses and giving me the thumbs up," Nagel said. "I realized he wasn't spitting it all out."

Did these people at the house on Queen Anne know they were at the beginning of something big? "It sure was momentous to me," Nagel said. "In this group of experts, I felt like a rookie." As they swished and swirled, it was clear Washington had arrived on the wine scene. "You could sense things were going to pop," said Wallace, who, already infected with wine fever, started Hinzerling Winery in Prosser the next year.

Several weeks later, the group presented the winners of their tasting at the very first wine festival of the Northwest Enological Society, which, to their surprise, drew a crowd of more than 300. Alongside a sumptuous dinner prepared by Seattle chefs Francois Kissel and Robert Rosellini, the guests tasted some of the winning wines from Associated Vintners, the forebear of Columbia Winery, a 1971 Chardonnay from Boordy Vineyards in Prosser—which closed in 1975—and a 1974 Johannesberg Riesling and 1972 Cabernet Sauvignon from Ste. Michelle Vineyards, now a major force in the American wine industry.

Washingtonians learned to grow wine grapes through the efforts of WSU researcher Walter Clore. But equally important is the man who taught Washington how to make and taste wine. Remember, 1975 was a time when Americans drank light European rosés, or possibly something more fortified. There were only six wineries in the state, and of them, only two survived.

Clore looked to Chas Nagel to turn the early grape efforts into wine and to encourage others to do the same. Nagel made the first two vintages in 1964 and 1965, then oversaw George Carter's winemaking at WSU's Prosser Research Station. At the same time, Nagel organized tasting panels in Pullman, training graduate students and community members, many of whom didn't drink wine at home, to find and diagnose the problems in the local vintages. Winemakers often turned to Nagel for advice. In fact, the plans for Arbor Crest Winery in Spokane were hatched by WSU alums C. Harold Mielke and his brother David at Nagel's dining room table. "We spent a lot of time with Chas," said C. Harold Mielke, who graduated from WSU in 1958 with a degree in zoology. "I would always bring the latest and greatest Chardonnay and cracked crab, and we would talk about the wine business."

Nagel took his expertise to the west side of the state, becoming one of the founding members of the Seattle-based Northwest Enological Society and offering courses on how to taste wine. He was very particular about how it should be done.

"Honey, he never even let you wear perfume or lipstick to the tasting," said his wife, Bea.

Walla Walla

Annette Bergevin is focused on a different kind of perfume. The co-owner of Walla Walla's Bergevin Lane notes that her new Columbia Valley Calico Red has a certain compelling flavor. "Can you guess what it is?" she asked, as she pours a taste into a glass. I sniff and swirl and take a sip as she leads the way into a cavernous room filled with oak casks and gleaming steel tanks.

Until a few years ago, Bergevin, who graduated from WSU in 1986 with a communications degree, had been living in the Bay Area of California in the thick of the telecom industry. But she dropped that fast-paced life for one at home in Walla Walla, where she could work with her family. She comes by wine through her father, an eastern Washington vineyard owner. With his help and the encouragement of her business partner Amber Lane, Bergevin started making wine. "We had a lot of support from folks around town," Bergevin said. That included help from well-known winemaker Rusty Figgins, who urged them to hire French enologist Virginie Bourgue. Bergevin Lane's first release was in 2001, and now they've made the wine lists of restaurants and resorts throughout the Northwest. Bergevin still can't believe her path. "I wake up every morning and I think, 'Are we really doing this?'"

The young winery owner is grateful to Walla Walla's pioneers such as Rick Small of Woodward Canyon and Leonetti's Gary Figgins, two men who put the appellation on the map in the 1970s. Their standards of quality have made a name for the small wine region; now it's up to the rest of the wineries to maintain that reputation, Bergevin said.

By this time, I've finished most of my Calico sample. It hits me. "Grapefruit!" Bergevin smiled.

Wine is changing Washington. Communities like Woodinville, Whidbey Island, and Walla Walla have caught the nation's attention, thanks to the high-quality vintages they're producing. And in the wake of their wines come elite chefs and high-end stores ready to cater to the wine-buying crowds.

Still, at 6 p.m. one Tuesday last summer, we struggled to find a place in Walla Walla for dinner. The two "hot" new restaurants were closed, the backup bistro had shut down for a wedding, and the sun-baked streets were nearly empty.

"One of the gaps we have is scope of amenities in wine country," said Ted Baseler, president and CEO of Ste. Michelle Wine Estates. "Look at Napa, the number and quality of restaurants, spas, hotels, shops, and galleries. It really makes it a great experience, whether you want to try the wine or not. That's where we're still falling a little short."

There are a few other sour notes. The long-time residents still strive to adjust to the lifestyles and tastes of the newcomers. People like Adelle Ganguet, who attended WSU briefly in 1940 before coming home to marry a farmer in Dixie, can hardly imagine paying $34 for a steak at one of the fancy new places when she can get it for $12 at her favorite spot. "Thirty-four dollars? I'd have to eat a lot of food for that," she said.

Ganguet, ever interested in the news of the community, keeps her ears open to the conflicts between the area's traditional wheat and onion farmers and the new folk planting vineyards and building tasting rooms. A few years ago grape growers filed a law suit against other farmers to stop the aerial application of an herbicide which was harming some of the grapes.

"Yeah, there's some tension there. It's just the tension of differences of use," said Jim Hayner, a Walla Walla-based attorney who graduated in 1972 from WSU with a degree in economics. Hayner handled the case of a New York investor who grew up in Walla Walla and wanted to come back and open a winery and tasting room near town. His plans ground to a halt when his neighbors argued it would bring too much traffic to a rural area.

In spite of the occasional resistance, this corner of the state produces a dazzling collection of good wines. The number of wineries in Walla Walla, Yakima, and the Columbia Valley has grown exponentially. In four years the number of Washington wineries has more than doubled from about 170 to 360.

Among the newcomers is Cougar Crest, a small company headed by winemaker Debbie Hansen and her husband, David, who manage 50 acres of vines. The couple, who both graduated from WSU—she in 1979 and he in 1977—started making wine in 2001. They've kept their day jobs, though maybe not for much longer.

Their past year was better than they could have imagined. The Cougar Crest 2002 Syrah scored a 94 in *Wine Spectator*. "I was kind of awestruck," said Debbie Hansen, who knew the wine was good, but didn't know how the marketplace would like it. "I submitted it in a lot of competitions just to see how it would measure up." Then the *Spectator* review came out last winter. "It was read by a lot more people than I ever thought." She didn't even have a subscription to the magazine. The orders started pouring in.

What Hansen learned at WSU gave her the science grounding she needed to make wine. She then polished her skills with winemaking classes in California. "You can walk right out of pharmacy school and right into enology," she said. "The rest of it is taste, experience, and good taste buds."

On the other side of town, where Highway 12 stretches west, 1969 WSU alum Rick Small has transformed his family wheat farm into a vintner's domain. Still, he has anything but the artifice one might expect from a lauded pioneer in the Walla Walla scene. On a busy weekend last spring he stood in the middle of his Woodward Canyon winery in a T-shirt, sandals, and shorts, chumming it up with the customers and sampling his latest Chardonnay. "It's pretty good," he said, grinning and swirling. Wine junkies surrounded him in everything from their best diamonds to funky grape-themed Hawaiian shirts.

While people milled by, eager to meet him, Small pondered why Washington wine is not more widespread. He set down his glass and moved to the door, where it was quieter. "I think our story is a harder story to tell," he said. "People don't know what we do best." He pointed to the Chardonnay, then mentioned the cabernets, the Syrahs, the Merlots, the Gewürztraminers, the Rieslings. "We have so many wines and grapes that we do well. People talk about Oregon and they mean Pinot, but they don't even know what the hell it is we do."

Well, a few do. On that spring release weekend, Small saw close to a thousand customers. As he talked, a limo drove by, and a private helicopter beat through the air over the winery and landed in a nearby field.

While the industry is growing fast now, Small hadn't expected it to take this long. He sees a future Washington with many more high-quality boutique wineries and a world-class reputation.

Yakima Valley

In the beginning was the Yakima River Valley, where the state's earliest vinifera was planted, thanks to the urging of scientists at the WSU Prosser Research Station.

As the Washington wine business aged, the valley changed. Like a wine, it lost its green flavor, deepened, and developed new characteristics. Last summer perhaps the biggest change was the increased focus on terroir, the French notion that place can affect the wine.

The Yakima Valley appellation is being broken up into specific American Viticultural Areas, a federal designation. Winemakers hope to use the new AVAs like Red Mountain, Horse Heaven Hills, and Wahluke Slope to express and market the distinct growing conditions of their areas, said Gail Puryear, owner and winemaker at Bonair Winery.

Puryear and his wife, Shirley, met as foreign language students at WSU in the late 1960s. They pursued jobs in education and social work in California. Two decades ago, they decided to move home and grow grapes on five acres of weeds and alfalfa near Toppenish. While they had good customers in the nearby wineries, just growing grapes wasn't satisfying. So they mortgaged their farm, started their own operation, and made their first batch in their bathroom. Today they have a full-blown winery, including one of the oldest vineyards in the state, which they purchased from the original owner. "It's not hard to make good wine around here. It's not rocket science. Just don't screw up," said Gail, the winemaker. They sometimes sit beneath a locust tree in front of the English Tudor-style tasting room and watch the cars come in, many with license plates from Oregon and California, noted Shirley one afternoon last summer.

Behind their tasting room and farther south across the Yakima River lies Horse Heaven Hills, Washington's seventh and newest AVA. It joins the Puget Sound, Yakima Valley, Walla Walla, Red Mountain, Columbia Gorge, and Columbia Valley appellations.

To the north of the valley is an area vying to be Wahluke Slope. And Bonair is right in the middle of what the Puryears hope will become the Rattlesnake Hills appellation. The area has nearly 30 growers, 23 wineries, and its own distinct set of weather, soil, water, and cultural conditions, Gail Puryear said.

So far the AVA movement has met little opposition. But some in the industry are cautious. "The only concern I have is that we don't want Washington growers and wineries pitting themselves against each other," said Ste. Michelle's Baseler. "Up to now, it has been such a collegial atmosphere." He fears that some may start declaring their appellation better than others. "Our position is this state offers so many kinds of terroir. And it's all good."

At the east end of the valley, where the Yakima River bends north around Red Mountain, the Williams family planted the first vines for Kiona Vineyards and Winery in 1975. Today, they still have some 30-year-old Cabernet vines in their 65 acres of grapes. The business was co-founded by WSU alumni John, who graduated in 1961, and Ann Williams, who graduated in 1963.

In jeans stained with grape juice and dust and with a sun-burned face, their son, Scott Williams, also a Coug, looks more like a farm hand than a recognized winemaker and winery manager. It would be hard to guess that he crafted the stunning Chenin Blanc ice wine that took the top award at the Northwest Enological Society judging last summer.

He has a real enthusiasm for his product, though he's quick to disclaim credit for it. "You don't have anything unless you have good grapes," he said. "Red Mountain grapes make very, very powerful, very structured wines with a lot of color and a lot of mouth feel." Most of the people who buy grapes from Red Mountain's vineyards use them as the backbone for their wines and then blend in other grapes, he said.

In many ways, the Williams family has been ahead of its time breaking sagebrush-covered land on Red Mountain and figuring out what to grow there. In others, the small operation is just now coming of age. Kiona's tasting room is still in the basement of John and Ann's house, but the family has plans to expand, with ground already broken on a new multi-million-dollar cellar and tasting room. And now they're watching as the land around is bought up by the likes of Hedges Cellars and Ste. Michelle. Since the 1970s, nine other wineries have popped up around them. And in ten years, Scott Williams predicted, the whole Red Mountain slope will be covered with grapes.

Seattle Again

Washington wine today is a tangle of trends. Pinot versus Merlot, Riesling back in style, new appellations sprouting across the landscape, and both growers and drinkers wondering what grape they should grow next.

But that's all good news for members of the now three-decade-old Northwest Enological Society, who hosted their latest wine judging in August. They're ever willing to support and sample from Washington's wealth of wines. This year they had bottles from 190 wineries to try, including some from WSU alumni-connected wineries like Alexandria Nicole Cellars, Kiona Vineyards and Winery, Kestrel Vintners, and newcomer Saint Laurent Winery. Among the submissions were Muscat, ice wine, and lemberger, as well as the traditional Chardonnays and Bordeaux blends.

They met early one morning last August on the 40th floor of the glass-encased Bank of America Building in downtown Seattle. While busloads of people on their way to work poured into the streets below, the attention upstairs focused on the judges silently tasting wines in their cardboard booths. The volunteers in an adjoining room, though busy opening bottles and prepping trays of glasses, did a little sampling of their own.

Sally Hooper picked a glass of Viognier, sipped, and raised her eyebrows. This was one of the perks of dedicating two long days of pouring, washing, and toting, a duty Hooper, a 1957 WSU alumna, and her husband, Paul, who graduated from WSU in 1953, have shared for the past decade. The couple joined the wine society in its second year at the urging of friends, but only ten years ago got into helping with the judging. "This is a tough job to get. Everyone wants to do it," said Paul Hooper, a retired transportation engineer.

In the other room, the five judges, including a wine writer from the *Washington Post* and a California winemaker, finished their rounds and then argued through what they thought deserved awards. Snippets of their talk filtered back to the prep room: the Merlots were too syrupy, none merited a gold. Later, word came that the Viogniers had some pleasant surprises, and the Syrahs were sublime.

That night, the Hoopers and a few hundred of their wine society friends heard the final rulings at Bellevue's Woodmark Hotel. Sitting beneath a white tent, with the waves of Lake Washington chopping behind them, they learned that three of the Syrahs had met the gold standard.

On the edge of his seat, Glenn Nelson made careful notes, limiting his enthusiasm to a smile when one of his favorites made the list. Others weren't so reserved, cheering and clapping at familiar names.

Nelson, who coordinates many of the wine society events during the year, and his wife, Judy, planned their week around this evening. They manage to fit wine into many of their activities, even tying trips to Walla Walla into WSU football weekends. "It just makes sense, doesn't it," said Judy, who was sampling a Cave B Merlot during the salad course. "We love wine. We love WSU."

Along with the state's wine industry, the Northwest Enological Society has matured over the past 30 years. Today, the group has chapters throughout the region, the largest being the Seattle Wine Society, which hosted the judging and dinner. The membership still numbers in the hundreds, but now the society competes with a growing number of other wine clubs based out of wine shops, wineries, and even Boeing, proving that Washingtonians have cultivated a real taste for wine. They'll be ready for the growth to come, say industry leaders.

In the past year, pieces about the state's fast-growing wine industry have appeared in the food and travel sections of most major papers and in periodicals such as *Town and Country, Time, Men's Health,* and *Newsweek.* The word has long been out that Walla Walla can produce world-class Cabernets, that in the beginning Riesling was king, and that today Washington is the second largest U.S. state in wine-production and grape acreage.

"But we've only scratched the surface," Baseler said. "I figure the state will have 40,000 to 45,000 acres of grapes over the next five years.

"We'll be the same size as Napa," he said. "Then it starts to get serious."

Outside In—Architecture of the Pacific Northwest

Hannelore Sudermann

It's a cool morning in October when the door to Rex Hohlbein's Fremont studio swings open. Four Washington State University architecture students crowd into the small entry looking at once curious and nervous.

Hohlbein, a 1981 WSU alum, solidly Seattle in a plaid shirt and fleece jacket, greets the group, which includes his daughter Jennifer. They have come to Seattle to make presentations in front of professional architects at a firm downtown. One carries an unwieldy printed display he needs to trim. Recalling his own days as an architecture student at WSU, Hohlbein urges him to open it up on the floor and crop it there.

In the meantime, he and Jennifer talk about the students' visit to the well-known Miller Hull Partnership that afternoon and the lecture they would attend that night. The other students soak in the office, visiting with one of Hohlbein's partners and glancing at photographs of the firm's completed homes on Vashon

Island, in Ellensburg, on Orcas Island, and at Yarrow Point. In one example, an island cabin makes practical use of plywood in the kitchen. In another an eastern Washington farmhouse radiates off a great room. In a third a traditional-style retreat nestles into a wooded hillside.

While the homes are all different, they share an aesthetic. There's warm wood detailing inside and out, expansive glass windows, exposed structural components, and deep overhangs—all details of what could be described as Northwest elements of style.

The students are even seeing elements of the style in the 1906 house Hohlbein renovated to serve as his studio. The place sits on a one-way street tucked up against the ship canal. One of his first improvements was a floor-to-ceiling picture window to bring in the subtle Seattle light and feature the view of the Burke-Gilman Trail and the water, people, and boats outside.

His design template includes natural materials, a simple and elegant aesthetic, and building in a way that is sensitive to the region, the neighborhood, and especially the site. It all comes out of the feeling he gets having grown up in the Northwest, he said later. "Seattle was a sleepy city most of my life. We're not flashy. We're quiet. We live in a gray world, with subdued, soft light. With such beautiful scenery around us, the thinking is 'Hey, let's be a little quieter. Let's go out and blend in and take it all in.'"

The Hinoki House, a new view home in Bellevue's 1950s Clyde Hill neighborhood, fits beautifully with the Northwest style. The owners themselves started with a list of classic Northwest desires that included creating an open-concept home within the older neighborhood, using natural materials, and capturing a stunning Lake Washington view.

"It was going to be a bigger house to begin with, but I said, 'Really, you should worry about it being too big,'" Hohlbein said. "There's a coziness and connectedness that would be lost."

While the view across the lake is stunning, Hohlbein didn't want the home to be just about the distant view. "We did not try to line everything up, and did not want to block the views of other people in the neighborhood." He spent time on the property exploring. It required an approach from a busy street, through an alley, and then a courtyard. He saw it as a migration from a public self to a private self. While the view is the big payoff, he worked to create beautiful spaces and experiences in the house before arriving at the view. "The house should be able to stand on its own."

A hallmark of the Hinoki house is walls made out of windows. It's a tradeoff, Hohlbein said. It is perhaps less energy-efficient, but it does different things in different spaces. In the kitchen, it lets in light and views of the trees. In the dining room, it provides a serene scene of the pond and courtyard. But the most wondrous effect is in the living room, where the windows slide away, and you feel as if you could walk right out onto the lake.

Hohlbein didn't come to WSU to study architecture. "But I just fell in love with drawing," he said. "At the end of that first year, I decided to switch." The new direction gave school new meaning. He lived for his classes and projects. "And I couldn't wait to get out and practice," he said.

He loves the process of working with residential clients. "You talk a lot about very personal and important decisions," he said. "Besides raising kids, building a house is probably the most intense thing adults will sustain. Their hearts and minds are fully engaged."

And if his clients are seeking to make a statement with their homes, he hopes that it is one of quiet, thoughtful design. "Houses and buildings should be backdrops to peoples' lives, and secondarily, buildings should be subservient to the landscape."

A Style of Our Own

Architecture in the Pacific Northwest has always had to contend with the environment.

In many parts of the country, the builders of great cities started with flat planes and created their landscapes out of brick and stone, steel and glass. But in the West, a land of mountains, water, forests, and views, the natural landscape usually came first. Here the early architects had to nestle their structures in valleys and along shorelines. Then their neighborhoods climbed the hills of cities like Spokane, Bellingham, Tacoma, and Seattle, always looking to the views around them.

The architects took climate into consideration, orienting to capture much-needed sunlight in winter, and designing sheltering overhangs to protect from the rain. Some might say they were building green long before the notion was in style.

When you see that iconic scenic photograph of the state's largest city, said Phil Gruen, associate professor at the WSU School of Architecture and Construction Management, it's the Space Needle with the mountains in the background. "Seattle is the metropolis in the natural environment," he said.

The same description could easily be extended to other Northwest cities, he adds. Spokane, for example, has the slogan: "Near nature, near perfect."

Gruen, who teaches history of architecture, is loath to describe one type of architecture as specifically "Northwest." For each detail there are many examples, and many exceptions. And some are not so great. Indoor shopping malls for an auto-centered culture, for example—Northgate Mall, which was built in 1950, was the first car-focused indoor mall in the country. It was an idea that first happened here, Gruen said. "But nobody would say that it is an example of the Pacific Northwest architecture."

Still, in other structures, there seems to be a Pacific Northwest idiom, Gruen admitted. It's a particular kind of consciousness that connects the materials, the structure, and the natural environment.

Architects from WSU like Hohlbein have had a hand in shaping the state's built environment, and in incorporating it into the Northwest landscape, for nearly a century. But it was almost not to be. Decades ago, the fledgling architecture program at Washington State was nearly crushed.

In 1907, Washington's agricultural college, now WSU, established one of the first programs to train architects on the West Coast—after the University of California at Berkeley. When the college's early leaders started their search for a chair, architects from the Midwest and East Coast were coming west to help build the new communities. Kirtland Cutter, from Ohio, was designing Arts and Crafts mansions throughout the state, and James Stephen, from Chicago, was creating school buildings in Seattle and Everett after designing Thompson Hall in Pullman in 1893. The four-story Victorian building was constructed out of brick made from clay deposits on campus.

In drafting a plan to train architects in Pullman, the college's leaders believed that architecture would fit in well among the mechanic arts. They also saw an economical route to building their campus. Rudolph Weaver was hired from the architectural staff of the University of Illinois and immediately took on the design of buildings for Pullman's campus. "We looked upon it also as a measure of economy to combine these instructional and professional functions in such a department," wrote President Enoch A. Bryan in his *Historical Sketch of the State College*.

Weaver's first project was the president's house. The thought, according to Bryan, was to try him out on a smaller, less essential structure. Its success is apparent since the Weaver-designed Wilson-Short and Carpenter halls followed in rapid succession. For a few years, both the program and the building progress held up.

But when Ernest O. Holland became president of Washington State College in 1916, the years of growth both for the curriculum and for campus were about to end. A legislative committee from Olympia had visited the college and was surprised to find graduate students in Pullman as well as strong liberal arts and architecture programs. Concerned that the state was already paying too much for higher education, the committee decided that the University of Washington should be acting as a university and that the college in Pullman be reduced to a trade school. To Holland's dismay, an old friend, the UW's president Henry Suzzallo, agreed.

Suzzallo and Holland started their friendship as students in 1909 at Columbia University. Holland was best man at Suzzallo's wedding in 1912. Suzzallo moved west to become president of UW in 1915 and almost immediately encouraged Holland in his pursuit of the Pullman job. At the same time, both men were urging an end to, in Bryan's words, the "petty rivalry" between the institutions.

But they were overtaken by politics. There were concerns that the schools were duplicating their offerings at great cost to the taxpayers.

In 1921, the state legislature created the Joint Board of Higher Curricula to oversee development of programs for the University of Washington and Washington State. In 1922, UW, which hadn't established its architecture department until 1914, challenged the state college's offering of an architecture major. As a result, it was one of several programs deemed "illegal" by the legislature, including commerce, journalism, and forestry.

But according to school records, Pullman found a way around it. By 1928 the degree in architecture became "architecture engineering." The students would study alongside the school's construction managers and civil engineers. Because they studied and competed with students in other disciplines, the architects who trained at WSC had a rigorous grounding in engineering—something alumni say made them sought-after assets to their firms.

It took some redesigning on the part of the state college to keep architecture in the mix, but it led to training many hundreds of architects for the state.

While all this was taking place, a Northwest architectural style was emerging, said Phil Jacobson, a 1952 WSU alum, retired Seattle architect, and professor emeritus of UW's architecture program. While much of the early building is derivative of architecture from around the country—with Arts and Crafts, Beaux Arts, and International styles—a Northwest aesthetic emerged in the timber framing, exposed wood beams, open spaces, and large windows designed to capture the Northwest light, he said. The developing style is also reflected in how the buildings fit within their site and landscape.

"There is a Northwest school for architecture," Jacobson said. "In my judgment, it is primarily in the area of residential design. It's much clearer there than anywhere else."

After World War II a strong Northwest vernacular really took shape, he explained. Families settled into the Puget Sound region and the demand for new housing skyrocketed. The local architects, unfettered by their clients' demands for a certain style, not limited to build within established neighborhoods, and freed to use new materials, started pushing further into the landscape. Some beautiful examples include Surrey Downs, a neighborhood of 1950s Northwest-style ranchers built with minimal disturbance to the land by architect Omer Mithün in Bellevue, said Jacobson. Others can be found in communities like Fircrest and University Place in Tacoma and the South Hill in Spokane.

Jacobson, who watched the movement develop, readily lists the key architects of the Northwest school. Among them: Paul Thiry, Omer Mithün, Paul Hayden Kirk, and Fred Bassetti.

Thiry, who is considered a father of modernism in the Pacific Northwest, started off in the 1930s with International-style homes and apartment buildings. As times changed, so did he. By the 1950s and early '60s his structures were like sculpture. He was the principal architect for the Seattle World's Fair and can be credited with the Pacific Science Center and the Coliseum. By the time of the 1962 fair, the Pacific Northwest was getting international recognition for its architecture and buildings that connected with the landscape, captured light, and had attention to detail.

While most of their work centers on Puget Sound, Thiry and a number of other architects are represented in Pullman, said WSU's Gruen. Thiry designed the Regents Hill buildings. Kirk's trademark bands of windows are evident in the American Institute of Architects award-winning red brick French Administration building. And Bassetti built Avery Hall to harmonize with the old quad.

The regional architecture that developed during that time used natural materials, brought in the outdoors, and incorporated some very early "green" practices like economy of materials and building to capture heat and sunlight, Jacobson said. It fits well with today's Northwest and sustainable aesthetic.

A Sustainable Aesthetic

All local cultures contain an essence that must be discovered or preserved and which expresses the uniqueness of a place. For architects in the Pacific Northwest, that essence is the fundamental understanding of the conditions of ecology and their effect on architectural values and meaning. Significant aspects of this essence lie in local geography, climate, and customs and involve the use and transformation of mimicking of vernacular forms ...

—1968 WSU alum David Miller, *Toward a New Regionalism, Environmental Architecture in the Pacific Northwest*

Late at night back when David Miller and Robert Hull were architecture students at WSU—they both graduated in 1968—they would sneak into the agricultural buildings around town. "We were interested in how those structures contrasted with the landscape," Miller said. "We were impressed by the toughness, economy, and directness of this kind of buildings."

"We wanted an understanding of why things are the way they are in any particular area," added Hull, who was fascinated not just with the technology of building the buildings, but how, with materials and orientation, people were adapting them to the area's hot summers and cold winters.

That and their separate tours in the Peace Corps creating buildings with local materials in Afghanistan and Brazil, helped them hone their practice of developing socially responsible, simple, innovative designs that respond to environmental demands. After working in separate firms for several years, the two in 1977 decided to create their own firm. Since then, it has grown to 50 employees and completed hundreds of projects, including the Shock Physics Lab at WSU and the Northwest Maritime Center in Port Townsend. They have received national recognition for their work. In 2003 the AIA gave them the Architecture Firm Award for producing distinguished architecture for more than a decade. "Miller | Hull has defined Pacific Northwest regional modernism in a way that inspires architects around the globe to respond to the unique characteristics of their own regions," wrote their nominator.

While Miller and Hull had to sneak into barns and grain elevators to look around, last year 18 WSU graduate students were given an assignment to follow in their footsteps. They turned their focus to a grain silo 12 miles south of Pullman in the town of Colton. The silo soon after blew down, said their instructor Taiji Miyasaka, who had been consulting with the owner to find alternatives for the structure. It had been slated to be dismantled and the wood reused in other projects, but it had more than 130,000 nails, too many for salvaging. "I was not trying to advocate that we have to save the building," Miyasaka said. "But it was an interesting space and interesting structure." So he sent the students out to document and measure it in different ways.

The 18, including Jennifer Hohlbein and her classmates, logged many hours there inside and out, thinking of ways people might approach and experience it. Two camped on the property for 24 hours to record how light changed at the silo throughout the day. In the end they were all asked to summarize their thoughts and ideas and present them to professional architects at Miller | Hull in Seattle. The nervous students carried their models and displays into the office, which occupies the entire sixth floor of the Polson Building downtown.

The studio project is designed to kick-start the students into their graduate thesis project, Miyasaka said. Their main objective is to just spend time on the site and get a feel for it. "These students are not contaminated by the practicality of a project. That gives them an opportunity to leap. It makes for some exciting ideas," he said.

"I try to get my students to explore by themselves," he said. "I just hope they keep exploring."

Significantly Washington

Adriana Janovich

Of course, Seattle's iconic Space Needle is on the list.

So is the Pacific Science Center, Smith Tower, and Seattle Central Library, along with the Amazon Spheres, multiple museums—of Flight, Glass, Pop Culture, and more—and several entire towns: the Bavarian-themed Leavenworth, Victorian seaport of Port Townsend, and company mill town of Port Gamble.

Washington State University made the cut, too.

The most difficult part of the project, said J. Philip "Phil" Gruen, was narrowing down the list to a hundred significant sites in the state. "There could have been a thousand sites," said Gruen, associate professor in the School of Design and Construction at WSU's Voiland College of Engineering and Architecture.

Gruen recently served as one of the coordinators of Washington's Classic Buildings for SAH Archipedia, an online encyclopedia produced by the Society of Architectural Historians. The site contains entries for more than 20,000 landscapes, structures, monuments, and buildings across America. Its open-access component, SAH Archipedia Classic Buildings, contains maps, photos, and peer-reviewed essays for more than 4,100 structures in all 50 states.

Gruen and Robert R. Franklin, who earned his master's degree in history from WSU in 2014, the other project coordinator and assistant director of the Hanford History Project at WSU Tri-Cities, were tasked in 2015 with selecting the most representative works of Washington state's built environment. They enlisted the help of 25 colleagues statewide—current and retired professors, graduate students, architecture professionals—to document each location's building materials, techniques, and styles, as well as social and political contexts.

"We could have made it easier on ourselves by just selecting old buildings or buildings designed by well-known architects," said Gruen, who teaches modern and vernacular architecture, historic preservation, the global history of design, and the built environment of the Pacific Northwest, including local and regional landscapes of the Palouse. He also serves on Pullman's Historic Preservation Commission and WSU's Historic Preservation Committee.

Instead, he and his collaborators considered contemporary as well as historical structures, famous and lesser-known designers, rural and urban locations, and variety in structure type—from private residences and places of worship to commercial buildings, including a tavern and a parking garage, to public spaces such as libraries, schools, and athletic arenas. Some of the sites that they considered don't house buildings at all, but bridges, roads, or elevated tracks such as the Seattle Monorail.

Ultimately, Gruen said, these sites "had to be representative of the state. For us, that meant sites related to the landscape of the Northwest in some fashion. Most places we chose had some connection to the landscape or the context in which they sat—be that sky, water, forest, mountains, or hills."

Gruen and his team made sure to include places that are important to indigenous and underrepresented peoples, including women. "In my view, almost everything is significant—if you're willing to work hard enough to talk to the people, to do the research, to dig up the archives, and to understand that the built environment is more than just famous old buildings designed by old White men. Looking at sites that way, I think, is a type of social justice architecture."

Geographical balance was also important and, in the end, Gruen and his team included sites in almost every county in Washington state. Some of the locations they chose contain multiple structures. In all, their list of 100 sites encompasses 235 separate entries, including 17 at WSU Pullman. Gruen and Franklin edited all of the entries, researched and wrote about four dozen entries, and photographed the bulk of them.

Above all, Gruen said, "we wanted to tell stories—stories about place, about culture, about people."

As a historian of the built environment, Gruen emphasizes interpretation and narrative as critical tools for reading human-made surroundings. His expertise lies in American architecture and urbanism of the nineteenth, twentieth, and twenty-first centuries.

"Historians tend to focus on design and style and names and dates. But, fundamentally, it's meaning. How did the designs resonate? The life inside the buildings—that's how people begin to bring meaning to buildings," Gruen said. "When we start to tell those stories, they become the architecture of the building, in many ways."

Ten significant examples
A few of the 235 structures in Washington's Classic Buildings

Seattle Central Library, Seattle
This is sleekness in Seattle, a library for the digital age, a dynamic, light-filled, and unconventional edifice with a distinctive diamond-shaped exterior grid of steel and glass. This is, wrote Jaime Lynn Rice, academic program manager in WSU's

School of Design and Construction, "one of the few buildings to place Seattle firmly on the international architectural map."

Completed in 2004 for nearly $170 million, the 11-story Seattle Central Library encompasses a full city block and more than 350,000 square feet. Its exterior planes resemble stacked volumes while interior spaces are open and flexible to adapt to changing needs. Rem Koolhaas and Joshua Prince-Ramus of the Rotterdam-based Office of Metropolitan Architecture designed the contemporary public space with exposed structural elements and dramatic uses of color. Escalators radiate an almost neon chartreuse. A spiral connects four floors of bookstacks via gently sloped ramps. A mixing chamber, modeled after trading rooms, holds more than 100 computers. A dumbwaiter carries books between the stacks and the chamber.

Stadium High School, Tacoma

Construction started in 1891 on what was to become a luxury hotel resembling a French chateau. When a financial crisis hit two years later, the unfinished hotel was used as railroad storage. By the time the Tacoma School District bought it in 1904, the building had been partially dismantled, having sustained heavy fire damage in 1898. Tacoma High School opened in 1906, was renamed in 1913, and has since been renovated several times. In 1999, Stadium High School served as the setting for *10 Things I Hate About You*. Its Stadium Bowl, also seen in the film, opened in 1910 with seating for 32,000 and breathtaking views of Commencement Bay. Presidents Theodore Roosevelt, Woodrow Wilson, and Warren G. Harding gave speeches there. John Phillip Sousa and Louis Armstrong performed there. And WSU's football team played there in 1917 against a team from Fort Lewis, in 1941 against Texas A&M, and in 1948 against Penn State.

Governor's Mansion, Olympia

This three-story, red-brick, Georgian Revival mansion, designed by the Tacoma-based firm of Russell & Babcock, was completed with 19 rooms in 1909. Governor Marion E. Hay, his wife, Lizzie, and their five children were the first inhabitants. The mansion continues to serve as the state's executive residence. A 1975 renovation added about 4,000 square feet to the back of the building. Since then, the home has only seen slight alterations.

Rothschild House Museum, Port Townsend

Washington's smallest state park encompasses a half-acre atop a bluff overlooking Port Townsend Bay. The heart of the property is a simple, two-story, Greek Revival home built in 1868 by one of Port Townsend's early merchants.

David C. H. "The Baron" Rothschild opened his downtown mercantile in 1858, living with his wife, Dorette, and their first three children above the business. Their last two children, Emilie and Eugene, were born in the eight-room uptown house, which includes a formal dining room, parlor, sewing room, and children's playroom. Emilie, Port Townsend's first librarian, lived there until her death in 1954. Eugene, who had long since moved to Seattle, deeded the property to the state five years later.

The Rothschild House Museum opened to the public in 1962, giving guests a glimpse into what life was like for a prominent family in Washington's Victorian seaport in the second half of the nineteenth century.

Cape Disappointment Lighthouse, Ilwaco

Washington's oldest operating lighthouse stands at the mouth of the Columbia River, the most dangerous entrance to a commercial waterway in the world. Since the late 1700s, more than 2,000 vessels have wrecked in the Columbia Bar's shifting sands, high seas, and heavy winds, including the *Oriole*, which, in 1853, was carrying building materials to erect a lighthouse to help other ships escape the same fate. Construction finally got underway after another supply ship arrived the following year. The Cape Disappointment Lighthouse was first lighted October 15, 1856. It stands 53 feet tall and tapers from a diameter of just over 14 feet to 10.5 feet at the lantern room. Its distinctive black horizontal band was added in 1930. The light was automated in 1973.

Rolling Huts, Mazama

Situated on the eastern edge of the North Cascades, this pack of six, two-hundred-square-foot, contemporary cabins offers an elevated Washington state-style camping experience. Their award-winning design features modular furniture and hardy, low-maintenance materials. The steel, glass, and wood structures, created by Tom Kundig and completed in 2007, stand three feet above the ground and are topped with butterfly roofs. Sliding glass doors and wraparound decks give campers spectacular views of the mountains, meadow, and trees. Set close to nature, the industrial-looking, minimalist huts are outfitted with wood-burning fireplaces, Wi-Fi, and microwaves, but no bathrooms.

Stonehenge Memorial, Goldendale

This concrete replica of England's famous Neolithic structure honors Klickitat County's World War I dead. Dedicated July 4, 1918, it's likely the oldest full-scale Stonehenge replica in the world. The Stonehenge Memorial stands on 5,300 acres purchased by affluent industrialist Sam Hill in 1907 with the dream of creating a Quaker farming community along the Columbia River. The remote location and lack of irrigation ultimately caused that project to fail. And, in 1914, work began on what was to be his hilltop Beaux Arts mansion; instead, Maryhill Museum of Art opened in 1940. The memorial, completed and rededicated in 1929, stands 16 feet tall and remembers 14 local men who lost their lives in the "war to end all wars."

Teapot Dome Service Station, Zillah

This teapot-shaped gas station—short, stout, handle, spout—originally sat along the highway between Zillah and Granger. Today, the roadside attraction serves as Zillah's visitor center and reminder of a hundred-year-old scandal.

In 1921, President Warren G. Harding transferred control of three oil fields, intended as emergency naval fuel supplies, from the US Navy to the US Department of Interior. Interior Secretary Albert Fall then leased the reserves to two oil companies at low rates without competitive bidding. An investigation found Fall received $400,000 in bribes, and he became the first to be convicted of committing a felony while holding a Cabinet post.

One reserve was at Teapot Dome, Wyoming, and the incident became known as the Teapot Dome Scandal. It inspired Jack Ainsworth, whose father had a general store in the Yakima Valley, to install a kettle-shaped gas station beside the mercantile. The younger Ainsworth designed and built the structure in 1922, dubbing it "Teapot Dome." The circular, wood-shingled edifice stands 14 feet in diameter with 10-foot ceilings, a decorative sheet-metal handle, and concrete spout that functioned as a stove pipe.

Monroe Street Bridge, Spokane

When it was completed in 1911, the Monroe Street Bridge was the longest self-supporting arch in America and the third largest in the world. It replaced a steel bridge, which had replaced a short-lived wooden bridge lost to fire. City engineers designed the structure, and Spokane architects Kirtland Cutter and Karl Malmgren designed its four pedestrian pavilions adorned with life-size, bas-relief, concrete bison skulls. After a two-and-a-half-year, $18 million restoration led by the engineering and construction management firm of David Evans and Associates, the bridge—a key link between downtown and the north side of the city—reopened in 2005.

Stevens Hall, Pullman

WSU's first all-women's dormitory, named for former Washington territorial governor Isaac Stevens and completed in 1896, is WSU's oldest residence hall and second-oldest surviving building. It has been in continuous use since its completion, save for a year-long closure for rehabilitation in 1958.

Designed by the Seattle architectural firm of James Stephen and Timotheus Josenhans, Stevens Hall, done in New England Shingle Style with Pacific Northwest touches, feels classic and dignified yet unpretentious and homey. Local basalt, red brick quarried from clay deposits on campus, and sawn cedar shingles were used in the original build.

During the college's formative years, the hall served as a social center, hosting receptions, readings, dinners, dances, and teas.

Foggy sunrise over the Skagit Valley tulip fields
near the WSU–Mount Vernon Research Center
Photo © Alan Majchrowicz

Around the Sound

Kayaking in Henderson Inlet
Photo Zachary Hawn

Washington's Marine Highway

Pat Caraher

The ferry system has allowed the state to grow and prosper. It will become more important in the future, providing access to where people choose to live and work, and where housing is available.

— Mike Thorne, Washington State Ferries director and CEO

Washington State didn't offer a ferry service until 1951, although a handful of private companies known as "The Mosquito Fleet" transported passengers and goods across Puget Sound in the early 1900s on small steamers. By the late 1920s, the industry consolidated into two companies. In 1935, the Kitsap County Transportation Company was forced out of business by a strike, leaving the Puget Sound Navigation Company, which became the Black Ball Line, to provide the bulk of the service.

In the late 1940s, labor unions representing the ferry workers successfully struck Black Ball for higher wages. The ferry line petitioned the state highway department to allow a 30 percent tariff increase. The request was denied. Black Ball tied up its boats, bringing much of the cross-sound ferry service to a halt.

Black Ball eventually sold its ferries and terminals in 1951 for $5 million to a newly created Washington Toll Bridge Authority, now Washington State Ferries. WSF intended to provide temporary service until a network of bridges could be built connecting Puget Sound's east and west sides. By 1959 the legislature rejected the plan for bridges. WSF continued to ferry people and vehicles across the sound as part of the Washington State Department of Transportation.

Sailing into the 21st Century

Today Washington operates the largest ferry system in the country. Twenty-nine ferries ply the inland waterways of Puget Sound. The boats deliver nearly 27 million passengers annually to 20 different terminals in eight Washington counties plus the province of British Columbia.

For daily commuters, commercial users, and tourists, Washington's marine highway provides a critical link between the greater Seattle area and expanding communities west of Puget Sound on the Kitsap Peninsula, as well as to Vashon, Kitsap County, Whidbey Island, and the San Juan Islands.

During fiscal 2001, WSF transported 11.5 million vehicles and 26.6 million riders. This compares with 28.4 million passengers at Seattle-Tacoma International Airport and 23.5 million patrons nationwide served by Amtrak during the same period.

Sailing into the 21st century, Washington State Ferries appeared to be in good financial shape. Reserves exceeded $110 million. Referendum 49, approved by state taxpayers in 1998, designated funds for needed passenger-only ferry service to Seattle from Kingston and Southworth. In fiscal 2001, 19,700 walk-on passengers, or 27 percent of ferry riders, benefited from the service. Referendum 49 allowed for the transfer of monies from the motor vehicle excise tax (MVET) to the state highway system, and the legislature appropriated a record $289 million of that to WSF.

Things were to change dramatically. In November 1999 voters approved Initiative 695. The backwash rippled through state transportation, reducing funds for roads, highways, bridges, and the ferries. In effect, I-695 abolished the bulk of the MVET, including an expected $111 million designated for the 1999–2001 biennium to help finance the expansion of the passenger-only ferry service. The plan to enhance that service had to be scrubbed. The timetable for replacing aging ferries and terminals also was pushed back.

Thorne Takes the Helm

The task of righting the ship fell to Mike Thorne. He was hired in January 2002 as WSF director and CEO. His credentials included more than a decade as director of the Port of Portland and 18 years as an Oregon state legislator. He grew up on a large wheat ranch in Pendleton, Oregon, and still kept a hand in the operation that his son now runs. Thorne earned a degree in agricultural mechanization from Washington State University in 1962.

Before he came aboard, WSF was instructed to take a close look at its way of doing business, specifically the relationship between the cost of providing service and the income generated from riders. In 2000, the legislature created the Joint Task Force on Ferries comprising legislators, citizens, ferry management, and workers. The group was charged with examining the WSF operation and recommending its future direction. One recommendation was that WSF increase fares throughout the system to 80 percent of operating cost and maintain the existing level of service. Historically fares had provided about 62 percent of operating costs.

"We can't capitalize the ferry system from fare box recovery alone," said Thorne, who wanted WSF to be "customer-minded and business-oriented."

In September 2002, nine months after he was hired, WSF introduced a new business and capital-funding plan, dubbed the "5+5+5" plan. It called for the ferry system to cut costs by 5 percent, increase general fares by 5 percent, and generate 5 percent in new revenues via a comprehensive retail, marketing, and advertising program. After designing and implementing the plan, Thorne estimated that fares should cover approximately three-quarters of operating cost by the end of 2003 and near 90 percent by 2008.

Had Referendum 51 not failed in November 2002, it would have provided approximately $750 million for new ferry construction over 10 years. But with the 5+5+5 plan in place, Thorne thought the ferry system was headed in a positive direction.

"We can do better."

WSF was looking at introducing small retail businesses, like gifts and books, and expanding concessions to include food and beverage items not currently available from galley service or vending machines on the ferry. "What best fits the needs of our customers," Thorne said in late July 2003 from his office near the Seattle Center.

He was confident savvy marketing would provide better visibility for WSF and attract more riders, both in-state and beyond.

"When you are pushing hard to make financial goals, it makes good sense to advertise on the ferry itself and in the terminal, if done discreetly," he said. Travel packages could be developed as an incentive for people to ride the ferry during non-peak-hour service to the San Juan Islands, or elsewhere. Ferries on some routes run one-fourth full. Passengers could be added without increasing costs to WSF.

Thorne said two core principles figured in decisions to reduce service: WSF wanted to impact the fewest number of riders and make changes only where riders have other transportation. Three vessels were idled in June 2000, before his watch. Ridership declined slightly in 2001 and likely will continue—without additional promotion—due to sustained cuts in service and ongoing fare hikes.

Immediately after I-695 passed, WSF conducted a thorough review of administrative and staff positions. Management and support staff were reduced by 29 percent, including 43 positions from the management side, representing 2.4 percent of WSF's 1,800 employees.

"We are at a level we would not want to go much (below)," Thorne said. "I think we can find efficiency in other areas of support." He also said he believed basic services were being met, and most riders agreed. But, he said, "We can do better."

Statistics showed that ferries completed 99.6 percent of 178,500 scheduled runs in fiscal 2001, the best record dating back to 1966, when WSF started tracking the reliability of its service.

Ferry schedules continued to be reviewed. For example, management concluded that more than an acceptable rate of overtime was being logged on one of the Seattle-Bainbridge runs. The situation was remedied by adjusting the schedule for that route.

Keeping WSF running on time, with safety and security, was all-important, Thorne said. "People use the ferry system as a way of supporting their livelihood."

While safe and serviceable, some ferries needed to be replaced. The average age of the fleet was 30 years old. Four ferries were built in 1927. Their commercial application was "far outdated."

They were designed to haul cars built in the 1920s and '30s, not wide-bodied trucks and long trailer rigs loaded with chips and logs.

Ferry terminals, too, were getting to the point where their pilings and underpinnings will soon be beyond usefulness. Long-term plans called for replacing several terminals on Puget Sound. Terminals at Edmonds and Mukilteo were planned as connection points for rail service extending into Seattle.

Despite the serious financial challenges facing WSF, Thorne remained positive. He was confident goals will be met, that riders will continue to find the service they need and expect. "If I hadn't believed that," he said, "I probably wouldn't have come here in January 2002."

Thorne's office was close to Puget Sound, and he rode the ferry. He intentionally scheduled meetings that took him to communities served by the WSF. "I go there so people don't have to come to me," he said. During his marine travels, he observed WSF employees carrying out their duties and sometimes visited with patrons.

What Commuters Say
Even in mid-afternoon, one sensed the pace picking up at Colman Dock. Foot passengers began to arrive, first in a trickle, then in a stream. Some grabbed the *Seattle Times* from a bank of newspaper vending machines in the elevated terminal. They flashed their tickets while passing through the gate or pay their fare at one of three ticket booths leading to the large, bench-filled waiting room.

Below, on the landing north of the terminal, vehicles fed into lanes 43 through 58, nine-deep, in parallel rows. The arrival of the *Wenatchee* from Bainbridge was still 15 minutes away. A Mack truck with an image of the Statue of Liberty painted on the side of its black hood stood out. It was burdened with bales of green hay. Ahead of the waiting vehicles, nine bicyclists pinched in near the steel ramp that will be lowered to meet the ferry.

If he had been in the terminal, Thorne might have met commuters like Mike Crotty, dressed in gray shorts and a matching T-shirt with "O'Dea Football" printed on the chest in purple letters. A teacher and coach at the high school on top of Seattle's First Hill, he made the nine-block hike to and from the ferry each day. He commuted from Bremerton like some of his students, others of whom come from Bainbridge.

Crotty used to live in Des Moines. Now he preferred "the slower pace of life" on the Kitsap Peninsula. "The cost of living is less, even with the commute," he said.

Tracy Hagbo was a WSF information agent at Colman Dock. Her work finished, she took in the foot traffic on the concourse outside her office through dark sunglasses. She lived in West Seattle. "When housing got high over here, people sought cheaper housing on the Kitsap Peninsula," she said. "They've still got to get across the water. That's the bottom line."

Another woman on the Seattle-Bainbridge run commuted three days a week—"a little over an hour door-to-door." It beat fighting freeway gridlock on I-5. One-third of her commuting neighbors felt the same way. She came to Seattle from Chicago, but moved to Bainbridge Island three years ago. The major appeals—a smaller community, more house and a little more property for the money, and quality schools. Even with two fare hikes in 18 months, the cost of riding the ferry was comparable to taking Seattle's Metro buses, she said.

Being tied to the ferry schedule, particularly missing a ferry or finding it full, can be frustrating, she admitted. "But there's always another one." She and most of her friends gave the ferry system good marks, although she said she'd like to see more retail businesses on the ferry or in the terminal—"shoe repair, dry cleaning, and a book store."

At the end of each run, the boat was cleared of all passengers for a cabin sweep. "We want to make sure the ferry is secure for the next trip," said blue-uniformed deckhand LeRoy Augustine, stepping aside to let passengers board at Bainbridge. "It's a Mariner crowd going to the game tonight."

"Every deckhand, galley personnel, and engineer has special duties during fire, abandon ship, and rescue drills," said chief mate Victor M. Lotorto. One drill was conducted weekly.

Here to Stay

Those who worked with Thorne described him as a man of "tremendous integrity," driven to be as good a public servant as he can be.

He was sometimes frustrated that things took so long to accomplish. Since early in his WSF tenure, he had wanted to transform Pier 52—Colman Dock—into a more retail-friendly establishment. The remodeling began in fall 2003.

For many it was "a very outward sign" that things were changing with the ferry system. WSF was also slated to build two new ferries over the next three to five years. A management team was charged with finding $120 million for that effort. The legislature was set to help fund a third ferry.

"If there's truly an interesting side of Mike Thorne, it is his willingness to stand up and be held accountable," said a colleague. "At a time when new taxes and revenues are not available, he's willing to do business a different way. He's moving the ferry system toward being as self-sufficient as possible. I think the ferry system can get it done, knowing what I know about Mike Thorne's leadership and commitment."

Public opinion regarding the ferry system was highly favorable in general. That was not to say there weren't opportunities for improvement, Thorne said. "We've identified where we want to make the system run more efficiently—and the general baseline support needed. The people who use the ferries know we don't just have an eye on raising fares."

In June 2002, Washington State Ferries celebrated its 50th anniversary. The occasion clearly signified its service and commitment and that the ferries were here to stay. "The ferry system has allowed the state to grow and prosper," Thorne said. "It will become more important in the future—providing access to where people choose to live and work, and where housing is available."

Did he have a wish list for WSF?

"Yes. We have to think in terms of being as efficient and cost effective as we can. We have to look outside the traditional processes that you find in state government and more in terms of being entrepreneurial in delivering this essential service."

If the WSF was realistic and successful in reaching its goals, he said, "We will have a system that will be worth talking about at the 100-year anniversary."

Friendly People: Bill Hewitt Built Tillicum Village on Northwest Traditions

Pat Caraher

Blake Island seems miles, even decades, removed from metropolitan Seattle. The island was once a popular gathering place for the Duwamish and Suquamish

Indians. There's evidence that Seattle's namesake, Chief Sealth, leader of the Suquamish, was born on Blake.

But the island is only eight miles from Seattle's Pier 55. The 45-minute charter trip across Puget Sound affords magnificent views of the Olympic and Cascade mountain ranges, as well as Seattle's skyline. Deer, otter, and other wildlife inhabit the 473-acre island. Carved totem poles, depicting bears, ravens, and eagles, stand like stiff, silent sentries protecting a sacred place. Clam nectar is ladled out of big pots and served to visitors as they reach the terraced lawn in front of Tillicum Village at the water's edge.

"That's the best appetizer I've had in years," said one woman. She crushes the clamshells with her foot before entering the longhouse's heavy wooden double doors. The building is constructed of cedar posts and crossbeams and sided with split cedar planks.

Tillicum Village—"Tillicum" means "friendly people" in Chinook—celebrated its 40th anniversary in 2002. It has built a reputation on fresh-baked salmon, prepared inside the longhouse on cedar stakes over alderwood fires in the traditional manner of the Northwest Coast Indians. Guests file past circular fire pits where orange-pink slabs of salmon have been baking for an hour. Generous portions are served buffet-style on fish-shaped trays. Following the meal, the lights dim. Patrons sit quietly at long tables at right angles to the stage anticipating "Dance on the Wind." Some 100,000 people a year visit the village with as many as three tours departing the Seattle waterfront daily in July and August.

Tillicum Village was the vision of William S. "Bill" Hewitt, who graduated from Washington State College in 1942 with a degree in home economics and hotel and restaurant administration. The Seattle native wanted to build and operate a unique restaurant and cultural center in a longhouse. He grew up in Bremerton, where his father owned a restaurant near the naval shipyards. While completing his degree, he opened The Cougar Den, a small eatery in downtown Pullman, to help pay for his education.

Hewitt's training in the food industry would pay dividends during World War II. Drafted into the Army, he was assigned to the general's mess hall in the rear echelon away from the firing lines at the Battle of the Bulge. "That was the best break I ever had," he said.

After the war, he returned to Seattle. He was hired as a relief manager for Clark's Restaurants and later worked for Western Hotels. For two years, he was food department manager at the Newhouse Hotel in Salt Lake City. Later, he opened Hewitt's Café on 4th Avenue in downtown Seattle, then launched Hewitt's Catering Service. Early on, he catered for youth and church groups. He learned to bake salmon Indian-style with the head and backbone removed, and prepared the first "potlatch-style salmon bake" for the Boeing Airplane Co. in 1958. It was a big success, and business grew. He began looking for a place to build a longhouse to showcase his service. Blake Island proved to be the ideal site.

Hewitt's plan was to open Tillicum Village in April 1962 to capitalize on the tourist trade generated by the Seattle World's Fair. He thought the village would turn a profit from the beginning, gain momentum, and become a magnet for local organizations and groups. The venture's continued growth would ensure prosperity for years to come.

But things didn't go quite as smoothly as hoped.

From the living room of his waterfront home near the Fauntleroy ferry landing in West Seattle, Bill Hewitt pointed out Blake Island, flanked by Vashon Island to the south and Bainbridge Island to the north.

"There was nothing out there when we started," Hewitt said of the site that is now Tillicum Village. If allowed to build on Blake Island State Park, he agreed to take care of the pit toilets.

Mark Hewitt, who succeeded his father as president in 1990, was 11 or 12 when the logs being towed across Puget Sound to be used in construction of the original building were scattered to kingdom come in a storm. He remembered playing on the logs after they were rounded up and stacked on the beach.

"It was a gamble," Bill Hewitt explained.

The original building cost about $400,000. Friends in the plumbing and electrical trades provided him in-kind services for stock. First-year gross sales of $25,000 came to only 5 percent of the expected sales volume. The seasonal nature of the business, confusion regarding docking facilities on the island, and the fact that another company controlled virtually all of Seattle's tourism compounded Hewitt's difficulties. Debts soared. He went to the Chamber of Commerce for advice. Those reviewing the project said his only option was to file for bankruptcy. He would not consider doing that.

"The catering business supported us at the start," he explained. Fortunately, the year after the World's Fair ended, he and two partners landed the catering contract at the Seattle Center. But nine months later, he sold his half interest to focus on Tillicum Village. With hard work, perseverance, and faith he managed to get the operation on a sound financial footing.

"It took nearly 15 years," he said.

"One thing we find challenging is the preconceived idea people have of what they will find at Tillicum Village," Mark said. "What we do well is share the Pacific Northwest, with its water, islands, mountains, salmon, clams, native culture, deer, and lowland forests."

"Visitors will tell you what sets our place apart is the people," the senior Hewitt added.

Tillicum Village employs about 10 people year-round in its Seattle office. Another 12 to 15 work on Blake Island. In the peak summer months the island staff swells to nearly 60, most of them Native Americans.

From the start, none were more important than Hyacinth and Winnefred David, Native American elders and longtime village employees. They instilled a great respect for Indian tradition in their large family. The two youngest sons, Joe and George, have provided leadership and inspiration to fellow artisans in expanding the boundaries of their classical art forms, including the village's totems, masks, and other carvings on display. Brothers Benny and Douglas also worked at the village.

The Native American Dance Program, which had remained virtually unchanged since Tillicum Village opened, took on a new presence in 1992. Greg Thompson Productions began working on a stage set and script based on individual dances of the Northwest Coast Indians.

"We wanted something more professional, including the timing of the show," Mark explained of the result, "Dance on the Wind." While individual tribal customs differ, the tribes share many of the same traditions passed on from elders to their children and grandchildren. The Paddle Dance welcomes visitors to the potlatch, the ceremonial Mask Dance comes from the West Coast of Vancouver Island, and the Blanket Dance from the Lummi. The Dance of The Terrible Beast is a favorite. It tells in story and dance of a mythical creature that could fly like a bird, swim like a fish, walk upright like a human, and disappears at will.

Over the years, Tillicum has baked salmon throughout the world: on top of Mount St. Helens, Greece, the United Arab Emirates, Japan, Mozambique, and Namibia—the latter during a celebration marking delivery of a new Boeing 747-400 to Air Namibia. But in 1993, the world came to Tillicum.

In November of that year, at the invitation of President Bill Clinton, the fifth ministerial meeting of the Asia Pacific Economic Cooperation (APEC) conference was held in Seattle. Leaders from 14 member countries convened at Tillicum Village for a day to discuss the future of trade throughout the Pacific Rim.

"We had two things going for us," Mark said, "a remote location that officials thought would be secure, and our ability to work with the White House and U.S. State Department in preparing the site during the week prior to the event."

Preparations for the November 20 meeting began in mid-summer. Nearly everything had to be removed from the village's front lobby and longhouse, stored in vans, and parked a quarter-mile away. New carpeting was installed. Special furniture was brought in. Selected Indian art from Tillicum's collection was displayed. Millions of dollars of electrical communications equipment was installed to provide satellite links throughout the world. Six hundred media representatives were housed under a huge tent erected on the island's northeast point near Tillicum Village. The president and APEC delegates arrived at 9:45 a.m. The meeting concluded mid-afternoon.

"That was a lot of work for one day," Hewitt said.

After relinquishing control to Mark, Bill Hewitt would visit the village several times on weekdays and nearly every Saturday and Sunday. He enjoyed collecting tickets, passing out plates in the buffet line, and answering questions about the village's history.

While those visits became less frequent over time, Hewitt was aboard the *Good Time* charter boat operated by Argosy Tours on April 28, a beautiful Sunday afternoon—the day before his 85th birthday. The previous evening's attendance had topped 600, and nearly 600 pounds of salmon had been prepared.

Hewitt sat quietly in the sun outside the longhouse taking in the scene and observing the people before entering the dining hall.

"It's a nice feeling to see people have a good time," he said.

On the Waterfront

Hannelore Sudermann

Lara Herrmann is a personal injury lawyer with a busy practice. She's also a new mother balancing her work and family. Still, she has spent the past year thinking about Tacoma's history and ecology, and its tideflats and toxins. Whether she's working on a case or walking her baby in a stroller, in the back of her mind she's mulling a plan to protect her city's seven-mile waterfront.

Herrmann and a group of friends and neighbors are intent on righting the city's historical wrongs, helping finish the clean-up of some of its most polluted sites, protecting precious salmon habitat, and connecting the community with one of its greatest natural assets.

The great notion, which she shares with a grassroots group called Walk the Waterfront, is to complete a pedestrian path that would wind along the south shore of Commencement Bay from the Tacoma Dome past downtown and the adjoining historic neighborhood and all the way north and west out to the vibrant, verdant 700-acre public treasure known as Point Defiance Park. Such a path would bring more people to the waterfront to socialize, exercise, enjoy the scenery, learn some history, and visit small businesses scattered along the way.

It would also pass through and maybe revive some of the city's oldest and most derelict industrial sites, said Herrmann, who graduated from Washington State University in 1995. We talk about this over coffee one morning this summer in the warm café at the Spar, Tacoma's oldest operating saloon. We're in the Old Town neighborhood just two blocks up from Ruston Way, the part of the waterfront that gets the most public use. The sun and seagulls are out, and the air smells of salt.

The two-mile segment below us has parks, public piers and docks, restaurants, a hotel, and a long promenade that skirts the turquoise water's edge. It's what Herrmann envisions for the whole seven miles. But there is still Tacoma's industrial past to overcome, she said. The rest of the route east to downtown is blocked by industrial uses as well as by Schuster Parkway, a busy automotive bypass. Go too far in the other direction and you run smack into the Asarco smelter site, which has left Tacoma with several million tons of toxic waste.

While she is describing the waterfront's history and pointing out its views of Mount Rainier and the Olympics, Herrmann has an inspiration. "You have to see this," she said as she rushes us out to her Prius and whisks us several blocks up the hill through Old Town Tacoma, where the city's first homesteads were built in the late 1800s. We stop in a manicured neighborhood of old and newly-remodeled homes. A large stone perches in the grass on one corner.

Herrmann waves me over to the monument and we lean forward to read the plaque. "I was amazed when I first saw this," she said of the text composed by the Women's Club of the Washington State Historical Society in 1920. It notes that just 600 feet to the east of the stone was the Tacoma Mill, built in 1868 on a site called the "Che-bau-lip." "I think that means 'shelter place,'" said Herrmann letting her finger land on the word. Besides being one of the first lumber mills in the community, could it also be that this was a special place for the Puyallup and Nisqually tribes? There's no other marker or really any official acknowledgment that this was once a place used by them, she said. "I wonder; are we losing this piece of our history?"

When Tacoma was still not much more than a cluster of houses and mills, it was dubbed "The City of Destiny," an optimistic moniker for its potential to be the center of business on the Sound. True, over the years Tacoma has had a place in the sun. At one point it was the fastest-growing community between Portland and Canada. But too often it has slipped back into the shadows while its residents struggled with economic downturns, crime, pollution, and trying to be more than just another one of Seattle's suburbs.

It is a town with many facets, a blend of assets and neglect, a former railroad hub, industrial seaport, and with Fort Lewis and McChord Air Force Base, a military center. Tacoma is in constant search of the right identity, according to historian Murray Morgan, who was born and raised there. In his book *Puget's Sound* he wrote that "the City of Destiny remains unsure of what its destiny should be."

But there are so many things it is and could be, said Herrmann. Tacoma's inhabitants just have to recognize and use what they have. "There's so much more to this area than what we know right now."

Tacoma Discovery

In the spring of 1792 the British sloop H.M.S. *Discovery* sailed into the Puget Sound and dropped anchor just off Bainbridge Island. From this harbor, the crew took expeditions in small boats to explore and map the shoreline around the sound. When, about 28 miles south, they neared the Dalco Passage, they were the first non-Native peoples to admire what would become Tacoma's waterfront. They noted the stunning aspect up the shoreline to a snow-capped mountain. In their diaries, Vancouver and several of his crew remarked on the area's beauty, the abundant woodlands, and the serene climate.

But that wasn't enough to lure pioneers. Because of the remoteness and the availability of fur and food in other places, the first settlers didn't arrive until 1864 when Job Carr filed a claim for 168 acres along the waterfront of what would become Old Tacoma. The area then started to draw residents of European extraction.

Soon others, including Carr's sons, bought up and platted the land and started clearing the dense timber to build a town. In 1873 Tacoma beat Seattle and Olympia to win Northern Pacific Railway's Puget Sound terminus. By the 1870s, Tacoma was a lively and growing metropolis, the center of the Sound. Anyone intending to travel between Portland, Olympia, Seattle, and Victoria had to pass through Tacoma where they would catch a steamboat or a train. Because of the wooded, hilly landscape around the Sound, what few roads there were could at times be impassible.

So Tacoma owes its existence to its waterfront. Its bay, a rare deep saltwater harbor, was ideal for a shipping-based economy. A hub for transportation, it also drew industry—fishing, logging, and boat building. In 1877, the city adopted a plan that filled the waterfront with railroad tracks, yards, and wharfs. By the 1890s warehouses, lumber mills, tall ships, and steamboats lined the shoreline. Tacoma was the state's key port for shipping eastern Washington wheat and western Washington hops, coal, and lumber, as well as for receiving goods from Asia including tea, silk, and rice.

The tide flats at the south end of the bay were filled in and channelized to create eight waterways, including the Thea Foss, which is closest to the city and named for a Norwegian immigrant who started a tugboat business on the bay. Foss, a savvy businesswoman, was the basis for the MGM movie character "Tugboat Annie."

For a few decades, Tacoma was the star of the Sound. Its downtown was a jewelry box of beautiful buildings including the Italianate-style Northern Pacific Building, built in the 1880s, and the 1893 brick and terracotta City Hall.

Then in the mid 1890s, everything fell apart. As the nation sunk into an economic depression many of the city's banks and businesses closed. By the end of it, the railroad had moved its hub to Seattle.

In the wake of losing its railroad focus, Tacoma turned to enhancing its industry along the water, which included shipbuilding, lumber, pulp and paper mills, oil refining, and chemical manufacturing and storage. There was a coal gasification plant and later an automotive recycling business. Construction pushed up the shoreline to the 67-acre site of the Asarco copper smelter.

While all these businesses brought jobs and money to Tacoma, they also contributed to the tars, acid, and other toxins along and in the water. By the 1980s, a century of heavy industry had made Tacoma an ecological disaster. In 1983 the 12 square miles of Commencement Bay were declared a federal Superfund site, one of the most polluted waterways in the country. At one end, the Asarco smelter had over the decades deposited 15 million tons of slag byproducts, including arsenic, cadmium, and lead, next to and into the Sound. At the other, the waterways' businesses had done their own share of polluting.

In the years since then, the government has made efforts to hold the polluters accountable, and well over $100 million has been spent to clean up Tacoma's waterways. Because of the oversight and involvement of local government and the Federal Environmental Protection Agency, Lara Herrmann hadn't thought much about the industrial site below her home until one night last year when she got up to feed her baby and realized her house was flooded with light. The source was a dock and two hulking military support ships just below the cliff that forms one side of her neighborhood. Herrmann started thinking more about it when she heard that the dock's owner was requesting permits to add two more ships. Just by looking over the hillside, she could tell much of the large dock had rotted and collapsed. With the exception of a built-up area along one side, it was unusable. And considering the noise, the light, and the black smoke that comes from the ships, Herrmann couldn't imagine that site would be allowed to expand.

"Of course my city, my government wouldn't allow two more super mega structures right along the waterfront, right next to a salmon habitat, perched between two schools and two parks," she said. "But I was wrong." At a public hearing, Herrmann discovered that the council didn't have much to say in the matter, the area was zoned properly, and it was a "quasi-judicial," issue, she said.

"I was so shocked. I realized if our community does not stand up and say enough, we're going to have a military shipyard right here on our working waterfront."

As Herrmann came to understand that the city couldn't stop the expansion in an area zoned for industrial use, her mission became clear. Tacoma has this great resource with its urban waterfront, she said. But it needs to be expanded and revitalized. It needs uses that are compatible with its urban and residential neighborhoods, as well as with the fragile ecology along the shoreline.

A grassroots group of Tacoma residents started meeting last fall to plan a campaign to unify and revitalize the waterfront. They settled on a catchy name "Walk the Waterfront" and began looking at other cities with waterfront issues. "Everything we're doing, none of it is original," said Herrmann, who is now president of the nonprofit organization.

The idea of using open space to revitalize cities has been around since the 1960s, said Jeffrey Sanders, an assistant professor in history at Washington State University. Sanders, who specializes in environmental and Pacific Northwest history, remembers driving along the Tacoma waterfront during his childhood in the 1970s and being shocked when the car went by the Asarco site. "I was blown away by the strange mixture of denuded landscape with what seemed to be a really beautiful scenic drive."

What's happening now in Tacoma makes sense, he said, especially with individuals from within the community pushing for more public space. It's now more democratic, with community groups and grassroots organizations helping the city decide how and where public spaces should develop, he said. The challenge is making sure all the voices, including those of lower income residents, are heard. "I'm all for revitalization…but you always have to ask the question, who is benefitting and who isn't from these changes," he said.

The Ruston Way portion of the waterfront draws residents from all over the city. That is a source of pride for Herrmann and her cohorts. On the weekday we visited, the path and parks were bustling. A large Russian family was out for a walk, a group of teens clustered under a tree to check out a friend's new guitar, and an older man rode by on a bicycle with a little boy, likely his grandson, perched sideways on the back. "This is our Central Park," said Herrmann.

Drawing on the Past

Twenty years ago, the City Club of Tacoma approached the city with a plan to unify the waterfront and build a walking path from the Tacoma Dome to Point Defiance. The club is a non-partisan, nonprofit organization. The painstakingly-researched report urged that the entire waterfront be redesigned as a people place—where the general public, rather than industry or business, is the primary component of the site. It even suggested rezoning the east size of the City

Waterway from 15th Street from port industrial and terminal use to mixed public and private use.

Herrmann was thrilled when a city hall worker handed her the document. "It was like a present just lands in your lap," she said. "I had it in my hands and I'm going 'Are you kidding me? This work is already done.'" Though it's two decades old, much of it is still relevant, said Herrmann.

But, whether the issue was money, land use, or property rights, the plan was never fully pursued, nor were plans from decades earlier. As early as the 1940s, the city was trying to preserve the waterfront. It had plans to make some of the unused industrial sites into parks and recreation areas. In 1965, another city recreation and open space plan provided for the city to buy up shore-side properties for future public use.

Still, a polluted, dangerous waterfront greeted Phyllis Harrison when she returned to Tacoma in 1988 to work on a maritime folk life project. After graduating from WSU in 1973, Harrison had gone on to earn a doctorate in folklore. Now she was coming home. With grants from the National Endowment for the Arts and the Institute of the North American West, she and a fisherman/boat builder named Mike Vlahovich had the mission of creating a traveling exhibit that would capture and preserve the culture of living and working on the water. "It was not just the history, but what was happening right then—predicting the weather, boat building, longshoring, and all the layers of tradition that went into them," she said.

The project was a particularly good fit for Tacoma with its maritime roots, Harrison said. "Tacoma was the capital of wooden boat building and repair in this area for a long time," she said. The exhibit was also extremely popular, taking up residence at Sea-Tac Airport for a number of years. In 1995 it found a permanent home on Tacoma's waterfront when the city agreed to lease out part of the Puget Sound Freight building on the Thea Foss Waterway. The site was no beauty, Harrison said. In fact, it had a squatter in residence, the toilets (which couldn't be used) emptied into the Sound, and half of the building was space for police-seized vehicles. It was a seedy sight. On the other hand, it was right on the water, Harrison said—the perfect location for a maritime museum.

Their timing was ideal. The cleanup of the Foss waterway had started, and plans were underway for a new, improved waterfront next to downtown. It paved the way for the now world-famous Museum of Glass, and a small collection of tony condominiums—with water and mountain views. But, said Harrison with pride, the very first thing to happen on the waterfront was the Working Waterfront Maritime Museum. Harrison remembers the day she learned their project would work: "It was so exciting to know that finally there was a public space where people could start coming and learning about the waterway."

Prior Tacoma city councils have made many investments in protecting the waterfront, and providing for safe public access to the Thea Foss Waterway, which is closest to downtown, said Tacoma City Councilman Jake Fey, who also works at Washington State University as director of the cooperative extension energy program.

"We really have an asset that's unique and attractive to people," he said. How the council and community take advantage of that and also use the space in the best way is the real challenge.

When Fey first ran for city council in 1995, he knew he was vying for one of the larger and more complex districts in the city. His territory includes the port, downtown, several business districts, historic neighborhoods, a suburban hillside, and the waterfront. He admits the size, variety, and demands of the district can sometimes be overwhelming. But he's also inspired by the interest and involvement of constituents like Herrmann. "Tacoma is a city, but it's not so big that individuals can't rise to the occasion and make a difference," he said.

It's not that the City Of Tacoma doesn't have a plan for the waterfront, Herrmann said. Actually it has many, including a shoreline plan, a waterfront trail plan, a Ruston Way plan, and a Foss Waterway plan. But they are piecemeal. "We need a plan that captures the entire waterfront, the owners, and the users who should have a voice," she said. "We can create something so spectacular that it would transform Tacoma."

And tying it into the city's history may be the key to getting it done. Herrmann's interest in local history started when she was a student at Tacoma Community College and wondered why the city didn't have a Chinatown when Seattle and Portland both did. In researching a paper, she learned that Tacoma once did have a thriving Chinese community. There was a neighborhood right on the waterfront called Little Canton that was filled with homes and businesses.

But during the economic downturn of the 1890s, after the railroad had been built, a mob led by Tacoma's leaders and business owners drove the Chinese residents out. Little Canton was burned to the ground. The brutal expulsion, later referred to as "The Tacoma Method," is a real stain on the community's past, said Herrmann. In recent years, the city has tried to make amends, by formally apologizing for the expulsion as well as dedicating a Chinese Reconciliation Park at the water's edge just outside of downtown.

The park is a great fit for the waterfront, Herrmann said. It has purpose and meaning and it is something that the community can use freely. That success has her thinking about the word "Che-bau-lip" and the Native American history in the area. At this point, Herrmann knows there are several spellings as well as explanations, a key one being that it is a Native American name of an area near the waterfront where the land slopes into the sound and where Job Carr built his cabin, the first structure in Old Tacoma. Many of the early settlers, including Carr, used the name for that location. According to historian Murray Morgan, a site below what is now the Stadium Way cliff had a Native American burial canoe and a boulder marked with petroglyphs, both now long-gone.

Members of the Puyallup tribe confirm the uses, noting that Native American history and legacy with this part of Tacoma have indeed at times been overlooked. Part of downtown, for example, was a village site, said tribal historian Judy Wright.

That's one more component of the waterfront that should be remembered, said Herrmann.

Considering urban waterfronts around the world, Herrmann wondered what characteristics Tacoma has that "makes our waterfront even better than your waterfront?" Well that's easy, she said. Besides the rich history specific to Tacoma, you have Mount Rainier. "You can't see Mount Rainier from Seattle's waterfront," she said. And on the other end, Point Defiance Park, a spectacular tree-covered park with trails, beaches, boat launches, museums, and even a zoo. "It's one of the best city parks in the country," Herrmann said.

In between, there's the cleaned-up Thea Foss Waterway, the Maritime Museum, a Chinese Reconciliation Park, the original Job Carr settlement, the Tahoma salt marsh, and a long stretch of parks and paths in front of Old Tacoma.

The city needs this new generation of citizens to care about the waterfront, Harrison said. "And the waterfront needs to be a resource not only for heritage reasons," she added. "But also because people should not spend all of their lives with their feet on concrete, especially if they live on the shores of Puget Sound."

Downtown to Point Defiance

Museum of Glass: One of the first projects in the rehabilitation of the Thea Foss Waterway, the museum opened in 2002. It features glass artwork from Northwest artists led by Dale Chihuly as well as work from world-famous artists from around the world. The museum can be reached from downtown via a 500-foot-long "bridge of glass" filled with Chihuly's sculptures.

Working Waterfront Maritime Museum: Whether it's a dose of history or a view of modern wooden boat building, the interactive museum provides the history, culture, and modern stories of Tacoma's waterfront. The museum is housed in a real piece of Old Tacoma—the near-century-old Balfour Dock Building.

Thea's Park: At the mouth of the Thea Foss Waterway, this 3.4-acre park has trails, picnic tables, and a view of the last immediate remnants of Tacoma's industrial past.

Chinese Reconciliation Park: The waterfront's newest park was dedicated in 2006 to commemorate the sad event of 1885 when Tacoma's leaders, blaming the

Chinese for the downturn in the economy, forcibly drove them out of the city and destroyed their homes and businesses.

Point Defiance Park: At 700 acres, it's one of the largest city parks in the country. Besides trees, trails, and waterfront, it holds a zoo, marina, lodge, and several historical and educational exhibits. Established 110 years ago, this park has long been the pride of the Tacoma community, making excellent use of the peninsula that juts out into the Sound.

Ozette Art and the Makah Canoe

Tim Steury

Many questions remain concerning the contents of the longhouses excavated at Ozette. One of the most intriguing is the nature of its art, which was pervasive. More than 400 artifacts stored at the Makah Cultural Center might be considered art. Although a few pieces, such as the well-known carved whale saddle, are (presumably) ritualistic, most are everyday objects, such as combs, bowls, clubs, embellished with designs.

Jeff Mauger, an archaeologist at Peninsula Community College in Port Angeles, earned his doctorate from Washington State University in 1978, analyzing the shed-roof style of the houses at Ozette and their relation to the style throughout the Northwest coast. Since then he has gradually left field work, turning instead to research and analysis—and to art. Besides his science, Mauger is a silversmith, creating jewelry inspired by Northwest Coast and Makah design.

"For whatever reasons," he wrote in an artist's statement, "tribal art has always evoked a deep emotional response within me and Northwest Coast Indian art traditions in particular are an early and continued passion."

Mauger's work is inspired by Makah designs. "I try to understand the structure and elements of those designs to produce art that falls in that tradition."

Individual designs are owned by families or individuals themselves. The design may have come to the creator in a dream. "It is a very personal and closed expression of their culture," said Mauger, "and there was this concern, they saw a lot of people doing Northwest coast art and benefitin commercially from it, who from a cultural perspective really had no business doing it.

"I have to say I was probably one of them, too," he said, referring to his early days before the truth dawned on him.

"To work within the tradition, which is what I try to do, you have to reach a level of technical competence and an appreciation and acknowledgment of where that art comes from."

Mauger is also now at work on a book about Ozette art. "Ozette gave us the largest single collection of southern Northwest coast art from a single place in a single period," he said. "Not only that, but you can look at variations between households and families. There's great potential."

But realizing that potential will not be easy. His first, monumental, task is simply documenting what's in the collection now stored at the Makah Cultural Center.

His second task is a structural analysis, determining patterns. In spite of the extraordinary preservation of the artifacts taken from Ozette, many of the patterns are faded by their 400-year burial. He discerns the designs through careful study and then drawing them.

He's developed a technique for abstracting the designs. "I enlarge images of Ozette art from digital photographs and see things you don't see from a macro perspective. Then I go back to the macro and there it is. One thing I looked at for 30 years, a comb, a wavy line." Once he enlarged it and outlined the design, he realized it was the outline of a whale. "So my technique for documenting actually became a method of discovery."

Finally, he determines how the pieces relate to other coastal art. This analysis is hardly straightforward.

Some of the pieces of art likely did not originate at Ozette. "That's to be expected," said Mauger. "Knowing what we know of ceremonial exchange and movement of stuff on the Northwest coast, there are things I'm sure were produced by Salish speakers and Nuu-chah-nulth (relatives of the Makah in British Columbia).

"The geometrics (design) may relate to are from around the Columbia River." The Makahs' long-time residence is at a very strategic location, said Mauger. Positioned at the mouth of the Strait of Juan de Fuca, the Makahs exerted cultural influence up and down the coasts of Washington and Oregon as well as Vancouver Island. Mauger considers their role as "almost brokers."

A fundamental element of Mauger's study is determining "Is it art?" Take canoe paddles, for example. "There are elegant canoe paddles, but there are clunky canoe paddles, too."

Does decoration in addition to a utilitarian function make it art? Or consider the wooden boxes found in the houses. They were made by scoring, then steam-bending thin cedar planks, then lacing on a bottom. They were so precisely constructed they were water-tight. The craftsmanship lends them an artistic elegance as well as function.

And is the extra work evident on some of them necessary for their function? "If not, then it's probably art," Mauger said.

Then again, interpreting a much different culture is tricky.

One of the more interesting artifacts in the Ozette collection is an inch-and-a-half-tall bone carving. I assumed, given the apparent head, torso, and limbs, it is a human abstraction.

Not so fast, Mauger said.

"I don't have any real information on the piece, one of the more intriguing in the collection," he wrote in an email exchange. "As for it being a stylized human, maybe, but I wouldn't even go that far. It is doubtlessly iconic and icons are very culture-bound. I am increasingly hesitant to project a 21st century, Western cultural, interpretation on such a piece; doing so probably tells us more about ourselves than the people or person who made it.

"On the other hand, on the purely structural level, it is an interesting construction of fairly typical Coast Salish style crescents, circles, and a trigon, using both positive and negative space. (Which is not to imply that it was made by a Coast Salish speaker—that is just the name of a widespread art style first noted in Coast Salish territory)."

But, he concluded, "Enough of the anthropology talk. I don't have a clue.."

Mauger's restraint is admirable, enabling him as both artist and scientist. It also gives credence to his answer to my question, "Has your definition of art changed?"

"Boy, that one caught me by surprise. Yeah, it's certainly because of Ozette that the way I look at art now is really different. I suppose that means my definition has changed. With the Ozette stuff, and any art from Indigenous people, there's that old axiom, that only English and a few other languages separate art out as a distinct thing, make art for art's sake.

"Art always has a function. I look at the Ozette stuff and more and more I realize its inseparably bound to the artifact and its use in the culture and what it meant in the culture and what it indicated in the social system and the kinship system.

"So in some ways art is an expression of a whole cultural system, that when we see the object, we're just looking at the surface. It's probably how an anthropologist would look at art anyhow, so maybe I'm just a late bloomer."

Think I knew that academically, but when it becomes part of your gut, it's no longer an academic definition. This is real stuff and real people we're talking about.

"That really comes home to you as an artist. When you're struggling with a design, making that paradigm shift, another way of looking at the universe, when a killer whale's fin doesn't have to be vertical on its back, where can you put it and still make a logic, though not the logic of your particular world view?

"One of the most satisfying experiences is when the whole world is reduced to a design."

Consider, for example, the canoe.

The Makah Cultural and Research Center houses two canoes, a canoe for hunting sea lions and seals and a larger whaling canoe. Traditionally, the canoes were carved from a single cedar trunk. In a sense, the canoe typifies a culture where art and function are indistinguishable. On the one hand, it signifies pure function. One senses merely from its presence and look that it is a match for the sea.

"They're the only real oceangoing canoe ever designed," Mauger said.

On the other hand, it is a craft of pure beauty.

Mauger immersed himself in the Makah canoe for a while, aiming to develop a prototype of a fiberglass model. He made seven canoes.

"With the seventh, I felt I was really starting to understand what the lines were about. They're simply amazing. There's nothing accidental. Every angle, every flair, has a reason. I don't pretend to understand what they're all about. But I was starting to understand the flair of the bow, the vertical stern.

"Which is odd," he added. "They're lousy in following seas."

But the reason for the strange chopped-off stern was their function. "These were work boats. That kind of stern worked well for working out of it."

That functional trait also reflects a deeper practicality. If a crew were caught in a following sea, they'd simply turn the canoe around and go backward.

This point in turn explains old photos of canoes pulled up on the beach, bows seaward.

"More glassy-eyed folks say they're ready to go. Jump in the canoe and go hunting whales.

"No, that's the way they came in through the surf, reversed. They came in stern first. But they achieved a practical double benefit in that they were ready to go."

Point of Reference

Brian Charles Clark

"There are oysters out there," Ed Bassett said. "And they are good."

Out there are the mudflats of Henderson Inlet where a thriving community shellfish garden supplies delicacies for neighborhood parties and celebrations. Bassett, a 1989 Washington State University graduate—his degree is in education—is standing in the eelgrass on the shoreline of WSU's Meyer's Point Environmental Field Station, established in 2003.

He's a science teacher at nearby Olympia High School, and he, his students in the OHS Earth Corps, and Meyer's Point facilities manager Chuck Cody, who earned his master's degree in horticulture from WSU in 1984, have been planting native trees here since then.

WSU environmental scientist Steve Bollens is the director of the station. He calls Meyer's Point a hidden gem and a too-well-kept secret. Bollens and his colleagues are determined to use the site to explore the urban-rural interface, that delicate balance between the resource-intensive and environmentally taxing human infrastructure of the built environment, and our growing awareness that things just aren't right without a healthy environment in which to play, meditate, and raise kids.

The 95-acre site has nearly half a mile of shoreline, acres of marshy wetland, and an expanding forest that climbs a steep slope. At the top of the property is a 12-acre hay field. For WSU researchers, the mix of agricultural land with forest and shoreline tantalizes mathematicians modeling forests, biogeochemists seeking to understand how fungi partner with plant communities, and archeologists who inform the present with lessons from ancient Native residents.

"There's something for everybody," Bollens said.

Bassett meanders through the restored forest; he offers a warning about the mud in his soft Georgia drawl: "You could find yourself in a seated position real fast."

Bassett has been best friends with Cody since the 1980s. "We hit it off the day I was unloading my U-Haul," said Bassett, "and Chuck stopped to help." Cody was a graduate student in Pullman, while Bassett had come to take a job with James Cook, a wheat root disease researcher. As soon as Bassett graduated with his teaching credential, he landed the job at OHS and has been there ever since. Sometime in 2003, he got a call from Cody.

"He said, 'I'm going to be in your neck of the woods. We have this property, and it needs a bit of work.'"

That, it turns out, was an understatement. What is now a 16-acre forest was then an abandoned dairy cow pasture that had been overrun by a vast tangle of blackberry vines. Where there weren't blackberries, there were red alders. Cody wanted to accelerate the process of succession, with the goal of restoring a mixed-species native climax forest. Successive waves of Bassett's Earth Corps students gave the old pasture many Saturdays over many years, tearing out berry brambles and replacing the alders with Douglas firs, grand firs, western red cedars, big leaf maple, Oregon ash, and, later, hemlocks that thrive in the protection of an established conifer forest.

The first planting, Cody said, was on Valentine's Day, 2004. Those saplings are now 30-foot-tall trees and one of Bassett's former students has her own virology lab at Brandeis University.

That's not the only success along Henderson Inlet. When Cody and Bassett first started coming to Meyer's Point, there was no shellfish garden; the water quality was too poor. But a concerted—and expensive—collaboration between local residents and various state and local government agencies and nonprofits led to an upgraded infrastructure, including better septic and stormwater runoff management systems. By 2017, and "after more than 20 years of work," according to a Washington Department of Ecology assessment, "the results of the Henderson Inlet watershed partnership are among the most positive results in any Washington watershed."

That dramatic improvement in water quality has meant that shellfish gardening could move to the southern end of the inlet, including at Meyer's Point. There, OHS students volunteer to help plant oysters in the local community garden. The Nisqually Tribe, too, garden and harvest the delicacies, which they sell to area restaurants.

Music of the Mists

Meyer's Point was a gift from Dr. Edward Meyer, who graduated from Washington State College in 1938 with a pharmacy degree. After medical school in Louisville, Kentucky, and service in the Second World War, Meyer returned to the area where he was raised to practice medicine. Doc Meyer's shingle still hangs from one of the buildings at the station. Meyer bequeathed the property to WSU before he died in 1993, asking that it be used for environmental and arts research and education.

He also left the university an endowment that established professorships in the arts and sciences. Composer and saxophonist Greg Yasinitsky is a former

Meyer Distinguished Professor, and he was also one of the first faculty members to visit the field station.

Yasinitsky visited Meyer's Point in the summer of 1995. He tromped around the property for a couple of days, shooting video and making audio recordings of wind, birds calling, shoes in mud, and the lapping of water. When he got back to Pullman that fall, he composed "Meyer's Point" for flute and piano. The one-movement piece is a challenging showcase for his wife, Ann Marie Yasinitsky, a virtuoso flutist, and perfectly evokes the ethereal mists that hover over the salt marshes and the tumbling sky that deepens the perspective up the long northward reach of the inlet.

Years later, the music still reflects the ecology of the site. As Bassett leads an expedition up into the woods, the soaring flute cadenzas seem to echo the sky-reaching trees, and the dramatic piano intervals capture the contrast of forest and marsh, of field and the murmur of streams running down slope.

On another day, Bassett might hear another sort of music: the whine of Nick Strigul's drone as it curls above the forest snapping high-resolution photographs.

A Silicon Forest

Strigul is a mathematician based at WSU Vancouver, 90 minutes south of the Meyer's Point station. "A big part of my work," he said, "is forest modeling, the self-organization of forest ecosystems." That's why his drone is circling the forest at Meyer's Point, collecting data that both informs and confirms his modeling efforts.

The trick, he explained, is to gather together all the individual studies of ecosystem components into "a single, highly complex model." A forest is not just trees: it is microbes in roots and branches, insects, birds, animals, forest-floor flora, all of which "operate on different time and space scales and yet interact in profound and important ways. The importance of bringing mathematics to bear is that it provides a path toward understanding the interactions and differing scales."

Getting all that data onto the same virtual page is just the first challenge. Any model, whether of climate or forest or shoreline, must be validated against reality.

"But to compare to reality, you need a data-intensive baseline to test against," Strigul said. "It's hard to find a particular place where you have sufficient data, where everything is measured. Where each individual tree, and all the fluxes of carbon, nitrogen, and trace gases, the soil nitrogen and carbon, where all that is known and measured."

Creating such a baseline is expensive and long term, he said. Harvard University has an experimental forest that has been monitored for decades. But there's not really anything like that in the Pacific Northwest. Perhaps, he mused, Meyer's Point could become a baseline for regional forest modeling.

Since the 1960s, he explained, researchers have been using computers to model forests. Foresters want to understand how to get maximum yields and wood quality, while ecologists wanted to grasp the entire system. Foresters aren't interested in tree mortality, because they'll harvest before a tree reaches the end of its natural life. And the same with pests: foresters try to wipe out the pest. But ecologists want the big picture. For decades, ecologists got the short end of the computing stick simply because processors simply couldn't handle the massive data required to model a real-world ecosystem.

Ecologists, Strigul said, "had to be very picky about what they put in their models. But now, computers are so powerful you can put all of it in there."

The value of a high-resolution model would be extraordinary. All manner of experiments could be run in silico, yielding quality results at the speed of microprocessors instead of consuming decades of real life. The effects of a warming climate, drought, fire, and much more could be modeled, informing decision makers and resource managers about particular courses of action.

Strigul said his goal is to "drive out the uncertainty" that exists in "models that do not completely reflect reality."

As Below, So Above

Harvesting and then harnessing data is the way to drive out uncertainty. Two WSU Tri-Cities scientists also see the Meyer's Point station as a prime candidate for collecting a wealth of information about the interactions of soils, microbes, plants, and their effects on ecosystem health.

Biologist Tanya Cheeke and her colleague, environmental scientist Sarah Roley, along with some of their students, have teamed up to collect and analyze soil samples from the up-slope hay field at Meyer's Point. The goal is to identify the particular mycorrhizal fungi that associate with plant roots and "create an intimate two-way exchange of nutrients," as undergraduate Ella Krinitsyn wrote in a recent presentation.

Understanding the symbiotic relationship between plant species and their fungal partners is critical to restoring native plant habitats. Those associations develop over time, but when soil is disturbed, as for a building project, that relationship can become threatened, to the detriment of native plants. That's one of the reasons weeds encroach on highway margins and building sites.

In the past, Thurston County managers have put major emphasis on maintaining and, where possible, improving environmental quality in the south Puget Sound region. Statements from the County Planning Commission indicate that sustaining a healthy economy and environment will be maintained in the future, aided in no small part by efforts to model forests and understand the role of fungi in soil and plant health.

Walking along the hay field and along the dense forest at the top of Meyer's Point, station director Bollens said that having an environmental field station "sited at the rural-urban interface is uncommon. There are a few truly urban field stations, but they're rare. There are many more that are as far away from humans as possible in order to maintain pristine habitats."

The north Sound is already densely populated and developed. "The south Sound is going that way, but is figuring it out. How do you provide opportunity for economic growth while maintaining ecosystems in a sustainable way?" That's a twenty-first-century challenge, he said, one WSU is perfectly situated to address.

A Backward Glance into the Future

WSU archeologist Colin Grier thinks a lot about 21st-century challenges and argues that what we face now and in the near future is nothing entirely new. Walking along the shoreline, he points out an archeological site that is at least 500 years old. It's a band of shells embedded in silt just a few meters above the high-tide line.

"That shell midden is a record of dinner by dinner decisions over 500 years. It's a fine-grained view of adaptation strategies." What Native peoples selected to harvest and what to leave for growth might be guides for shellfish gardeners today.

The Coast Salish peoples, Grier said, "had a system of proprietorship, rather than ownership, so it was a system of responsibility rather than exploitation. You own it in some sense, but you have a responsibility to manage it for the greater good."

There's an ancient campsite just up shore from the shell midden. A bowl-shaped hearth of fire-altered silt and rock has a bone sticking out of it. People have been camping along these inlets for thousands of years, Grier said, as they moved up and down the coasts between major settlements.

"It's no coincidence that a lot of modern settlement is right on top of indigenous settlement. The places that are amenable to the way we live our lives, 15,000 years ago as well as today, involve a lot of the same decisions. People want access to transportation, to food and resources, to neighbors.

"So this is sort of a microcosm of all the sustainability issues on Puget Sound," Grier continued. "Looking back to see what the baselines are, looking forward to what they should be, and trying to preserve the record that has all that information: that's why I think shorelines are so interesting. They're the nexus of all these dynamic issues and processes, past and present, coming together."

As he picks his way across the mud and dices around pools of salt water, Grier's boots squish and squeak. It's the music of Meyer's Point, a metronome that sometimes skips beats but that always comes back around, a rhythmic cycle of interconnection that Grier sees in both the contemporary philosopher of science, Bruno Latour, and "the indigenous view of the world, that everything is connected and that there are all these complex relationships that are beyond human control."

As he looks north, up Henderson Inlet toward Dionisio Point on Georgia Strait, where he's been excavating and collaborating with indigenous Salish Sea tribes for 20 years, Grier said, "One thing I ask my students to think about is this: what do the ancient Greeks, the Romans, the Mesopotamians, the Maya, the Inca, what do all these cultures have in common? They are gone! What they left behind is as close to a laboratory as archeologists are going to get, and it's a window on the interaction of ecology, politics, economics, technology." Those interactions are precisely those we, too, must contend with in the present.

Shoring Up

Puget Sound is the third largest estuary system in the United States, after the bays of Chesapeake and San Francisco. It's a young environment, with gravelly soils ground up and laid down by glaciers. Fifteen thousand years ago, the Vashon Glacier buried this region under thousands of feet of ice. The massive glacier shoved south of Olympia at its greatest extent. As the planet entered the warming Holocene, the glacier retreated, melting, filling the finger-like fjords of the Sound with water. Plants and animals rushed back in to the newly hospitable environment; biology abhors a vacuum.

Now, as the climate is changing again, Bollens and others consider how this jewel-like spot of earth might help us meet our future with grace. One of the values of Meyer's Point is that it inspires awe and a love of nature. And that inspiration is a timely remedy to the angst and fear that permeates discussions about climate change. And while that fear is in some sense justifiable—if we're not to burden today's children with a grim, superstorm-ridden future, time is indeed short to make meaningful change—fear also paralyzes while love of nature energizes and motivates constructive action.

Someday, Bollens speculated, a trail system might connect the field station to other ecological reserves on Henderson Inlet. But, he cautioned, public access has to be balanced with maintaining the integrity of ecological and archeological research sites. Bringing together the missions of research and public education in a place this fragile, Bollens said, "is a balancing act."

"Virtually every field station has this tension between maintaining resources for researchers and wanting to open things up for the public," he explained. "Some are so remote it's a moot point." Not Meyer's Point, here in the midst of millions of people.

Is that balancing act daunting? Standing next to his car at the entrance gate, Bollens looked back down the slope to the shoreline and said, "It's daunting in that it takes millions of dollars to build facilities and infrastructure. But this is a fabulous site and is already drawing support."

Bassett was leaving, too. All the volunteer hours students have given this place, he said, have also taught them the principles of ecological succession, how species change over time. That time frame might be millennia, as after a glacial recession, or it might happen in the decades after a volcano or fire has devastated a landscape.

But most of all, he said, is they just wanted to clean the place up and have it full of native plants and wildlife. Overhead, birds on the Pacific flyway call and then, as the sound of departing cars fades away, everything is quiet except for the music of the wind in the trees.

Lonely, Beautiful, and Threatened—Willapa Bay

Eric Apalategui

Charlie Stenvall skims an airboat across Willapa Bay on a placid summer morning, rousing 15 Canada geese whose complaints sound like an unsupervised junior high band practice.

Ahead, flocks of western sandpipers flash white and gray, as the shorebirds turn away from the approaching boat in choreographed waves of wings. Nearby, a Caspian tern dives into shallows after small fish, while in the distance two peregrine falcons flush wading birds off open mudflats. A bald eagle perches in a snag on the shore of the bay's forested Long Island, watching the boat pass below.

With a turn of the giant fan, Stenvall slides the boat down an alley of inch-deep water and enters an expanse of grass growing thicker than field corn.

Stenvall, manager of the Willapa National Wildlife Refuge, steers into a pocket of water enclosed in a wall of green. He cuts the airboat's engine, and the rumble of the fan blades whirs to a stop. Then, near silence. The honking of geese and screech of raptors fade into the light breeze, replaced by the faint *scritch* of swaying blades of grass.

To the newcomer, the lush meadows, broken only by vein-like channels that gather the outgoing tide, might seem like some of nature's best work. But to

Stenvall, the silent savanna sends an earsplitting message that precious Willapa Bay—tucked into Washington's rainy southwestern pocket—is in peril.

The culprit isn't the belching factories, agricultural runoff, and urban sprawl that endanger most of the nation's great bays. Instead, the scariest threat to Willapa is this spreading carpet of grass, *Spartina alterniflora*.

"We have sort of an idyllic estuary"

Willapa Bay, also known as Shoalwater, is the largest estuary between San Francisco and Puget Sound. It boasts one of the least-spoiled environments and the healthiest salmon runs south of Canada, produces one in every four oysters farmed in the United States, and is a favorite pit stop for tens of thousands of migratory birds.

And it's in trouble.

The infestation of *Spartina*, imported by accident from the East Coast, collects enough silt to raise the bay floor by up to a foot, turning much of Willapa's enviably productive tidal zone into a giant, unkempt lawn. At the same time, other introduced plants and animals and two opportunistic species of native shrimp also threaten to spoil the pristine bay.

"If you lose Willapa Bay, it's of both state and national significance," said Kim Patten, who earned his doctorate in horticulture from Washington State University in 1983. The WSU researcher and associate professor of horticulture is a leader in the battle for the bay.

"I think it's a national treasure, because every estuary in North America would try to emulate it. There's no other estuary out there like it," Patten said. "We have sort of an idyllic estuary. It's not perfect, but for all intents and purposes, it's a very functioning estuary. You don't get better than that."

Environmentally, aquatic landscapes from Chesapeake Bay to San Francisco Bay are infamous for what they've lost. Willapa Bay's protectors want to make it renowned for what it kept. They're starting to get noticed.

Last June, the National Audubon Society ranked Willapa Bay second—just behind part of Florida's Everglades—in its *Cooling the Hot Spots* report detailing wildlife areas threatened by invasive species. That followed a similar listing in the National Wildlife Refuge Association's 2002 report, *Silent Invasion*. And the Nature Conservancy has made protecting the bay and its rich watershed one of its highest Washington priorities.

Senator Patty Murray, who graduated from WSU in 1972 with a degree in recreation, and her colleagues helped secure another $1 million in federal funding for this season's work, the second in a six-year, multi-partner plan to eradicate *Spartina*. The state is pitching in hundreds of thousands more.

"It's so common for us to not realize what we've got until we lost it," said U.S. Representative Brian Baird, D-Vancouver. "This wonderful bay faces some real threats. *Spartina*, for example, is a nightmare. It can turn the Willapa Bay into the Willapa Prairie."

In a Lonely Wooded Place

Willapa Bay didn't always garner so much attention, and many of its residents—human and animal both—embraced the quiet life.

For generations, Native Americans gathered shellfish, caught salmon, and built sheltered winter villages on the shores of Willapa, pronounced "WIL-uh-puh." The name comes from the Indian Kwalhioqua, or "in a lonely wooded place."

That description still fit the bay in November 1805, when Corps of Discovery explorer Captain William Clark, scouting the "low pondey countrey" north of the Columbia, missed it entirely.

Fifty years later, just after the start of California's gold rush, early White settlers found treasure of their own in Willapa: oysters. Towns such as Oysterville and the now-defunct Diamond City—named for a bleached mountain of shells piled at the northern tip of Long Island that glistened when the sun pierced the cloud cover—sprang up at mid-century to ship oysters by the hundreds of millions to San Francisco. The salmon canneries came too, spawning more villages, and the bay buzzed with commerce.

But in the 19th century, Willapa Bay again became a lonelier place. The native Olympia oysters and salmon runs dwindled. Many people left, and some of their towns have long since rotted into the woods. Oystermen spared their livelihoods by importing large Pacific oysters, which to this day they farm like a crop, as their neighbors grow cranberries and timber on Willapa's sparsely developed shores.

Oyster growers of the late 1800s may have unwittingly imported an unseen menace that would haunt their great-grandchildren: *Spartina*. For generations, the new plants were mere tufts on the bay's 47,000 acres of tidal flats. Over time, however, the grass quietly adapted to an environment with no natural predators. By last summer, *Spartina* had infested 12,000 acres and was expanding 20 percent a year. It already had pushed shorebirds off some of their best foraging grounds and was poised to elbow out oyster growers.

"All I'm doing is killing stuff"

For a bunch of bird-loving, oysters-on-the-half-shell types, the language used for ridding Willapa Bay of *Spartina* is downright militaristic.

"All I'm doing is killing stuff," said Jonathan Bates, an equipment operator for the wildlife refuge, one day last July. At the time, he was rumbling across

Spartina meadows aboard a tank-like tractor outfitted with sprayer nozzles to mist the grass with Rodeo herbicide.

Closer to the tide line, where smaller *Spartina* bunches called "clones" hadn't yet formed meadows, airboat crews drew herbicide pistols and blasted the grass with blue-dyed herbicide.

"The plan," said airboat crew leader Darrin Zavodsky, "was to divide and conquer."

The tractors all are armed with GPS units to map their progress, and at least one has infrared sensors that signal the sprayer nozzles to fire only when it detects plant matter.

Last summer, the wildlife refuge, the Washington State Department of Agriculture, and the bay's oyster growers treated *Spartina* on 5,000 acres in the bay. It was a landmark year: they killed nearly 10 times more grass than any previous year and, for the first time, gained ground against *Spartina*. This summer, partners including WSU and the University of Washington have mapped out a strategy to treat another 3,000 acres while mopping up new shoots on mudflats they treated in 2003.

Until 2003, more than a decade of spraying, mowing, and tilling *Spartina* had proven futile, while a UW study of plant-eating insects remains unproven. Stenvall, the wildlife refuge chief, credits WSU researcher Patten, whom he jokes is Willapa's own "mad scientist," with finding a way to make common herbicides kill the pesky grass in harsh conditions—without harming the bay's fragile ecosystem.

This year, Patten's work should bring a new weapon to their arsenal: federal and state agencies' expected approval of imazapyr for use in the bay after Patten exhaustively tested the herbicide. Imazapyr, compared to Rodeo, requires less chemical and shorter drying times to kill *Spartina*.

Stepping Stone for Birds

Patten, an expert in small-fruit horticulture, naturally spends many workdays in the greenhouses and bogs at the Cranberry Research Station on the Long Beach Peninsula, the 25-mile finger of land that separates Willapa Bay from the Pacific Ocean. At other times, he's testing ways to kill *Spartina* or burrowing shrimp that plague the oyster industry.

On a spring day last year, however, Patten was up to his wader-encased shins in Willapa Bay mud off Porter Point—counting bird poop. The whitish plops, along with stick-like footprints, are helping Patten document where migrating birds feed during stopovers at Willapa Bay. He also employs high-tech surveillance cameras mounted on platforms in the bay and lower-tech surveys with binocular-armed volunteers to collect his data.

Patten's research isn't complete, but his aim is to scientifically document what he and various bird experts already know from observation: shorebirds, whether dunlins and dowitchers or sandpipers and plovers, HATE *Spartina*.

"You still have skeptics out there that do not believe *Spartina* affects shorebirds," Patten said.

President Franklin D. Roosevelt established Willapa National Wildlife Refuge in 1937 to protect habitat for migrating birds. But as *Spartina* has thickened, Willapa's legions of shorebirds have thinned.

Shorebirds flock to unspoiled tidal flats to peck for worms, midges, nematodes, and other critters that make up the "groceries" that fuel the birds' long migrations along the West Coast. Some also will forage among the stubble and wrack of dead *Spartina*, but they won't venture into living meadows where predators might lurk.

"Willapa Bay is one of the few stepping-stones of habitat left for migrating birds from South and Central America to Canada and Alaska," said Nina Carter, policy director for Audubon Washington. She helped lobby her national organization to train a spotlight on Willapa's disappearing habitat for short-billed dowitchers and tens of thousands of other shorebirds that migrate through each year.

Environmentalists to a Point

The sun rises through a September mist that covers Willapa Bay like a down comforter.

John Herrold eases the family boat, the *Tokeland*, over submerged oyster beds marked only by spindly branches poking into the mud 14 feet beneath the bay's surface. He flips a lever to winch an oyster "bag"—a heavy-gauge metal basket hanging from steel cable—off the port side, until the bag's open mouth dredges against the soft bay floor. He lowers a twin bag off the starboard side.

Three and a half minutes later, Herrold pushes the lever again, and the port-side bag rises with a groan of the winch, slightly tilting the 95-year-old boat toward the bag as it emerges from the water, chock-full of oysters.

His brother, Roy, grasps the bag in gloved hands and, in one quick motion, swings the load toward the boat's cabin and unlatches the basket. Six hundred pounds of oysters crash to the deck. Roy plucks an orange starfish out of the pile, as his brother lowers the empty bag back into the bay.

"It's not scientific at all," John said, reaching for the starboard lever.

An hour and 360 bushels of oysters later, the Herrolds steer the *Tokeland* toward the family home on Cougar Bend, where the Naselle River pours into Willapa Bay. The brothers are third-generation oystermen, not uncommon at Willapa, and one branch of their family tree stretches back to the Chinook tribe that foraged for shellfish before Europeans arrived.

"It's always the same around here," mused Roy, "but it's always different."

"The big change is *Spartina*," John said. "I've seen it (go) from nothing to what it is now. For the most part we've kept our beds clear," he added, pointing out some of their tidelands where the grasses have taken over the higher elevations but have been painstakingly cleared closer to the water. "We do everything it takes."

As with *Spartina*, the oyster industry—worth about $32 million a year to the region—suffers the brunt of any environmental imbalance on the bay. Leaky septic fields and unknown bacteria sources harm water quality, while some of the bay's 40 invasive species—including voracious European green crabs and deadly oyster drills—threaten their wallets.

"Oyster growers have always been environmentalists to a point. We have to be, because we need clean water," John said.

Growers also are battling the "political nightmare" of burrowing shrimp. Unlike *Spartina*, the shrimp are natives. But they have been multiplying out of control since the 1950s—perhaps in response to declining predators such as salmon and sturgeon and the damming of the nearby Columbia River, which historically flushed the bay with fresh water, killing salt-loving shrimp.

Last year, oyster growers agreed to phase out their controversial, 40-year-old practice of controlling shrimp with carbaryl, a pesticide found in flea powder. The decision settled a costly legal battle with environmental groups, but it also left growers without an effective, affordable way to keep the shrimp in check. Patten and other scientists are helping growers try to find the solution, as the carbaryl clock ticks out by 2012.

Meanwhile, as with *Spartina*, overpopulated shrimp threaten more than just oysters and clams. They destroy tidal wildlife habitats for many species.

"*Spartina* has been devastating to the birds," said Dick Wilson, a Bay Center oyster grower and bird-watcher, "but so have the burrowing shrimp."

Nahcotta oystermen Dick and Brian Sheldon are working on both problems, but it costs plenty. For example, they figure in the past few years they've spent $6,000 an acre to clear the *Spartina* from just one of their 90-acre plots on the bay. The land is only worth $200 an acre, and it's in a spot that's frankly better for feeding birds than fattening oysters.

"Most of us have a family history of up to 100 years in the bay," Dick Sheldon said. "As an oysterman, as a person, I just couldn't see the bay going down the toilet."

Eating Well to Save the Sound

Tim Steury

Here on the gravel shore of Little Skookum Inlet, just south of Shelton, Brett Bishop shucks another native Olympia oyster and hands it to me. The Olympia is the Northwest's only native oyster. It is also fabulously unprofitable.

"They're exquisitely sensitive," said Bishop. In fact, they're downright wimpy when it comes to temperature extremes. Worse for the grower, if not the gourmand, they take forever to grow. While clams and other oysters reach market size in two years or less, the Olympia can take four to five years. Even then, they're still quite small.

Olympia oysters are a very small part of Bishop's family's business, Little Skookum Shellfish. Clams are far more lucrative and make up 85 percent of their sales. From a business perspective, Olympia oysters are mainly a labor of love.

But boy, are they good. Save your frying or stewing or grilling for their introduced inferiors, the Pacifics and Kumamotos. And no Tabasco or lemon, please, nor anything to mask their amazing taste. Olympias should be eaten just as they are, raw from the shell with their liquor. And preferably right next to the water from which they came.

"They have an intense, complex flavor," said Bishop. "Japanese oysters basically taste like what you cook them in."

There's an oniony taste toward the end, I notice.

"Yeah," said Bishop, "and a nutty flavor, too."

Yes, sir, I have found heaven here on Little Skookum Inlet.

So has Bishop.

True, there's a downside to raising shellfish. Puget Sound has two high and two low tides every day. Shellfish are generally harvested during the dominant low tide. But the dominant low tide in summer is during the day, and the dominant low tide in winter is at night.

"You can recognize a shellfish grower," said Bishop. They're dazed and confused, with large coffees in hand. "My family is just getting up when I'm going to bed.

"But it's worth it. I'd suffer something twice as bad to do it. I love this place, I love this way of life. And I love growing food of this quality and sharing it with people."

Bishop is a lucky man, in more ways than one.

The water in the Little Skookum Inlet of Puget Sound might well be cleaner than the last glass of water you drank. The quality standard as measured by fecal coliform count is more restrictive in Washington for shellfish-growing waters than they are for drinking water.

Shellfish themselves really don't mind a little fecal coliform. They're perfectly happy to ingest your waste. But shellfish that have been dining on such would not go down well with you. Shellfish are filter feeders. They feed continuously, sucking in water, filtering out the meaty stuff, then spurting it back out. A mature oyster can filter 50 to 60 gallons of water a day.

Unfortunately, Little Skookum is the exception, rather than the rule, on Puget Sound. The area has good zoning laws, said Bishop, restricting subdivision development to one unit per five acres. Also, much of the Little Skookum Creek watershed is timberland, owned largely by Port Blakely and Simpson timber companies. Port Blakely has determined it will not sell any of its land for development, except for schools or parks.

It's development, of course, that threatens Puget Sound. The area's 3.8 million population is expected to grow to 5.2 million within the next 15 years.

Even in his protected inlet, Bishop is well aware of a fundamental equation that will determine the fate of his livelihood and, ultimately, of Puget Sound. The variables include the number of people in the watershed, the number of acres of impervious surfaces versus absorbent soils, the ability of the marine environment to process pollutants and rejuvenate itself, and many other complex factors that a great number of scientists and public officials are puzzling over.

"Here in this bay," said Bishop, "I'm optimistic that my children will be able to grow shellfish. Maybe another generation."

But move out through Totten Inlet into the greater Puget Sound, and Bishop has grave concerns.

In testimony before the U.S. Commission on Ocean Policy in 2002, Robin Downey, executive director of the Pacific Coast Shellfish Growers Association, said that since 1985 the western United States has lost 29 percent of shellfish-growing areas to non-point pollution—"from failing septic systems, increased impervious surfaces and road runoff, and agricultural wastes."

So can anything be done, or should we just succumb to growth and forget about eating raw Olympias from the Puget Sound and wave goodbye to the orcas and steelhead and all the other critters affected by the increased human population pressure?

Bishop is surprisingly optimistic, and yes, he does know exactly what can be done.

"Two things," he said. "Education and technology."

Karen Lippy, a 1981 Washington State University alum, watches, bemused, as a couple of students swish nets around in the small stream we're standing next to. They're just starting to hone their technique for gathering benthic (bottom-living) invertebrates. Lippy gives them some brief instruction. "And tomorrow grab the bigger nets."

Regardless, invertebrates are showing up in the inadequate nets. "I got bunches of bugs," one boy said.

"Mayflies," said Lippy, picking them out of the net.

"This stream had no salmon in it when we came down here," she said.

"Here" is the Theler Wetlands Education Center in Belfair, at the head of Hood Canal. Sam Theler had left his land to the North Mason School District. Originally this spot was to be a ball field. But that was nixed by the Corps of Engineers, because it would have involved filling in a wetland. So it became instead the current 155-acre education site with what is now a salmon-bearing stream which, due to the efforts of Lippy's aquatic biology students, has ten years of data affixed to it.

The stream is only a mile or so long. But now there's a hatchery upstream run by the Belfair Elementary School, which annually sends over 100,000 chum downstream into Hood Canal. Lippy and her students started putting salmon carcasses in the stream, as nutrient sources, and now the Coho have come back naturally.

It wasn't long ago in geologic time that this area of Puget Sound was scoured by glaciers. Twelve or fifteen thousand years is scant time to build soil from rock. "We're actually standing on material from Canada," said Lippy, referring to the nutrient-poor glacial soil of the area.

What little soil nutrients that had built up over the last few thousand years were generally depleted in early logging of the area. Clearcutting was traditionally followed by burning.

The only nutrient sources for the local ecosystem are the alder tree, which is nitrogen-fixing, and salmon. The salmon carcass as a nutrient source moves through the whole system through animals, said Lippy. Analyses have shown evidence of marine-derived nutrients in 137 species. So the health of the system, she said, is directly related to the health of the salmon runs that come back up the streams to spawn. Salmon don't do well swimming up a foodless stream. When the salmon nutrients were returned to this stream, so followed the live salmon.

Herein lies the irony of Hood Canal. Whereas the land surrounding Hood Canal is nutrient deficient, the canal itself appears to be too nutrient rich, causing the algal blooms that plague it in the summer. When the algae die, they sink to the bottom and rot, consuming oxygen in the process, leading, with other factors, to the dearth of dissolved oxygen that suffocates fish.

Likely culprits such as septic system contamination and agricultural runoff aside, assessing the absolute cause of the problems of Hood Canal is difficult because of its peculiar nature. It is actually not a canal at all, but a glacier-carved fjord, a long, narrow inlet of Puget Sound.

What keeps the main Sound as clean as it is, in spite of its 3.8 million residents, is the continuous exchange of water between the Sound and the Pacific, the twice-a-day tidal flush. Most inlets benefit from this flush also. But the flush of tides in Hood Canal is partially blocked by a massive sill near its mouth. Although the canal is deep, because of that sill only so much water can flow in and out with the tides. So deeper portions of the canal, particularly below the sharp elbow where it turns back east, suffer from low dissolved oxygen.

There arises then the major question of whether this low dissolved oxygen would be a problem, even if the canal were not lined with thousands of homes and their septic tanks and lawn fertilizers. Or if storm runoff weren't flushing automobile-deposited hydrocarbons off the roads and parking lots around it. In spite of those thousands of homes, there is no sewage treatment plant anywhere on Hood Canal—except at Alderbrook, the luxury resort owned by Jeff and Tricia Raikes. She's a 1978 WSU grad.

A well-functioning septic tank with a well-functioning drainfield in suitable soil works pretty well at containing the more directly pathogenic parts of human sewage. What a conventional septic system does not do, said Bob Simmons, is stop most of the nitrogen in the waste from filtering downstream and percolating through the groundwater. Simmons is chair of Mason County Extension and a water-quality educator. Nitrogen, which makes up 78 percent of the atmosphere, is good stuff in appropriate forms and amounts. But where it accumulates in too great a quantity in plant-accessible forms, it causes major problems, such as eutrophication and the resulting low dissolved oxygen.

About half of the students in the North Mason School District will go through the classes taught at the Theler wetlands.

"This class depends on the weather," Lippy said. "In the winter we do things like build nitrogen-cycle models. We'll go from this unit into water-quality studies for about three weeks. They'll learn how to analyze data, how to take data, and become certified in the lab."

Even though Lippy pointedly keeps politics out of the classroom, still, once her students have finished counting benthic invertebrates as water-quality indicators, they pretty well understand how things work in such an ecosystem. She runs through the phases of environmental education. First thing, she said, you have to have this basic awareness that it's there. Understanding leads to valuing. And finally, stewardship.

Does that understanding make its way into the community, where knowledge can be converted to action and prevention?

"It's difficult to measure what students do once they leave school and the effects they have on their families' practices," she said. "We suspect it is positive, even if it cannot be measured."

Regardless, she is undaunted. And a remarkable number of her students have gone on to be scientists.

We've left the creek and have moved to the edge of the wetlands near the head of the canal. One of the students has brought Lippy a dragonfly nymph, which she identifies.

"That's a dragonfly?" said the student. "I thought they were pretty."

I'm having breakfast at the Little Creek Casino near Shelton with Bob Simmons, Emily Piper, and Duane Fagergren. Like Simmons, Piper is a water-resource educator with Washington State University Extension. Fagergren is the director of special programs for the Puget Sound Action Team, an organization connected to the governor's office that coordinates research and education activities having to do with the health of Puget Sound. He is also a small-scale shellfish grower.

Fagergren is talking about the relationship between shellfish and water quality. And of Justin Taylor, the patriarch and founder of Taylor Shellfish, the biggest shellfish grower in the state.

"One of (his) theories is that because we have not relied on Hood Canal producing and harvesting wild set oysters, a lot of oysters just stay on the beach and are never harvested out of the system. That's where you get the benefit of natural filtration."

"So we take it out of the system and eat it?" I pause briefly over my plate of oysters and eggs. Which, by the way, are very good. Even though I don't gamble, I've enjoyed my stay at the casino, eating oysters every meal so far. But now I can't help but wonder what they've been eating.

Everyone nods, pleased that I'm getting it. They're not eating oysters, for some reason. But Simmons reassures me: "So it doesn't turn into nitrogenous waste." What he means is the non-toxic (to me, the oyster eater) nutrients. (The Department of Health is quite careful about keeping toxic bacteria from reaching my plate.) Generally the way it works is, nutrients flowing into the Hood Canal encourage the growth of phytoplankton, which the shellfish gobble up. What we want to do, I'm realizing, is, if we can't keep the nutrients from flowing into the canal, then we're just going to have to take them back out. And one of the best ways to do that is by harvesting shellfish. And that means, I realize virtuously, I need to do my part and eat more shellfish.

Obviously, increased gastronomic possibilities are only a part of the needed solution. Everything involved would be better off if some of that nutrient flow were slowed. In fact, even from the perspective of shellfish, the health of Puget Sound and Hood Canal is a conundrum. Yes, their filtration powers are impressive. Shellfish can remove nearly 17 grams of nitrogen from estuaries for every kilogram of shellfish meat harvested.

But the water has to be sufficiently free of toxicity to support them and other life in the Puget Sound waters. What are you going to do with millions of harvested shellfish if you can't eat them, store them on the Hanford Reservation?

The effort to remedy the Sound's afflictions has been taken on by a myriad of organizations, both public and nonprofit. Coordination is kind of organic, said Fagergren. "There's so much to do, and we know the strengths of each other. As long as somebody doesn't claim overall leadership, I think we're far better off."

Much of that coordination, however, is through the Puget Sound Action Team. Under its broad umbrella are many nonprofit and government groups, including UW Sea Grant, the maritime version of the land-grant system. And, of course, Extension. Most of the Puget Sound counties have water-resource educators like Simmons and Piper.

"I think it's great having both major university systems working on the same problem," said Fagergren, "and doing what each of them does best."

After breakfast Simmons, Piper, and I head down to Oakland Bay to meet Bill Dewey of Taylor Shellfish. Oakland Bay is one of Taylor Shellfish's major growing areas. Other than the hum of machines on the dock, the bay is serene. Across the bay are native Olympia oyster dikes built in the late 1800s. Between us and the dikes is a group of clam diggers, part of Taylor's crew. The tide is still going out, and not all of the flats are exposed yet.

"This is probably the most productive Manila clam beach for us anywhere in Puget Sound," said Dewey. "The flat we're looking at produces about a million pounds of clams a year. It's an incredibly productive area."

Such was not always the case. In fact, not too long ago, Oakland Bay was dead, killed off by the effluent from the pulp mill in Shelton.

"There was nothing," said Dewey. "No barnacles, no crabs, no marine life out here at all. People used to bring their boats here, store them for the winter to kill the fouling on the bottom of their boats."

Before the effluent killed it, Oakland Bay was the seed source for much of the shellfish industry in Washington. In an effort to survive the effects of the pulp mill, the industry switched to the hardier Pacific oyster. But finally, everything in this bay died. The mill bought up all the tidelands to mitigate complaints from the oyster industry.

Finally, the mill shut down in 1958. Justin Taylor, in an act of foresight that must have seemed crazed to many, bought the tidelands from Rayonier.

"Gradually," said Dewey, "the bay has come back."

The Clean Water Act of 1972 eliminated point sources of pollution in Puget Sound along with the rest of the country.

Now the problems facing Puget Sound are far less defined, if not greater.

Dewey is worried about another area of Oakland Bay.

"Another productive area, around that point, is Chapman's Cove," he said. "Sampling results at one of the water quality sampling stations up there since May have been off the chart, really bad."

If the samples don't improve, the Department of Health may reclassify the area, said Dewey, which would mean a massive economic hit to Taylor.

As is the case throughout the Puget Sound, the problem with Chapman's Cove is not specific. "It's nonpoint pollution," Dewey said.

Any number of things contribute, including failing septic systems and domestic animals. In the more urban regions, a major problem is stormwater runoff. Roadways and parking lots block rainwater from soaking into the soil, so it washes quickly into the Sound, along with whatever pollutants it picks up on the way.

Shellfish-growing areas are classified in two ways, Dewey said. Every 12 years, inspectors walk the shoreline of the whole growing area and investigate every potential pollution source and test all tributaries coming into the Sound for fecal coliform. Much more frequently, the Department of Health samples the water. Following heavy rainfall, areas can be shut down temporarily. But consistently high levels of fecal coliform can lead to a growing area being reclassified.

"Once an area goes down," Dewey said, "the best turnaround I've seen is four years."

Nutrient loading, of course, is also on Dewey's mind. "We've got oyster beds in a number of inlets in the south Sound that are growing oysters in half the time they did just six years ago. It's not a miracle of genetics. It's just so much damn food.

"I hate to kick a gift horse in the mouth," he joked.

Miraculous growth is not a good trade.

"What's happening," he said, "there's so much plankton production that's going unconsumed, when those blooms die, they settle out. This time of year, they smother the beds. Inches of dead algae pile up in a matter of days.

"It's always been a problem for us. But it's worse this year. We've had huge losses.

"These are not problems we're going to solve overnight," Dewey said. "These are lifestyle changes that have to happen for the whole population. We have to go to everyone in Puget Sound watershed and get them to change their lives."

Now what about that "technology" that Bishop mentioned? As Bob Simmons indicated, one of the weaknesses of conventional septic systems is they don't sort out the nutrients. New septic technology can boost nitrogen removal, through natural processes, to 80 percent. But these systems are pricey. When a conventional system can cost upwards of $10,000, the homeowner understandably draws the line at just getting the toxic stuff out.

Plus, there are plenty of sources of excess nitrogen other than human sewage. Animal waste, yard waste, garbage. If it finds its way into the Sound, it's more excess nutrient.

The answer that keeps popping up in conversation wherever I go is the "anaerobic digester."

There's nothing new about anaerobic digesters in general. They're used throughout the developing world to generate methane. At its simplest, an anaerobic digester is a sealed container with a gas valve into which a family can throw its waste, including manure from animals.

Bacteria digest the waste, producing methane, which can be tapped as cooking fuel or to produce electricity. When the bacteria are done with their handiwork and the volatile organic compounds have been stabilized, what's left is a fine residue that can then be used as a soil amendment and liquid fertilizer.

"It's not a magic bullet," said Shulin Chen, the WSU engineer who's been tweaking the technology and consulting with a project in Mason County. "But it's a good candidate."

Once its basic virtues sink in, all sorts of possibilities start popping up, particularly along the flood-prone Skokomish River Valley, which empties into Hood Canal. Those possibilities were clear to Governor Gregoire, who budgeted better than half a million dollars for the Mason County Conservation District to build a digester.

Shannon Kirby, an environmental specialist, and Richard Geiger, an engineer with the conservation district, completed a report in December regarding the potential for a community digester in Mason County. One immediately clear use would be to process the thousands of chum salmon carcasses discarded by the Skokomish tribe after they harvested the roe. Until recently, the tribe was simply dumping between 16 and 24 tons of carcasses back into Hood Canal, a natural enough thing. However, that practice was halted once it became clear what a major source of nutrient they were adding to Hood Canal. The carcasses are currently being composted. Anaerobic digestion will be better, said Chen. Not only will it circumvent the odor associated with composting fish, but it would produce methane for fuel.

The carcass production is seasonal, however, and anaerobic digesters work best with a steady and continuous flow of feedstock, just one of the kinks that Chen and Geiger are working on.

Another source of feedstock for the digester is the 1,060 cattle and horses, 500 poultry, 32 goats, eight llamas, and five pigs that live in the Skokomish Valley. That's not a huge livestock population, but still it means some pretty serious poop, at least if it washes down river into the Canal. It could mean some serious methane if it were gathered and digested. Kirby and Geiger envision gathering that resource as well as, possibly, digesting it, selling the remains as fertilizer, converting the methane to electricity or sellable gas, and everybody's happy.

At least if those byproducts result in sufficient income to pay for the digester, beyond the governor's subsidy.

And there's one of Chen's primary goals. "We can get a system working, no problem," he said. "Our challenge is, how can we reduce the cost?"

Once that cost is lowered, the digesters will be more attractive to individual farmers, such as Judy and Darryl Vander Haak of Whatcom County, who believed enough in the technology to build a digester on their farm. Their 1,500 dairy cows produce enough manure to generate electricity to power 180 homes.

So far, theirs is the only digester operating in Washington. But that should change soon. Chen is testing a digester on the WSU dairy farm, and Mason County is planning to go ahead with its digester this summer.

Now, if everyone around the Sound will take Bill Dewey's advice and change their lives, the future of the Sound ecosystem looks downright rosy.

Streaming Solutions

Rebecca Phillips

High in the Cascade and Olympic Mountain snowfields, pristine rivulets trickle into brooks that descend through forest, farmland, and town. Streams merge into rivers and sweep through cities until finally breaking into Puget Sound and the marine waters of the Pacific. There, in the southern arm of the Salish Sea, the waters mingle in a fertile estuary teeming with biodiversity.

"Looking out at the waters of Puget Sound, you see the sunset, the beautiful mountains, and people think, 'Everything is good, we've got the orca.' But we have invisible problems," said Chrys Bertolotto, natural resource programs manager at the Washington State University Snohomish County Extension office in Everett.

Indeed, the region's rich natural resources have attracted a booming population complete with homes, schools, industry, and the inevitable waste products they generate. Much of it, unfortunately, ends up in the Sound. At least 63,000 pounds of toxic chemicals *each day*.

Before the passage of the 1972 Clean Water Act, unfiltered wastewater from smelters, pulp mills, and sewage treatment plants was freely discharged into the Duwamish River and other Sound waterways. Regulations and permits have successfully decreased industrial pollution but a dozen or so Superfund sites remain in remediation.

Today, it is estimated that 75 percent of Sound contamination is unwittingly produced by citizens. Hidden residues from everyday activities are carried by stormwater runoff over miles of paved highways, paths, and parking lots that have essentially become an extensive new system of "rivers."

With every rainfall, a toxic slew of animal manure, roofing materials, vehicle debris, home and garden chemicals, and sewage from failing septic tanks is washed down those conduits into the Sound.

The estuary also suffers from a slow rate of water exchange, allowing chemicals and bacteria to linger in bays and inlets. It all adds up to an ailing ecosystem, with negative effects on plants, wildlife, and humans alike. Rivers and streams once thick with Coho and Chinook salmon now see a fraction returning to spawn. Bacterial contamination of shellfish beds and swimming beaches is common. Water supplies are vulnerable.

In 2007, an alliance of concerned citizens and organizations formed a state agency called the Puget Sound Partnership whose goal is to restore the Sound to health by 2020 and safeguard it for future generations.

Their progress can be tracked by a "Vital Signs" wheel that colorfully highlights six major areas of concern, each with specific indicators of the Sound's health such as eelgrass habitat and economic vitality.

It's an enormous undertaking that relies heavily on regional and local efforts. Hundreds of state, federal, municipal, tribal, and nonprofit organizations work together to keep recovery on track. Among those participating is WSU Extension.

From Puyallup to Bremerton, Port Townsend to Everett, WSU Extension and research centers are immersed in Puget Sound revitalization through a combination of investigation, stewardship, and educational outreach programs.

Bertolotto, who directs the Snohomish County Beach Watchers program, is just one of many Extension agents who use the latest scientific discoveries to design locally relevant community projects and train volunteers to become citizen scientists.

It may be surprising that WSU, whose original campus is 300 miles away in dryland farming country, can be a partner in marine and freshwater recovery efforts.

But as Bertolotto said, "We're a well-kept secret."

On a sunny day at the Puyallup Research and Extension Center, tulips and even the grass seem jubilant as John Stark walks out of the tidy brick admin building en route to his outdoor laboratory.

The New York native and WSU professor of ecotoxicology is one of the original members of the Puget Sound Partnership Science Panel and helped design the Vital Signs wheel.

"Every slot on the wheel is very important," he said. "We try to cover all major issues affecting quality of life in the Sound, from scientific to social impacts."

The panel advises Partnership directors on the best ways to protect the Sound while improving ecosystem health. The panel was key in pinpointing stormwater as today's biggest source of contamination.

Much of that data came from the Washington Stormwater Center—a collaboration between WSU Puyallup and the University of Washington Tacoma since 2010. Stark, who directs the center, leads Puyallup researchers in the study of low-impact development emphasizing conservation and the use of natural features.

Instead of traditional gray stormwater measures like pipes, sewers, and manholes, Stark's team uses green stormwater techniques to slow rainwater runoff and allow it to filter naturally into the ground.

"We're studying things like bioswales—gently-sloped roadside drainage ditches—rain gardens, and permeable pavements," he said.

Permeable concrete and asphalt are made of porous materials that allow water to percolate through to the earth rather than glide over the surface. The materials also trap sediment and filter out pollutants.

Stark said rain gardens use a similar principle. The shallow pond-like areas are filled with a mixture of soil and compost that filters runoff from rooftops, driveways, and other hard surfaces.

"People ask me if our stormwater facilities will be a toxic dump in 30 years—are the chemicals and other pollutants building up in the soil?" he said. "But, no, it's a living system of algae, bacteria, fungi, and other microbes that eat and break down the pollutants."

Some of those pollutants are analyzed indoors at a lab containing an unsettling smorgasbord of toxic vehicle debris. "Every time you hit the brakes, copper dust and asbestos are expelled," Stark said. "Tires wear down, spewing carbon black, hydrocarbons, and metals. They're all really toxic. Then there are bits of oil and radiator fluid that drip on the catalytic converter and drop cadmium, another toxic metal, on the road."

He also analyzes roofing materials and the contaminants they release during storms.

It all amounts to a recipe that takes a heavy toll on salmon and other aquatic species. The evidence was recently confirmed by Stark and aquatic toxicologist Jenifer McIntyre together with NOAA Fisheries and the U.S. Fish and Wildlife Service. Their studies showed that 60 to 90 percent of stream-spawning salmon like Coho die before laying their eggs due to stormwater pollution.

"Untreated stormwater from Seattle freeways is extremely toxic to fish and the aquatic insects they eat," he said. "But allowing water to run through rain gardens completely eliminates that toxicity.

"The number one reason the Puget Sound Partnership was established was in response to the decline of wild salmon populations. It's a fact that certain species are threatened or endangered."

With continued funding from the Environmental Protection Agency and other organizations, Stark hopes to discover ever better ways to control stormwater. For example, using carbon fiber from jet wings to strengthen permeable pavements.

His research findings not only impact state policy decisions but are also reflected in many Extension programs around Puget Sound.

Set in the shadow of the Olympic Mountains, the Kitsap County Extension office in Bremerton is home to both WSU land-grant and University of Washington Sea Grant programs. Their mutual goal is to enhance public outreach efforts.

"We have a unique partnership here—one of only a couple in the state to share an office and expertise," said Renee Johnson, water stewardship program coordinator for Kitsap County Extension.

Her UW counterpart is Jeff Adams, a marine ecologist with the Washington Sea Grant program. He is also a coordinator for the Beach Naturalists program. Johnson said Kitsap County is very progressive when it comes to stormwater management with city and county leadership taking a big-picture watershed approach. "The health of Puget Sound begins in the watersheds," she said. "Our small lowland streams have been called the lungs of the Sound."

That thinking is evident in the city of Silverdale, a mecca of low-impact development where rain gardens, permeable asphalt, and permeable paving stones are common and even adorn a local roundabout. The latest in green engineering techniques are also on display at the Clear Creek restoration site, where the long-neglected stream is getting a massive overhaul.

Kitsap Extension supports these efforts through a palette of environmental stewardship programs. Stream Stewards, for example, trains volunteers to restore and monitor the health of freshwater habitats like Clear Creek. One way they do that is by sampling aquatic insects. The types and numbers they find are related to the amount of pollution in the waterway.

"Stream bugs are a sentinel for stream health," Johnson said. "If we find many pollution-sensitive species, like mayflies, it can mean the water quality is better." It's also better for the salmon who depend on those insects for food. In fact, monitoring bugs is an easy way to help gauge the general health of salmon populations.

Clear Creek eventually empties into the estuary at Dyes Inlet on Puget Sound. It is here that Johnson visits homeowners with information about the Shore Friendly program for removing beachfront retaining walls known as bulkheads.

"The shoreline is part of a delicate ecosystem and when it's blocked with a bulkhead, it can't function properly," she said.

Bulkheads are placed to prevent bluff erosion. But, Johnson said, the sea walls can actually increase beach erosion as well as disrupt natural shoreline habitat. Shade plants are lost along with terrestrial insects that feed juvenile salmon. Changes in beach sediment also block forage fish like smelt from spawning which leads to a subsequent decrease in the salmon who eat them.

"The cumulative effect on Puget Sound is big," Johnson said. "But once you remove bulkheads, the beach can recover to a more natural sand-gravel mix that fish and other creatures can dig into."

The health of those marine creatures is of keen interest to Adams, who leads volunteers in the Beach Naturalists program. At the Bremerton public marina, he points out a few while lying on his stomach on the dock. He calls it "belly biology."

There, just below the water's surface, hundreds of fluffy white anemones wave their tentacles. Sea squirts join a montage of feather duster worms, giant barnacles, sea slugs, and one red rock crab eating a mussel.

"These aggressive crabs are an important defense against the invasion of European green crabs," Adams said. "On the east coast, green crabs damaged the soft-shell clam industry—they eat everything including eelgrass and smaller crabs."

Adams trains Beach Naturalists to trap and identify native crabs in hopes of finding and eliminating nonnative invaders. Just this spring, more than 50 green crabs were discovered near Sequim on the Olympic Peninsula. The fear is that, once established, the crabs could disrupt the Puget Sound ecosystem.

He also monitors sea stars. "We used to have hundreds of purple stars on this pier," Adams said. "Now, if you search, you might find one."

The paucity stems from a devastating viral outbreak of sea star wasting that began in 2013 and has killed many millions of starfish along the west coast. Although die-offs have occurred in the past, Adams said they were never of this magnitude. Researchers suspect warming waters played a role.

"A year and a half ago, we saw lots of sea star babies and got excited but they all disappeared and we haven't seen many since," he said. "In the past, populations have recovered in a number of years.

"Sea stars play a big role in the ecosystem; they eat barnacles, mussels, clams, even dead mammals. If they disappear, it changes the ecology of the area—all the way down to the plankton."

At the far end of the dock, he finally spots one lonely starfish clinging to a post—it's a giant pink star, one of the largest species in the world.

Near a beach in Port Townsend, the Jefferson County Extension office stands guard over Puget Sound like a blustery outpost. The white clapboard building is sea weathered and quaintly topped with a cupola.

Inside, Bob Simmons, associate professor of water resources, pores over a map showing where he and his team have installed local rain gardens.

Simmons's office, like Kitsap Extension, places a major emphasis on stormwater management and watershed protection with programs specifically geared toward the needs of rural communities.

Small hobby farms are common in Jefferson County and manure is easily washed into streams by rainfall. Rural areas also rely on septic systems of which 5 to 10 percent can be failing at any given moment, spilling coliform bacteria into waterways and eventually the Sound.

"Government can't do it all. It really needs to be addressed at the individual level if we're going to make a difference," said Simmons.

It also takes an extensive partnership with nonprofit organizations, tribes, and local city and county governments. Those rain gardens, for example, were built with support from Master Gardeners, the city of Port Townsend, and the local Marine Resources Committee.

"We provide the time and expertise to train people to put a rain garden together," Simmons said "But we're really building the capacity of the community to tackle these projects on their own."

Like Kitsap County, they also offer a Beach Naturalists program, led by Cheryl Lowe. The six-week, entry-level course provides scientific training taught by regional experts. Once certified, trainees commit to 40 hours of volunteer service with local marine-related programs.

Two of those volunteers, Amy Does and John Conley, are visiting the beach at Fort Townsend State Park. Both became Beach Naturalists in 2013—an adventure, they say, that enriches their lives and communities as well as the health of the Sound.

Does is a retired community college biology instructor who tackles projects ranging from green crab and sea star monitoring to forage fish egg sampling and Olympia oyster restoration work.

"It only takes a few days a month. It's not a huge commitment," she said. One of the perks Does enjoys is meeting citizen scientists from all walks of life—IT, engineering, social work, and more. Each connects with a web of other volunteers to ultimately form a very large network.

Conley, a retired public health director, puts his training to use as a docent at the Marine Science Center where he shares his enthusiasm for marine life with schoolchildren.

He also works with SoundToxins, a monitoring program that gives early warning of toxic algal blooms. Puget Sound is home to several species of algae that produce poisons that can harm humans and wildlife.

"The program augments the resources of local health departments," he said. "We provide data that helps the department decide whether or not to close a beach to shellfish harvesting due to biotoxins.

"It's fascinating. It's so much fun to sit for a couple hours with a microscope and plankton," he said. "It's particularly gratifying to people like me who love to eat shellfish and are happy to be part of a program monitoring their safety for eating."

While Conley is analyzing plankton, Does takes part in a similar project with the Puget Sound Restoration Fund. She is on one of seventy teams that collect and test mussels for paralytic shellfish poisoning through the State Department of Health. She said volunteer help is critical to effective widespread monitoring.

In Edmonds, Snohomish County Extension volunteer Rick Albright swaps a federal science career for his new role as a Beach Watcher. To say he's enthusiastic is an understatement.

"When I first heard about the program, I thought it was too good to be true," he said. "It's getting me back to my roots with marine biology."

Recently retired, Albright was a staff biologist at UW before joining the Environmental Protection Agency Region 10 office in Seattle, where he directed the hazardous waste program and, later, the Superfund program that oversees the Lower Duwamish Waterway cleanup plan.

"The opportunity to get involved with Beach Watchers refreshed me," Albright said. "It's a deep passion of mine. It's more than I expected, and I think WSU deserves a lot of credit for conceiving this program and supporting it."

The program is directed by Bertolotto and coordinated by Yolimar Rivera Vazquez.

Beach Watchers is a step up from Beach Naturalists, with volunteers receiving an extensive, 80-hour training course. They also agree to 80 hours in service over the next two years.

Albright volunteers on "beach patrol" where he tells stories and answers questions about things like sea star wasting and ocean acidification. He also maps profiles of intertidal beaches, monitors water quality, and conducts rain garden assessments.

He and Bertolotto also hope to team up with UW to study eelgrass, a Vital Signs indicator for healthy marine habitats. The aptly-named sea grass grows near the shoreline, providing an important food source for tiny organisms as well as cover for juvenile salmon, molting crabs, forage fish, and more.

Bertolotto said one of Beach Watcher's main priorities is to introduce people to the outdoors, especially the intertidal areas where volunteers explain the beach creatures, their life cycles, and environmental sensitivities. "We're hoping to build a lifelong love and appreciation for Puget Sound and its resources," she said.

That includes story time and activities for children. "Research shows that preschool is the age when humans start making connections to the outside world, so it's an important age to reach out to," Bertolotto said.

Indeed. Big hands, little hands. All lifting, measuring, teaching, counting, repairing, cleaning, building, planting, healing. The work is far from over.

In the latest Vital Signs report, statistics show that Puget Sound interventions have made some progress, at least on local levels. Several indicators have improved, but others, such as salmon and orca populations, remain uncertain or in decline. Unfortunately, few indicators are on target to meet their 2020 goals.

Guardians of the Sound are more crucial now than ever. Bit by bit, their hands help stem beach erosion so surf smelt can spawn in the sand. Watershed creeks are restored and more salmon survive the trip upstream to nest. Shellfish harvests stay open a few days longer and crabs can safely molt in the eelgrass.

The efforts accumulate and with enough time and care, even the sea stars could return to brighten the rocks and pilings of America's second largest estuary.

Bulbs and Blooms

Pat Caraher

If their ten children weren't sick, in school, doing their homework, or playing sports, William and Helen Roozen expected them to be working. There was no sitting around watching television. The five sons and five daughters were to be up early in the morning. For role models, they had to look only as far as their parents.

"Hard work never hurt anyone," William Roozen used to tell his children, including Leo Roozen, who succeeded him in 1985 as president and official spokesman for the Washington Bulb Co., Inc., of Mount Vernon.

William knows something about work—and bulbs. His roots in the bulb business date back to Holland, the land of his birth. His ancestors began raising tulips there in the late 1600s. On an early sales trip to the United States, he discovered two things. He didn't like selling, and he didn't like the East Coast. When he finally immigrated to Washington in 1947, he decided to settle in the Skagit Valley.

The valley's fertile soil and maritime climate made it the perfect place to grow tulip, daffodil, and iris bulbs and flowers. Early on, Roozen put his strong back and hands to work for other farmers. Then in 1950, with five acres, he decided to strike out on his own. Alongside a few hired hands, he toiled long hours in the fields. Meetings were held in a garage. To save money, he acquired used tractors and farm machinery.

In 1955, he purchased the Washington Bulb Co., a small but successful business, from two of Mount Vernon's first bulb farmers—Joe Berger and Cornelius Roozekrans.

Now the Roozen family-owned business is the largest tulip bulb grower in North America. The company employs 125 full-time workers. That number exceeds 300 during a peak nine- to ten-month period, making the company one of the major employers in the Skagit Valley.

In terms of volume, the Washington Bulb Co. ships more than 50 million cut flowers and tens of millions of bulbs throughout the United States and Canada annually. The name Roozen means "roses" in Dutch.

"He was a grower at heart," Leo said of his father. Seventeen years ago, William passed ownership of the company on to his sons, all Washington State University alumni, and a daughter, Bernadette Roozen Miller, who died in 1996.

William, 82, and Helen Roozen, 81, married for 54 years, "did everything together," Leo said. A strong sense of family and a solid work ethic have always been important to the senior Roozens. So is religion and love for their adopted country. On their arrival in the States, they quickly became aware of the "immense opportunity" that America presents immigrants. As soon as they could, they became U.S. citizens.

"Dad is a real up-front guy," Leo said. "You never have to guess what he is saying or thinking."

In a perfect world, the Roozens would have wanted all their children involved in the family business. But William left the door open to other options. He encouraged the children to think on their own, to make their own decisions. He expected only one thing: "If you're going to do something, you should be the best no matter what it is."

The Roozen children took the message to heart and followed William's lead. Then, in the mid '80s, William had to face reality. He knew if he wanted to control the business forever, the rest of the family members likely wouldn't stay.

"We had our own goals," said Leo. He speaks not only for himself, but also for his partners John, William, Richard, and Michael. "I have to respect Ma and Pa for that. Maybe they stepped out before he (Dad) was ready."

The sons still value their parents' opinions. But once the decision was made—for better or for worse—the business was handed over to the next generation of Roozens. There was no turning back. William and Helen knew that.

The Washington Bulb Co. farms nearly 2,500 acres, mainly daffodils (550 acres), tulips (450 acres) and iris (200 acres). In season, 1,100 to 1,200 acres are devoted to bulbs. Winter wheat (400 acres) and green peas for processing (240 acres) also figure in the crop rotation. Area farmers, however, are turning away from peas, replacing them with corn, potatoes, pumpkins, and berries.

Bulbs and cut flowers are two different operations under the Washington Bulb Co. umbrella. With almost 625,000 square feet of flowers under cover in glass, double poly, and fabric greenhouses as well as Quonset huts, the company cuts flowers 365 days a year.

Most of the company's products—bulbs and cut flowers alike—are sold in the contiguous 48 states, as well as in Hawai'i and Alaska. "There's a ton of opportunity here (in the U.S.). There's plenty of business in our own backyard," Leo said. He and his partners believe that the Washington Bulb Co. is strongest when it has more control over the variables. That doesn't mean the company ignores the world market. Markets change. So does the company's marketing, which has grown from printed catalogs to use of online ordering. At one time, the largest percent of WBC's gross revenue came from bulbs. Now more than half comes from cut flowers.

Leo travels a fair amount, usually within the United States for business meetings and to meet with associates in the bulb and cut flower industries. He'd prefer never to leave the farm, but acknowledges that's no longer the way the business works.

In an 18-month period ending fall 2001, Richard, who oversees the farm operation, including greenhouses and warehouse, traveled to Holland at least four times.

"We get on a plane, go for what we have to do, and then come back," Leo said of company travel and efforts to stay abreast of competition and the market. WBC sells its products mainly to domestic wholesale distributors, large supermarket chains, and mass merchandisers. He declines to name names. Time-sensitive cut flowers are delivered to Sea-Tac International Airport daily by refrigerator trucks for shipment. All bulbs are shipped on the ground via tractor-trailers. Trucks reach the east coast every four days.

On a global scale, bulb growers are found in Western Europe, England, France, Holland, and in various locations in the Southern Hemisphere. For cut flowers, suppliers are mainly in Western Europe, Canada, Mexico, and Central America.

As growers, farmers, and businessmen, the Roozens want to control as many variables as possible regarding their products. This means they have to be "good at finance, planning, scheduling, human relations, personnel, production, efficiency, and management," said Leo, rattling off the litany.

"We all have to do that." And the company has to plan for the norms in weather. There's always concern about the elements—particularly in November and December, when Skagit Valley farmers have witnessed "some goofy things." For example, bulb growers suffered heavy losses in 1990, when flooding put many acres under water. There was nothing they could do about it.

"You have dry years, cold years," Leo explained. "But when you have a severe frost or flood after the crops are in the ground, that can really set you back."

Asked to comment on how tasks and responsibilities are determined in the family business, Leo responds shyly. He's not sure that he is president of the company, "because none of my brothers wanted the position." Regardless, he and his partners don't put much emphasis on titles. But as president, he makes the final decision if it comes down to that.

In general terms, Richard is responsible for the farm operation. William's responsibilities include planting and harvesting of all crops and cut flowers in the field. Michael, the youngest, is the controller. John, the eldest, oversees buildings, machinery, and equipment. He also is a tireless worker in the community, attends many meetings, and deals with issues related to chemicals, and land and water use.

Sometimes the other brothers defer to Leo, because "it's been the easiest way," he said. After all, they are partners. They make decisions together. At times, however, the volume goes up during business discussions, but they never lose sight of what is best for the company.

"If that means I eat crow, I eat crow, or someone else eats crow," Leo said. "Sometimes your ego gets kicked. But that works. What the heck. We wouldn't be successful if we all walked into a room and always agreed on everything.

"We challenge each other's thought process on a daily basis—sometimes more than we wish to admit."

The late Bernadette Roozen Miller was the only one of the four sisters involved in the Washington Bulb Co. In 1985, she left her career in bank management to build a dream she called RoozenGaarde. The three-acre show garden with Dutch windmill is planted in the fall. Each spring, the more than 200,000 tulip, daffodil, and iris bulbs blossom in a rainbow of colors.

RoozenGaarde is an official sponsor of the Skagit Valley Tulip Festival. The early spring event attracts thousands of visitors from around the world to the family garden and to the tulip fields of the Roozens and other growers. Bernadette lost a long battle with a rare disease known as amyloidosis in 1996. Her memory lives on in RoozenGaarde and the company's retail store she helped shape.

While it may have been a forgone conclusion that the sons would wind up in the family business, where they have worked since they were six or seven, the brothers also know the value of education.

"For me, and I think I can speak for my partners, the Washington State University experience was outstanding," said Leo. "We loved the school, the courses and academic disciplines it had to offer, and the area."

John and Leo graduated in agriculture in 1974 and 1975, respectively. William, a member of the Class of 1977, followed the same route. Richard and Michael earned degrees in business administration, with an emphasis in accounting, in 1978 and 1985, respectively

"We probably learned as much out of the classroom as in it. That's part of education. You mature. You grow up. You form great relationships that you can fall back on the rest of your life," Leo said

In 1989, the Washington Bulb Co. donated 2,000 tulip bulbs to WSU as part of the University's centennial celebration. That year also marked the opening of the Lewis Alumni Centre, and many of the bulbs were used to landscape the grounds around the historic livestock barn that had been renovated and enlarged.

"The Roozen family has been very loyal and generous in providing us with bulbs on at least three occasions," said Pullman alumnus Bob Smawley, who has assumed the duties of planting the bulbs and maintaining the flowerbeds around the center. He reports that the WSU Horticulture Club also has received gift bulbs, probably in an equal amount, from the Washington Bulb Co. to beautify the campus. Other bulbs have been made available to the Pullman Civic Trust on a low-cost basis for planting in city parks and gardens.

The Washington Bulb Co. also cooperates with WSU Extension researchers and scientists, mainly in Puyallup and Mount Vernon.

"We work closely with them on problems that pertain to our business," Leo said. The brothers have constructed and donated equipment, as well as bulbs, for research. WSU scientists are allowed to conduct field trials on WBC land and its greenhouses.

"They (WSU researchers) do a percentage of the work here and monitor the results," the company president said. "You can't leave out those research and extension stations throughout the state. They are vital to WSU and its future."

He reflects on his early days in the field and what the experience has taught him and his siblings. If they wanted things, their father told them, "Here's an opportunity to work." They learned early the value of money, earning enough to pay for their own baseball gloves and bikes, and later their education at WSU.

During his years with Washington Bulb Co., Leo has seen his role change and now as president is involved more than ever in the business end of things. He likes working for himself, as do his brothers, and they enjoy working together.

"The quality of life is higher when you like what you are doing," he said, "and when you can make a decent living at it."

Back to the City

Hannelore Sudermann

The landscape around the Puget Sound has been in flux since the pioneers felled the forests to open up the bottomlands for agriculture. These loamy soils drew some of the earliest farmers, who were delighted to find the region suited a wide variety of crops.

The South Park neighborhood in South Seattle sprang up on fertile, level farmland adjacent to the Duwamish River. According to historian David Wilma, before the settlers arrived, the spot was occupied by Indians, who grew potatoes, fished, and harvested berries there.

In the 1900s this neighborhood became home to "Contadini," Italian immigrants who had been born into farming in their native country. This is where Carmine Marra and his wife Maria bought land in 1920 and set up a truck farm that for years to come would be a center for the community. Besides producing a bounty of food to sell in Seattle at Pike Place Market, the farm was a place to meet at the end of the day or play bocce on weekends.

Today the neighborhood is still home to immigrant communities, but much has changed. It sits just behind one of the most industrial and most toxic areas of the city. The Marra Farm, which survived as a community garden, is the only agricultural land left. It seemed inevitable. Development had started before the Contadini arrived. The river was redirected and channelized for improved shipping access. In the 1920s Boeing's air plant sprang up on the east side of the river, followed by recycling plants, concrete plants, rendering operations, and a foundry.

Besides the pressure of Boeing's expansions and increased industrial use of the neighborhood, by the 1940s the local farmers were finding it hard to compete with the large-scale California produce farmers. All the while, "the farmlands themselves were becoming too valuable for agricultural use," wrote the Marras' nephew Fred Marra.

While the story of the lower Duwamish is extreme, a similar tale can be told for many other fertile areas of the Sound.

Kent, once home to hops farms, dairies, and acres of produce, was known in the 1920s as the Lettuce Capital of the World. The area started to change in the 1960s after the Howard Hanson Dam on the Green River stopped the valley from regularly flooding. The Boeing Aerospace Center was followed by other industry and technology businesses. Today, the valley is clogged with warehouses, trucks, and storage units. It is also home to a variety of corporate headquarters including Oberto Sausage Company and Recreational Equipment Incorporated REI.

To the east, along the Snoqualmie River, developers are pushing the question of what is a farm by packing the rolling hills with mini-estates complete with their own horse paddocks. Larry Pickering who grew up among the 40-some dairy farms near Fall City and graduated from Washington State University in 1968, watches with dismay as these multi-million-dollar homes cover the land around him. "We took it so for granted," he said. "We didn't know what we had."

Back in the 1960s, Larry Pickering enrolled at WSU with plans to study animal science and prepare to run the family dairy. But dairy farming was changing, and the farms were growing to hold hundreds of cows. "I could see that I would have to become a manager rather than a farmer," he said. So he changed his course and became a veterinarian. "I figured I could switch to horses and have the life I wanted."

He watched in the 1980s as King County spent $50 million to preserve agricultural land, and then watched that farmland dissolve into one-acre horse estates. "Thirty years ago, we assumed if you couldn't put development on land, you would have to farm it," he said. But that proved wrong. "Now they put a $5 million home on it and some horses and it's lost to agriculture."

North of Seattle, in Everett, a similar story plays out along the Snohomish River. And south along the Puyallup, farms have given way to housing developments, warehouses, and shopping malls. In recent years, according to a USDA Natural Resources Inventory report, the state has lost an average of 23,720 acres of farmland per year, an amount about the size of Lake Washington.

But in this river of expansion there's a countercurrent, a push of agriculture back into the urban and suburban areas around the Sound. Farms are sprouting up on land where industry has stalled. In some areas, instead of selling off to development, old 50- to 100-acre farms are carved up into 10-acre operations that deal directly with consumers.

Farms are spreading back onto lands that have been rezoned for industry. No one's building warehouses right now, said WSU extension agent Chris Benedict. That means in places like the Green Valley, Renton, and Kent, people are farming again. "From Renton to Puyallup it's really helter-skelter amongst the warehouses," he said.

And within the larger urban populations, consumers are more interested in eating local food and knowing the farmer. Whether they're trying to shrink their carbon footprint or have more control over the sources and safety of their food, people are much more interested in where what they eat is coming from, said Benedict.

And their public leaders are hearing them. This is the year the Seattle City Council has proclaimed the Year of Urban Agriculture. "We are committed to making changes that are better for people and better for the environment," Mayor Mike McGinn announced in February. "This means making it easier to garden and grow food, to ensure that good food is available in all neighborhoods, and to find innovative ways to encourage local and regional food production."

It's not just happening through farm stands and farmers markets. Grocery stores are offering classes on how to find food produced closer to home. And some, like PCC Natural Markets, have established trusts to preserve ag land and support new farmers.

In her 1970 book *The Economy of Cities*, author and urban theorist Jane Jacobs hypothesized that cities came first, and rural economies, including agriculture, were built upon city economies. She also pointed out that the most urbanized countries "are precisely those that produce food most abundantly." Growing, healthy cities, she argued, carry rural and agricultural productivity in their wake.

Japan, after World War II, reinvented its agriculture, noted Jacobs. It did so on a foundation of city productivity. The result was a more diverse and abundant food supply. It is something other countries could do as well, she suggested.

This time shares much with the early 1970s, when Seattle saw its first community gardens and people were interested in fresh, local food. A new generation of farmers had come to the Northwest to drop out of the industrial culture and get back to the land. The public garden movement started when the families like the Marras sold their land to the city so the people living nearby could garden and grow food there.

Today, the sounds of the Marra farm include the roar of airplanes and traffic as well as the voices of children tending their grade school P-patches and buzzing of bees in the hives on the west side of the farm. Here in the city on bits of farmland, neighbors meet over rhubarb plants, tomato seedlings, and rows of lettuce and beans. Since the 1970s these gardens have taken root all over Seattle—Ballard, the 1.3-acre Danny Woo Community Garden in the International District, and Jackson Park to name a few. And thanks to a recent flush of new gardens, Seattle's list of public P-patches numbers more than 80.

The city's P-patches provide food for those who garden there, and for food banks and schools. Depending on which garden, the land is owned by the city, the Seattle Housing Authority, King County, a P-Patch Trust, and private interests. The city estimates that more than 4,000 people are gardening in the community plots, with nearly 2,000 more on waiting lists. At the highest-demand sites like Queen Anne, Fremont, and Capitol Hill, the wait may take three years.

The question today, as agriculture is pushing into the cities, is whether we have returned to a period like the health-food conscious, back-to-the-land 1970s. Or is this something else?

From the perch of her farm above the Skagit Valley, Anne Schwartz, who graduated from WSU in 1978, has watched agriculture and consumer demand from the time she harvested her first crop of organic vegetables. Back in the late 1970s, the new farmers were politically active and intent in finding a way to help save the world from industrialization. "In the '70s it was a general rebellion from things," she said. Today, when people go back to the land, it's much more complicated, she said.

Besides running a farm and supplying produce to farmers markets and directly to consumers, Schwartz has ventured into public policy and organized activism. She has served as president of Tilth Producers of Washington and participates in local and state farm and legislative advisory committees.

That movement from the 1970s didn't disappear, said Schwartz. It matured. The original issues are still in play, but they have broadened to include countering global climate change, protecting farmland from development, securing the food supply, and instilling a sense of community.

"There certainly is enough of a public upswelling," she said. Add to it that the downturn in the economy is stalling development and that there's a greater public awareness of the need to preserve farmland. Then factor in a greater desire for fresh, local food. It has all worked together to put farming back near and into cities, she said. "It's a little bit of a perfect storm."

The New Farmers

A few miles uphill from the Marra Farm into West Seattle, right in the middle of a brand-new neighborhood, is the High Point Market Garden—where small-scale farmers can raise produce on public land that they sell at farmers markets and through Community Supported Agriculture subscriptions.

High Point is a born-again neighborhood. In 2003, working-class and immigrant families were moved out of the 60-year-old community and all the roads, homes, and utilities were removed. They were replaced with a mix of 1,600 low-income rentals, single family homes, condominiums, and town homes. And small farms and gardens.

The mixed-income community was completed this year. It houses about 4,000 people including new immigrants and refugees. On a warm spring morning, two Cambodian women water and weed in the High Point Market Garden. As one walks the hose around a raised bed, the other sits down for a break. They tend their portions of more than 70 raised beds. Here none of the soil is sacrificed to weeds. In this brand new farm in this brand new neighborhood, these women and their fellow farmers are using intensive cropping to grow enough produce to fulfill orders of weekly produce for 50 households.

These new farmers are bringing labor and energy to our cities, said Bee Cha, WSU's small farms agent who works directly with Hmong and refugee and immigrant farmers.

When Cha was 15, his family moved from Laos to Washington. Almost immediately he and his parents and siblings went to work on farms. Among other things, Cha helped his family earn money by picking strawberries. Though they farmed in Laos, "everything is different here—the crops, the system. The only thing that is the same is the willingness to farm and the energy."

A family member had started farming through WSU's Indochinese Farm Project and by the late 1980s was turning decent profits. That prompted Cha's father to grow his own crops in the Sammamish area. For Cha's family and the nearly 100 Hmong families who are now farming in Washington, agriculture was a means of making a living in their new country. Some of what they did went against their culture and traditions, said Cha. Growing flowers for example—

in Seattle, the Hmong farmers are famous for providing gorgeous, affordable bouquets at places like Pike Place Market. "In Laos flowers are considered a nuisance," said Cha.

It is not a love of their beauty or a decision to provide an alternative crop at the market that causes Hmong farmers to grow the flowers. It's a simple equation of labor and economics, said Cha. "Vegetables are much more labor intensive," he said. They're harder to pick, you have to be more aggressive with weeds and insects, and you need things like water to irrigate and wash them and to have storage structures, probably cold storage, on site. Flowers, until you get to the market and have to start arranging them, are much easier, he said.

Cha's understanding of what it means to be a new immigrant, his language skills, and his knowledge of farming gives him a perspective for helping the newest refugees figure out farming in the Puget Sound region. One day this spring he drives down to Kent where a dozen East African farmers are waiting. It's Cha's day to teach them how to assemble and use a small seed planting machine. Back at the refugee camp in Somalia they planted everything by hand—and grew food to supplement their rations. Here they're trying to feed themselves as well as sell produce through small grocery stores.

The refugees' farm is a ten-acre lot at the base of a hill. At one end is a ramshackle blue shed. At the other, a home and yard littered with cars and appliances. Two groups of refugees are using these acres—a group from Somalia and a group from Burundi. The men gather around as Cha pulls the seeder in parts out of a medium-sized cardboard box. Celestine Sibomana, the farm manager for the project, follows Cha's instructions and uses the tool to sow a row of beets. "Part of the challenge for them," said Cha, "is just learning how to farm in the Pacific Northwest."

Back to the Farm
On the day the African farmers in Kent are trying out their seeder, 30 miles north along the Snoqualmie River Siri Erickson-Brown and Jason Salvo spend their morning planting lettuces, tomatoes, and other seedlings.

Salvo and Erickson-Brown are both city kids, graduates of Garfield High School who seemed destined for urban lives. After college, Erickson-Brown went to graduate school in public affairs and Salvo headed to law school. But then while Salvo was studying for the bar, Erickson-Brown interned at a local farm. Why not? Not only did she enjoy farming, Salvo did too. A year later they found a landowner willing to farm with them and broke ground on his property along the Snoqualmie River.

At the same time, points out WSU extension agent Andrew Corbin, they live in one of Seattle's oldest and most urban neighborhoods, Capitol Hill, and drive a reverse commute out to the farm near Carnation.

"We're Local Roots in all its meanings," said Salvo, explaining that when they started selling their produce, they reached out to friends and family in the city. They sold subscriptions for weekly delivery of their produce simply by sending an invitation to everyone on Erickson-Brown's email address list. "It's our parents, our relatives, our friends, their friends, and so on," she said. They also sell their produce to about a dozen Seattle-area restaurants.

They aren't the small-scale farmers of the 1970s, though, noted Corbin. Their outreach goes beyond farm and family. Each year they take on interns, training the next batch of new farmers. This year, more than 60 people applied for just six positions. Salvo and Erickson-Brown also participate in regional government advisory panels and nonprofit organizations supporting local food systems. And they keep an online blog on the challenges (slug and deer damage) and the pleasures (selling out at the market) of farming.

More and more 10- to 30-acre farms with hundreds of varieties of vegetables and specialty livestock are moving in, said Steve Evans, King County's farm specialist.

Over the years he has seen established farms disappear for a variety of reasons—including encroaching development and increased environmental regulations. But as things like dairies die off, land is now available for smaller farms with high-value crops.

Despite the trend to more small farms, the future of agriculture in King County is uncertain, notes the county's 2009 Farms Report. While the conversion of farmland has been slowed, agriculture is still threatened by population growth and upslope development that increases the risk of floods in the farmlands. Rezoning and real estate speculation drive up land prices. Still, enough land remains open in King County to grow sufficient produce for its entire population, Evans said.

The push to bring agriculture into the cities is quite organized. Schools are teaching children to grow their own food and nonprofits like Seattle Tilth, Lettuce Link, and City Fruit, a group that harvests fruit from neglected trees throughout the city, are advocating the local production of food. The nonprofit Cascade Harvest Coalition is a collective of farmers, chefs, teachers, land managers, and others who grouped together in 1999 to "re-localize" the food system in Washington.

The movement is pushing south into Pierce County and Tacoma, "which is a good indicator of changes beyond the primary tier consumer," said WSU extension agent Chris Benedict. In Seattle people will pay more and drive farther to get fresh, local food. In Tacoma, where the median income is lower, "it has to be much more economically competitive," he said.

Terry and Dick Carkner—Dick graduated from WSU in 1965—have managed to maintain their organic berry and produce farm in Tacoma for more than 25 years while the farmland around them has been swallowed up by housing developments, warehouses, and a truck driving school. They've watched demand increase for their food and have expanded their business by selling CSA shares for their crops.

They're being joined by new urban farmers, as the City of Tacoma is converting seven city parcels into community gardens with the goal of someday being the city with the most community gardens per capita.

This growth of new farms and the revival of old ones is a pleasing sight to Larry Pickering, who serves on the King County Agricultural Advisory Committee. It's not just a phase, he said. When diesel reaches $10 a gallon and produce imported from California and beyond becomes too expensive, everything is going to change, he said.

"Local producers close a lot of loops," said Pickering. They give our region independence from the vagaries of the world market, he added: "This is going to take off like crazy."

Call It the Urban Extension

David Wasson

The massive Oso landslide killed 43 people, caused extensive flooding, and destroyed a key highway north of Everett in 2014, pushing the communities of Arlington and Darrington to their breaking point.

For months, grieving residents and community leaders remained so immersed in the search and recovery demands that nearly everything else had to be put on hold. That's why, when they were invited to participate in a national competition that could funnel up to $3 million or more toward desperately needed economic revitalization efforts, Arlington Mayor Barb Tolbert was practically on the verge of tears, again.

"It was this rare opportunity but we had no one left," Tolbert recalled, explaining economic revitalization has been a top priority for the once-thriving logging communities trying to forge their place in Puget Sound's ever-expanding urban reach. "It couldn't have come at a worse time. Our capacity was tapped."

At Washington State University offices in Seattle, Everett, and Pullman, though, an idea was taking shape. The University already was assisting with various recovery efforts, and it sent a team from WSU Extension to help with the competition as well.

What followed was a joint Arlington and Darrington entry that has survived two elimination rounds, already brought in more than $150,000 in grants, and is among just eight of the more than 350 original entries still in contention for the top prize.

"I never, ever had any inclination of the resources that were available at my fingertips," Tolbert said.

Call it the Urban Extension.

Long recognized as the authority on everything from gardening and vegetable canning to livestock care and other staples of a traditionally rural lifestyle, WSU Extension is evolving for a new era marked by rapid urban growth.

Now, Extension is helping research more efficient strategies for protecting natural resources and assisting communities dealing with socioeconomic challenges ranging from poverty and homelessness to wage stagnation and economic diversification.

"The root of Extension is in our link to the University's knowledge base and having a way to effectively reach into and deliver that to the communities we serve," explained Richard Koenig, associate dean and director of WSU Extension. "Considering what Extension was built on, its origins, we're vastly different today and we're continuing to evolve."

The goal is to make sure WSU, as the state's land-grant university, continues to provide practical and relevant expertise communities need, particularly as they face diverse and increasingly complex challenges.

Formally established in 1913, the WSU Extension service grew from an earlier state-funded effort to deliver practical knowledge through what were known as traveling Farmer's Institutes. It put Washington at the forefront of the applied research movement, having an organizational structure and key staff already in place when federal legislation authorizing Extension outreach programs was approved by Congress in 1914.

At the time, one of the greatest challenges nearly every community faced was developing and maintaining a reliable food supply, which is why much of the early Extension focus was on agricultural issues.

Then, as reliability and yields increased, many communities also saw greater economic stability and Extension's outreach began to include programs focused on the family and communities, such as nutrition, parenting, and youth development through the 4-H program.

"A lot of what Extension did historically was community and economic development," Koenig said. "We just didn't call it that."

Meanwhile, the population of America's cities continued to swell, creating large and complex metropolitan regions. Globally, the number of people living in cities overtook the rural population for the first time in 2008, according to the United Nations. That shift is even more pronounced in developed nations, where an estimated 86 percent of the population is expected to live in urban areas by 2050.

In the Pacific Northwest, specifically the Puget Sound region, community leaders grappled with the environmental and social strains of increasingly dense population centers. Suburbs sprawled, and new cities sprung up, creating a patchwork of local governing and policy-setting boards.

Extension offices in urban areas adapted. WSU, for example, modified programs to focus on topics seen as more relevant to big city lifestyles, such as small-scale farming, container gardening, and other urban horticultural pursuits. Additionally, Extension began teaming up with other agencies to focus on improving nutrition and healthy lifestyles, while launching awareness initiatives to bring greater public attention to the importance of preserving clean water and forest resources.

"That emphasis started about 20 years ago and has been well received," Koenig said.

But it remains tightly intertwined, both in practice and in public perception, with Extension's agricultural origins.

To fully evolve, Extension leaders realized in 2009 they needed a new, separate framework that would complement traditional programs while improving community access to the expertise available within all 11 of WSU's colleges.

"Extension has always been about our direct connection to the end user," explained Brad Gaolach, who is leading WSU's metropolitan Extension effort. "What we needed was a way to bring applied research benefits from throughout the University to new groups of end users."

Among them are state lawmakers, city councils, school districts, nonprofit and other community organizations—all with policy-developing roles that can sometimes conflict or overlap. King County alone is home to 39 separate cities and towns, for example, and while Extension has long enjoyed healthy working relationships with the state's counties, its connections to other governing boards are less developed.

The first major step toward that new approach came earlier this year. The WSU Board of Regents authorized development of the new Metropolitan Center for Applied Research and Extension.

Based at WSU North Puget Sound at Everett, it's built on the university's experience with delivering practical research directly to those who can most benefit from it. Unlike traditional Extension services, the Metro Center focuses on targeted projects rather than the development of ongoing programs.

"Land-grant universities understand the importance of applied research. It's what we do," said Gaolach, who served as Extension director in King and Pierce Counties before being named director of the new Metro Center. "Urban problems can be incredibly complex and, given the historical perceptions of Extension, we need to make sure we're recognized as a valuable resource to metropolitan communities."

Awareness of Extension's evolving metropolitan services already is beginning to grow in neighborhoods such as Seattle's historic Beacon Hill, where a vibrant community herb and vegetable garden thrives alongside a renovated commercial office building.

It was inside that office building over the summer that Donna O'Connor, a financial coach with a nonprofit organization serving low-income families, got a first-hand look at Extension's urban focus.

Growing up, she and her brothers helped raise livestock as members of a 4-H group operated by the county Extension office. They'd learned how to plant a garden, turn fruit into jam, and how to safely preserve food for winter.

So when she showed up for a half-day poverty immersion workshop designed to help boost awareness among community leaders of the challenges faced by the working poor, it came as a bit of a surprise when she heard it was being conducted by the Extension service.

"To me, Extension was always about 4-H and agriculture…rural kinds of things," O'Connor said. "But what they were able to do here in one afternoon, simulating the kinds of stress and difficult choices that have to be made—without any time to fully think things through—is incredibly valuable for understanding what's going on with so many people right now."

The simulations are led by Martha Aitken, the Metro Center's project specialist, who conducts the workshops in an effort to raise awareness of how policies can affect vulnerable, often-overlooked populations. She usually opens each workshop with an introduction to WSU Extension and its commitment to metropolitan issues.

"Land-grant universities are the people's universities," she explained. "We generate knowledge, interpret knowledge, and disseminate knowledge."

The city of Renton is among the municipalities that has brought in Aitken and her colleagues to work with department managers.

"It was something I thought could help raise our awareness…which it has," explained Preeti Shridhar, who oversees Renton's inclusion efforts. "Whether it's affordable housing or homelessness, these are all things that cities are dealing with."

Elsewhere, WSU researchers as part of a potential Extension-based project are preparing to help evaluate strains on the Puget Sound region's food, energy, and water resources. All three are linked, meaning any policy changes designed to influence one will affect the others.

And, efforts are underway to help track impacts of differing municipal minimum wage requirements on restaurant and catering companies that operate in multiple Puget Sound cities.

"We can provide the research and information that enables data-driven decisions," Gaolach said. "The WSU faculty has a wealth of expertise."

Developing an effective urban Extension model has been a major topic among land-grant universities nationwide.

The first push came in the 1980s, followed by another in the 1990s, recalled Fred Schlutt, vice provost for Extension and outreach at the University of Alaska and chairman of a key policy-setting committee with the Association of Public and Land-grant Universities.

Extension leaders began to notice differences in the types of services eastern and western U.S. programs identified as critical to urban areas.

In the eastern United States, the major challenges involved combating urban decay, while metropolitan regions across the west were struggling to manage growth. Additionally, many western U.S. population centers still are surrounded by vast rural areas.

"It's evolved in stages," Schlutt said. "All of us are trying to figure out how Extension adapts for big cities while still continuing to deliver our traditional services."

WSU already had a potential plan taking shape in Seattle that appealed to western land-grant universities because it took an "urban engagement" approach, Schlutt said.

The transformation in Seattle began during the economic downturn that followed the collapse of the nation's real estate markets, forcing state and local governments to cut spending to help balance their budgets. One target of those cuts was Extension services.

Although WSU provides the Extension staff and administration, each of Washington's counties typically contribute toward a portion of the local costs.

The deepest cuts in local contributions came in urban counties, where Gaolach and others were told by government leaders that, in the painful budget-balancing decisions, there was a feeling that Extension services no longer were as relevant to metropolitan lifestyles.

Gaolach, who had helped spearhead many of the early efforts to develop urban-style programming in Pierce and King Counties, said it was then that he realized the struggle was as much about metropolitan perceptions of Extension as economic uncertainty.

With help from Ron Sims, who served as King County executive at the time, local allocations for Extension services began to rebuild. But as plans for a new metropolitan-focused Extension service started to take shape in 2009 they were abruptly stopped after Sims, now a member of the WSU Board of Regents, was tapped by President Obama to serve as deputy secretary of Housing and Urban Development.

"We continued to work toward a new model but when Ron Sims left, that put things on hold for a while," Gaolach said.

By 2011, though, the push was extending beyond the Northwest. The Western Extension Directors Association was aware of WSU's efforts in Puget Sound, and by 2014 land-grant universities in Alaska, California, Colorado, Idaho, and Oregon teamed up with WSU to create a regional research center focused on metropolitan issues.

"I think it's important to invest in it," Schlutt said. "We no longer can be the lone ranger."

Also eager to continue transforming Extension services is WSU's new president, Kirk Schulz.

"In the last 15 years there've been some substantial cutbacks in Extension across the country," said Schulz, who has a long history with land-grant universities. "We're having to evolve…and at Washington State we'll continue to evolve."

That evolution already is obvious to many in Arlington and Darrington.

Tolbert, the Arlington mayor, recalled an early conversation with Bob Drewel, then a senior advisor at WSU North Puget Sound at Everett who was helping coordinate the university's various assistance efforts following the landslide.

He told her about Extension's expertise with community and economic development, and suggested it might be a way to take advantage of the invitation to participate in the America's Best Communities competition without pulling city staff away from landslide recovery efforts. Tolbert and others agreed.

Extension sent them Aitken, who along with others reviewed economic revitalization ideas that were being discussed before the landslide, and met with leaders in both communities to get a better sense of how they hoped to preserve their quality of life as they diversified for the future.

Although the history of both communities is tied deeply to the region's natural resources, their economies have become increasingly intertwined with Puget Sound's technology and aerospace industries. Overall economic recovery, however, has been much slower on the urban fringes, and community leaders have struggled to find the best ways to move forward while preserving their own sense of place.

The proposed plan that WSU Extension helped develop would encourage, among other things, continued diversification along an economic corridor, and left many feeling that even if they lost out on the competition's $3 million top prize, they finally had a solid vision to help guide them forward.

"When I look back on it and think about the work that was done, in the timeframe that it was done, if anyone had told us that's what we'd be doing I'd have said, 'Great, where are the magic beans?'" Tolbert laughed.

"WSU was the magic beans. They brought this depth and breadth that I don't think any of us realized was available to us all along."

Wood Takes Wing

Brian Charles Clark

The most complex chemistry lab on the planet is growing in your neighborhood. There might be a tree in your own backyard, cranking out chemicals as it converts sunlight to food, wards off pests, and circulates water and nutrients through its roots, branches, and leaves.

So diverse is the chemical compendium produced by trees that we get aspirin (willow bark is a natural source of salicylic acid and has been used to treat pain since ancient times), the ink Leonardo used in his notebooks (from leaf galls produced by wasp larvae), and natural antibacterials (the fiber in cedar chips is used to make hospital gowns).

And now we get jet fuel from trees. (Indeed, Alaska Airlines in November 2016 flew a cross-country flight on NARA-produced jet fuel.)

That's been the mission of NARA, the Northwest Advanced Renewables Alliance, a $40 million, USDA-funded project led by Washington State

University. Using readily available biomass from timber in the Pacific Northwest, this international collaboration of private industry and research universities has spent the past five years figuring out how to bootstrap a bioeconomy into existence—one that would fuel our jets, meet our needs for plastics, medicines, and fabrics, and teach us new ways to sustainably manage our forests.

Regionally based chemical and energy production will also do wonders for the American economy, as we revitalize old mills, and repurpose refineries to process plants grown locally. One such biorefinery in Cosmopolis could herald the timber industry's future.

The story of NARA's five-year journey, its challenges, and its successes begins more than a hundred years ago, when timber towns like those in the Grays Harbor area were in their heyday.

Natural Plastics

A hundred or more years ago, we had plastic—but it wasn't a byproduct of the petroleum industry, it was made from cellulose. And cellulose comes from trees.

Like cow horns, elephant tusks, turtle shells, and your muscles and skin, cellulose is a polymer. Susan Freinkel, in her book *Plastic*, described these ubiquitous and essential substances as "long, flexing chains of atoms or small molecules bonded in a repeating pattern into one gloriously gigantic molecule." She continued, "Whether a polymer is natural or synthetic, chances are its backbone is composed of carbon, a strong, stable, glad-handing atom that is ideally suited to forming molecular bonds."

It's that glad-handing carbon that we're trying to get, well, a handle on. As carbon dioxide, methane, and a host of other gases, carbon is creating a way-too-cozy blanket in the earth's atmosphere and warming the whole place up. One cause of this greenhouse effect is the ancient carbon we're taking out of the ground—as oil and coal—and turning into fertilizers to grow our food; pesticides to keep bugs, fungi, and bacteria from getting our food before we do; fuel for our cars, trucks, boats, and planes; and plastics plus a million other useful chemicals. With plants, though, we are recycling carbon already in circulation in the biosphere.

All those products and chemicals we depend on can come from trees and other plants. Cellulose is full of sugar, and sugar is a great source of easily accessed carbon. Sugars can be used to make medicines, plastics, fuels, fabrics, and a lot more. If you show a pile of sugars to a horde of hungry yeast, you'll soon have a tank full of alcohol to, say, produce the fuel to fly a jet.

The New Wood Working

I sat down with NARA director Mike Wolcott in his office in the PACCAR Environmental Technology Building on the Pullman campus to talk about the

NARA project. Wolcott's a big guy with big ideas, and he's known as one of the top wood composites people in the world. That's saying something at WSU, considering researchers here commercialized or invented plywood and many other types of composite wood materials that are now staples of the building industry.

With NARA, "we've come full circle," said Wolcott, a Regents professor in civil and environmental engineering.

Jet fuel from forest slash—the residues made up of the branches, bark, and other bits left after logs are harvested—recombines two major threads of the Pacific Northwest economy: aviation and forest products. Recombines because, as Wolcott points out, the first planes were made of spruce grown in Washington.

"Any industry," he said, referring to a broad swath of them, from forest products and the building trades to aviation, "that stays around for generations and generations cannot continue to just do the same thing. Because society doesn't sit still."

We've always relied on forests for their solid products—for timber and pulp. Wolcott recalled seeing an educational poster used in classrooms that describes the many uses of timber, "and molecules were always on the tail end of that."

The thing about energy, as both a topic and an industry, Wolcott said, is that it is fiercely political because it is so essential to who we are and the way we live. Getting traction for change is difficult and requires "a lot of activation energy."

He argued that the Pacific Northwest has the resources, knowledge base, appetite, and passion to make change happen and to lead the world into a bio-based future.

Wolcott riffed on that idea, saying, "One of the strong outcomes of NARA has been huge support within the region" for a more bio-based economy. "It's resulting in actions like SeaTac Airport and Boeing and Alaska Airlines going forth and saying, 'We are going to develop infrastructure to handle biofuels at SeaTac. We're making this investment now because this has to be part of our future.'"

The economics of bioenergy, specifically, but a bioeconomy more generally, are tricky. "The chemical needs are a lot more plausible than the energy needs because we artificially keep energy cheap," Wolcott said.

That means an emergent bioeconomy must find value in areas other than fuels. "And that's exactly what the oil industry does. It makes chemicals, it makes plastics—that's the value chain."

Five years ago, when oil was around $100 a barrel, it looked liked a fuel-centric bioeconomy could get off the ground. Now, the push is to make wood the new black—to mimic, in a sense, the business model of the petroleum industry. That's why USDA's National Institute for Food and Agriculture (NIFA) funds projects for "bioproducts that enable the fuels development," Wolcott said.

The sugars in cellulose make fuels and other chemicals, but lignins are also available to make a wide variety of coproducts, as they are known in the NARA world. Lignins are the scaffolds that allow plants to defy gravity, grow vertically, and compete for sunlight. They're the woodiness of wood, critical in the evolution of plants as they moved from aquatic to terrestrial environments.

Lignins are used in a huge range of chemical products in industrial and agricultural processes, including dispersants, surfactants, adhesives, emulsifiers, binders, thermosets, as well as, in highly purified forms, cosmetic and food additives.

Simo Sarkanen, a NARA team member and a professor of bioproducts and biosystems engineering at the University of Minnesota, has figured out how to make "materials that are better than polystyrene" with lignins. Polystyrene is used in packing materials, DVD cases, to-go boxes and millions more products.

As we transition from an oil-based economy to the new bioeconomy, we're going to need to retool and reopen the currently shuttered infrastructure of the old timber industry. It could restore a lot of jobs in regions that were hit hard by the long, slow deindustrialization of America.

Pulp Nonfiction
I am riding around in a pickup with Larry Davis, director of fiber resources for Cosmo Specialty Fiber, a NARA partner. Davis is telling me about Cosmo's operation, which uses locally sourced hemlock chips to make cellulosic raw materials for manufacturers.

We pass a church on a corner, and the marquee proclaims, "God is not mad at you." In Aberdeen, Cosmopolis, and Hoquiam, we roll past shuttered mills and deserted brownfields where once flourishing mills were ripped out by their roots. God's not mad but you can see why people might be harboring doubts.

When you drive into Kurt Cobain's hometown, a large sign with his lyric greets you: "Come as you are." Another fifty yards down the highway is a much smaller sign. It reads, "Aberdeen, lumber capital of the world."

Davis drives along the Chehalis River, pointing out the rotting pilings sticking out of the water. "This really was once the timber capital of the world," he said.

"A hundred years ago," he continued, "those pilings would have supported decks. And the decks would have been piled high with logs." In Grays Harbor alone, between 1906 and 1907, nearly 500 million board feet of timber shipped out on 600 steam and sail-powered ships. Millions more board feet moved east on railroads. In 1935, at the peak of the Depression, unions in the region attracted some 70,000 timber workers. By the 1990s, timber employment in the region had declined by about 50,000 jobs.

If there's a cloud hanging over the Grays Harbor area, Cosmo is a silver lining. In 2006, Weyerhaeuser owned this pulp mill in the heart of Cosmopolis—and then shut it down. In 2011, an equity firm bought the mill, reopened it, and created about 200 jobs, many for workers who'd been laid off when the mill closed a few years earlier.

The mill takes wood chips and makes "dissolving pulp," Cosmo's contracting and purchasing manager Sandy Corrion told me. It's not made into paper. Instead, this pulp is dissolved into a homogenous solution, making it ideal for subsequent processes requiring a high cellulose content. Cosmo sells their pulp to manufacturers who spin it into textile fibers, mainly viscose, as well as other products.

I'd heard her talk at a NARA-hosted biofuels and coproducts conference a couple months before we meet and was fascinated by the concept of "byproduct synergy" she presented. It turns out that not all waste is trash. Like the logging residuals the NARA partnership turns into fuel and coproducts, Corrion wants Cosmo's residual outputs to be another company's raw materials.

For Cosmo, moving into the biochemicals market is smart. They've got valuable sugars in their waste stream. Finding ways to get those sugars into the market would increase revenues and reduce effluent treatment costs.

Getting Real

"Sustainability cannot be studied in a laboratory because it is inherently a function of communities," Wolcott said.

It can't be taught in a classroom, either, which is why WSU's Integrated Design Experience (IDX) tackles real-world projects in a community-based course. IDX brings together students and faculty from landscape architecture, interior design, architecture, the engineering disciplines and construction management, business, bioregional planning, and agriculture with community members.

Working with NARA researchers, IDX students from WSU and the University of Idaho analyzed regional supply chains for biofuels. As the Pacific Northwest continues to move toward a bioeconomy, where will mills and biorefineries be sited? And where will raw materials be extracted and gathered? And do locals even want that once thriving infrastructure brought back to life?

Undergraduate and graduate students, along with faculty and industry mentors, gathered and presented findings on everything from how government policy affects an emerging industrial bioeconomy to recommendations for mill and depot siting.

Students interviewed community members in likely refinery and depot locations to ascertain local willingness to support retooled mills. Most communities are enthusiastic about breathing new life into those facilities.

Wolcott makes a couple great points about involving IDX students in NARA's work. First, he said, who doesn't want to help a student? "Giving back to students is motherhood and apple pie. So students can waltz in and get people's attention and assistance far better than I can." Community members move from passive clients to involved partners in the project.

Plus, Wolcott said students don't see the same limits as seasoned professionals.

"We're hampered by what we think is possible—and what we think we can't do," Wolcott said. "So students come in with this incredibly refreshing point of view because they don't know they can't do something! And everybody is quite tolerant to let them play around. But, every time, something comes from the students' work that I never thought of."

Not that the IDX students' work is just playing around. The product of the class is innovation, Wolcott said. But, "innovation has to be articulated in the language of the discipline. So if you're an engineer, you've got to do enough calculations and enough design around that to show that you're not a wacko, that it's not just an idea you're writing down on a piece of paper. You're showing that there is actual merit behind the idea."

Fuel for the Future

NARA's capstone project was to produce a thousand gallons of jet fuel and have a major airline fly a commercial flight with it. It was a daunting task, because previous "proof of concept" work was at the lab-bench scale.

NARA's commercial-scale production partners had to get creative by tweaking machines and processes. Critically, too, the fuel had to be certified by an international standards board. And, finally, NARA had to find an airline willing to fly on the stuff.

It's all coming together. The fuel was made. The fuel was certified. And Alaska Airlines has agreed to fly from Seattle to Washington, D.C., to demonstrate that Pacific Northwest wood can indeed once again take wing.

But a commercial flight is really just the leading edge of something much more important and world changing.

Massive amounts of brainpower, along with private and public money, have gone into investigating plants' abilities to supply us with fuel and the starter chemicals required by key industries. The prospects are positive, both economically and environmentally. We can produce fuels and chemicals that won't compete with food production.

The market for alternative fuels is growing. The U.S. military wants to steam a green fleet and fly a green air force on biofuels. Airlines want alternative fuels in order to continue offering service to countries, like those in the European Union, with increasingly stringent carbon-footprint regulations. Environmentalists want alternatives to cumulative toxins released by the manufacture and degradation of plastics. Communities throughout the United States, like Aberdeen, want stable and sustainable economic foundations that offer living wages.

Bill Goldner, USDA-NIFA's acting director for sustainable bioenergy, said, "I've got a six-year-old. When I look at the future of everything we're doing, we're doing it because of them. We want them to have a world that's worth living in, environmentally.

"We want them to understand that food doesn't just come from a supermarket, and fuel doesn't just come from a gas pump. We want them to understand there are social and environmental costs for whatever you do."

Wolcott runs a hand through his shock of pale-as-spruce hair, and reflects on the winding path that brought him to this project. Like Goldner, he said his kids are at an age where they are asking themselves, "What am I going to do?" Their musings bring his own past to mind.

"I've always been a maker," he said, but with a strong love of the environment, too. Wolcott was gradually pushed and pulled toward trees' inner chemistry set and wood's energy potential. From work in forestry, "I finally went into materials engineering and got more interested in making a variety of things from that raw material rather than this," he said, rapping the wooden top of his desk.

That's a familiar refrain among members of the NARA project. Doug Rivers, director of research and development for Kansas-based biorefinery ICM, a NARA partner, recently said that when he worked for Gulf Oil in the 1970s, they built a prototype biorefinery because they were not going to be held hostage by anybody. Wolcott, too, talks about the oil embargo of the 1970s as a strong motivator of the course of his own and others' careers.

All over the United States, NARA and similar USDA-funded projects explore the use of available biomass for energy production: pines killed by beetles in the Rockies, energy cane (a variety of sugar cane bred for high fiber content) and sweet sorghum in the Southeast, switch grass in the Midwest, shrub willow and other woody crops in the Northeast.

The USDA didn't just pump money into research but put millions into education on energy literacy, as well. "We want young people to know about this stuff from an early age, and to think about careers, not just as scientists, but also as practitioners, farmers, and processors," Goldner said.

The next time you walk past a tree in your neighborhood, maybe you'll look at it in a new way. Trees—and, more generally, plants of many kinds—provide the renewable resources that bring us pleasant shade, treehouses for our children, and tall timber buildings for our businesses, as well as the chemicals we need to maintain our energy-intensive civilization.

It Happened at the World's Fair

Tim Steury

Seattle, 1960. The latest census had pushed the city's population over half a million. Labor leader (and former University of Washington regent) Dave Beck was on his way to prison on corruption charges. Otherwise, things were pretty good. Those who knew about Seattle recognized it as sitting in the middle of a glorious natural playground. People had jobs. But Boeing, lucrative as it was, was the only industry in town, and some worried that the city had become complacent. Governor Albert Rosellini thought that Seattle suffered from negativism, "too much inclination to suppress the confidence that lies naturally in many of the people."

But then two things happened, perhaps not quite of equal import. But they were related.

First, the Seattle World's Fair, officially known as Century 21 Exposition, had emerged as a shaky reality, not just a pipe dream.

Second, Jay Rockey returned home to take over as the fair's publicist.

As great an idea as the fair was in hindsight, convincing Seattle that it should, even could, be done was something of a miraculous feat.

Originating at a legendary, and perhaps apocryphal, martini lunch at the Washington Athletic Club in 1955, the idea of a fair soon took the form of a resolution before the city council. Interestingly, as Murray Morgan points out in his lively and idiosyncratic history, *Century 21*, there was no mention of funding in the proposal, which suggested a 50th-anniversary celebration of the Alaska-Yukon-Pacific Exposition.

Fortunately, the idea had legs and made its way to the legislature. Then-governor Arthur B. Langlie signed, with little apparent enthusiasm, a bill calling for a feasibility study. But if he had wished the idea would go away, he made a historic mistake. He appointed longtime friend and UW frat brother Eddie Carlson to chair the committee that would explore the feasibility of a world's fair in Seattle.

Carlson, who would soon become president of the Western Hotel chain, was dogged and bright. Maybe he couldn't walk across Puget Sound, but he had the determination, connections, and charisma to bring the fair to reality, against the odds and in spite of what some saw as a significant part of Seattle's population that was determined to stay small and out of the limelight.

Things proceeded. A commission was formed. Money was designated and eventually raised. A director, Ewen Dingwall, was appointed. Century 21 Exposition became a nonprofit corporation. Seattle was on its way to being presented to the world with a fair that was not only fabulous, but made money for the city and investors.

But maybe that's moving a bit too quickly. What started as a bold vision hit a wall in 1957. A group of civic leaders, including all the members of the Century 21 Corporation, met for a preview of the fair. The preview was indeed impressive. But the estimate for what was proposed came in at $32 million dollars more than had been promised the corporation by the city and state. Their dismay precipitated what Morgan depicted as "great waves of discontent, threatening disaster" during 1959 and 1960.

Let's now return to our second significant event.

Jay Rockey had grown up in Olympia, enlisted in the U.S. Navy during the last days of World War II, then went off to Washington State College to major in English and journalism, play second-string basketball, and sing in a quartet called the Spectacles.

After graduation in 1950, he returned to the Navy for the Korean War, then worked for a while for the United Press, covering the state legislature. Next to him sat Jim Faber, with the Associated Press. Eight hours a day, for four months. They got to be good friends.

Through a college friend's father who was regional public relations director for Alcoa, he landed a PR job with Alcoa in Vancouver. There he met Retha Ingraham, and they married. They headed East, where Jay manned Alcoa's New York office. He loved it—the job, the city, everything about it. But after five or six years and three children, he and Retha started thinking about moving back West, where their family was.

One day, Jack Ryan, formerly with the *Seattle Times*, now working the finance section of the *New York Times*, called and said there's a press conference you ought to be interested in. Washington governor Rosellini was giving a press conference over the phone. The guy directing the conference from Washington was Jay's old friend Faber. Rosellini announced that Seattle was going to host an exposition.

"I called (Faber)," Rockey said. "He was actually working for the fair."

A little later, Faber was in New York. Rockey took him to Sardi's, and they talked. Then Rockey flew to Seattle, just to check out the job scene. He had a meeting with Faber at the fair's planning headquarters.

He walked in and asked the receptionist for Faber, but was told Faber had quit the night before. But, she said, let me check with Mr. Dingwall, who invited Rockey into his office.

"Half an hour later they offered me a job," Rockey said. "And I said, 'Are you kidding?' I wanted to work for Boeing or Weyerhaeuser."

But as Rockey left for the airport, Dingwall said, let's keep talking.

That was January 1960. In May, he drove into Seattle with his family, ready to spread the word about Century 21.

Shortly after they arrived, the *PI* ran an editorial claiming it could not see how the fair could possibly make it. "Do you really know what you're doing?" Retha asked Jay.

Now, from an actual 21st-century perspective, we realize that the fair left Seattle with much more than the Space Needle, the Monorail (at least, the elevated track), and one of Elvis's less-memorable movies. Nearly ten million people visited the fair the summer of 1962. Somehow, Rockey got the fair on the cover of *Life*. Twice. And on a postage stamp, to boot.

After a six-month run, Seattle found itself discovered. (As a fourth-grader in Indiana, I'd have been hard-pressed to locate Seattle, until my teacher sent me and my classmates postcards of the Space Needle from the World's Fair.)

In other words, the fair was a fabulous success, and Seattle had joined the ranks of the world's great cities. Rockey, of course, did not do it by himself. But he got everybody to notice.

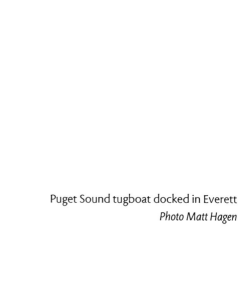

Puget Sound tugboat docked in Everett
Photo Matt Hagen

Along the River

What's the Catch?

Eric Sorensen

If the rainbow trout is now the world's most successful and popular fish, what's the catch?

Jim Parsons works near a waterfall above the Puyallup River, where the Puget lowlands mash-up of highways and warehouses starts giving way to pastures, the foothills of Mount Rainier, and swatches of dense, primeval-looking Northwest forest. Above our heads, a steady meteorological drip is soaking the firs and cedars and us. At our feet, a steady stream, funneled by a lava tube from Rainier's mantle of glaciers and snowfields, is pouring out of the woods. It's mesmerizing—clean, dark, and roiling out at a steady 4,500 gallons per minute and a breathtaking 48 degrees Fahrenheit.

Then there are the fish, tens of thousands of them, calling to mind legendary boasts of runs so dense you could walk across a stream on the creatures' backs. They're spectral, their colors having evolved to obscure them from all angles: dusky gray from above, matching the darkness of the water; white from below, matching a cloudy sky; black-spotted from the side, simulating a pebbled shoreline. But now and then a fish is jostled by the crowd on to its side, revealing the rosy band that gave rise to the name: rainbow trout.

If one animal might lay claim to being the Northwest's preeminent fish, this is it. Sure, that's a Chinook salmon leaping on the state quarter, but only about half a million might run up the Columbia and its tributaries. Meanwhile, three million-plus rainbows get stocked in state lakes, and the 300,000 people who turn out to catch them make the lowland lakes trout opener the state's most popular outdoor sporting event.

It's a survivor, weathering millions of years of geologic turmoil and climate change to establish niches around the Pacific Rim, from northern Mexico to eastern Russia's Kamchatka Peninsula. It's versatile. The red-striped ten-inch fish that a kid reels in on Seattle's Green Lake is very much the same as the silvery 29.5-pound behemoth that Port Townsend's Peter Harrison landed on the Hoh River two years ago. In one of nature's great option plays, Harrison's catch had taken a sea-running form. It is more commonly called a steelhead, our state fish, but by any name, it is still *Oncorhynchus mykiss*.

Other fish evolved for more specific niches, but the rainbow's tolerance for warmer temperatures and poorer waters has helped it thrive. Indeed, if an animal's prime directive is to proliferate, the rainbow's success is up there with the planet's hundreds of millions of dogs. The rainbow has so straddled the worlds of nature and nurture, exploiting the utility belt of its genes and the ministrations of hatcheries and aquaculture, that it has become what Gary Thorgaard, a professor in Washington State University's School of Biological Sciences, calls "a world fish."

And like the domestic dog, said Thorgaard, the rainbow now cultivated on six continents is a different beast from its wild relatives.

"From a genetic standpoint, with the fish that have been propagated for a long time, many generations in a hatchery, you're essentially selecting for a very different animal," he said. "The wolf-dog analogy is a good one. Essentially, we're creating a race of dogs that thrive around people but if you release them into nature, they're not going to survive as well as a wolf would."

This has significant conservation implications for native rainbows, as well as fish with whom they compete and even breed. Their global expansion has created a messy pile of genetic pickup sticks that Thorgaard and others are starting to sort out.

Meanwhile, the rainbow is securely established as a key player in the worlds of sport fishing and aquaculture.

In Washington alone, recreational anglers spent $900 million on trips and equipment in 2006, according to the state Department of Fish and Wildlife. The largest single group of them were angling for trout.

Raising rainbow trout for food is now an international industry worth more than $2 billion. Sales in the United States approach $100 million. Three-fourths of that comes from more than 100 facilities on a 45-mile stretch of the Snake River in southern Idaho.

Jim Parsons used to work there. Now he is with Troutlodge, near the waterfall above the Puyallup River, between Bonney Lake and Orting. It's a $10 million business and the world's largest provider of fertilized rainbow trout eggs, which are packed in Styrofoam and ice and flown to fish farmers in some 60 countries. The 60,000 or so fish writhing nearby are rainbows that Parsons has been breeding, mostly for fast growth, since he arrived from southern Idaho.

It's a prime spot. The fish are started in warmer waters near the company's birthplace in Ephrata, then moved here, where the colder Rainier-fed spring makes for a more consistent spawn and better quality eggs.

"Plus," Parsons said, "we're closer to the airport."

Good Genes

Parsons started as a fish rancher, hatching salmon and releasing them to the ocean with the hope of harvesting them on their return. One company he worked for was an Oregon-based subsidiary of Weyerhaeuser.

"Then Weyerhaeuser was in a transition point," he said, "where they were taking their research dollars and investing in something that we thought was ridiculous called a disposable diaper. How could that make money over fishing? That was my first business lesson."

As it was, salmon ranching wasn't all that dependable. The fish would hatch and smolt, but the ranchers who wanted to harvest fish on their return from the ocean had to get in line behind predators, sport and commercial fishermen, and the fates of ocean-going life. Meanwhile, Parsons wondered if he might learn more about the salmonid's inner workings.

"It became really clear to me that we were expecting these fish to do all these things in these environments," he said, "and we didn't know a thing about genetics of the animals that we were working with."

He ended up studying with a young Gary Thorgaard, fishing with him on the Snake and Grande Ronde Rivers and working on chromosomal manipulations. After graduation, he worked in Idaho raising brood stock and developing a better understanding of the role genetic traits have in the rainbow's production, growth rates, and disease resistance.

His work there reinforced his impression, as he puts it, "of what a remarkable animal it is. It can tolerate all of our mistakes pretty well." He credits this to the rainbow's genetics, and particularly the "tetraploid event"—a moment or moments 25 to 100 million years ago that produced large numbers of extra genes.

"It basically duplicated all of the genes that were present in the animal, in the historical ancestor," said Parsons. "So now all of a sudden there are all of these, not free genes, but excess genes that can be selected upon and still keep the basic animal intact."

He joined Troutlodge in 1998, overseeing technical programs and research. It's an intense operation with numerous WSU connections. Thousands of fish swim in each of dozens of long, concrete bound raceways that look like so many narrow Olympic-sized swimming pools. An independent veterinarian routinely sends tissue samples to WSU's Washington Animal Disease Diagnostic Laboratory to screen for seven viruses, four bacteria, and two parasites. The quality of water leaving the site is closely monitored for ammonia, organic compounds, and solids. Fish carcasses are recycled as fertilizer for local organic farms.

Meanwhile, workers standing in the frigid waters check some 30,000 fish each week for signs of spawning. Geneticists, including 2008 WSU graduate Kyle Martin, track genetic markers with the help of WSU scientists, who sequence the fish DNA. Rice-grain-sized transponder tags ensure that no fish goes undocumented.

"We monitor the performance of each individual," said Parsons as he stands in a wet lab capable of developing more than 2 million fertilized eggs. "Once they reach a one-kilogram size we'll collect all the final data off all the fish and run that into a program that takes into account their relative performance, their grandparents' performance, cousins, uncles, whatever, and generates a statistical value, a 'breeding value,' for each animal. Then we'll select the top 15 to 20 percent of the population to produce the next generation."

He's been at it for five generations now. In each one, he has improved their growth by 15 percent.

For the most part, the eggs that leave Troutlodge go on to be a fairly sustainable fish. Monterey Bay Aquarium's Seafood Watch, which rates the ecological impact of wild-caught and farmed seafood, ranks farmed rainbow trout as a "best choice."

The company's eyed eggs also make a significant contribution to the roughly half a million tons of trout farmed around the world each year.

But the relatives of these fish now swimming in streams on five continents are having a more questionable impact.

Dumb Fish

In a windowless basement room on WSU's Pullman campus, Kristy Bellinger runs a speed trap for fish.

It's a clear plastic tank, more than a meter long, filled with water and fitted with electronic sensors. Bellinger, a doctoral student in the School of Biological Sciences, recently spent 15 weeks repeatedly running 100 hatchery-raised and semi-wild rainbow trout through the tank, clocking their speed as they went.

"The more domesticated fish, when I try to startle them, they kind of mosey on down," she said. "They don't really have the burst of performance as much as the wild ones."

The slower the trout, the easier the prey. It's one of several shortfalls of the hatchery trout, say Bellinger and her advisor, Associate Professor Patrick Carter.

"That is a reputation that hatchery fish have," said Carter, "that they're slower, stupider, not as much fun to catch. Certainly I feel that way when I go. If you go trout fishing and catch a hatchery rainbow trout, to me the meat is kind of mealy. They're not very interesting to catch. I'd much rather go somewhere you can have a chance of catching wild fish."

Starting in the late 19th century, a national fishing movement helped spur the raising and releasing of rainbow trout across America and around the world. Its advocates ranged from acclimatization groups, who spread exotic species around the globe, to the early environmentalist John Muir, who advocated fish stocking in California's Sierra Nevada. But in recent decades, anglers and biologists have started worrying about the effect non-native and hatchery-reared trout have on the ecology of lakes and streams, particularly those with wild fish.

"The question is: Are we damaging the wild populations by releasing the hatchery fish?" said Carter. "And if we are, what does that mean? Are we going to drive the wild populations extinct through this? Or are we going to inject genes into them, at least domesticated genes into them, that may make them become slower and less able to live in the wild?"

The problem is fundamental. The rainbow and other salmonids have evolved over millions of years to survive in varied but particular circumstances in the wild. The hatchery rainbow flourishes in its relatively new, artificial surroundings, but its acquired skill set—like swimming near the surface and viewing anything on it as a fish pellet—compromises the meticulously worded survival manual of its genes.

"All hereditary changes brought about by artificial selection for more efficient rearing in fish culture are contrary to natural selection, where the sole criterion is survival to reproduction in the wild," writes Robert Behnke in *About Trout*.

In the Northwest, said Behnke, hatchery steelhead are less well adapted and die more easily than their native relatives. But before dying, as many as half stay in freshwater and compete for food and space with wild juveniles, suppressing their numbers.

The westslope cutthroat trout was once the most widely distributed trout in North America. But hatchery rainbows and other raised fish cross-bred with them so much that one study said the cutthroat is "threatened by genomic extinction."

In the long run, a shrinking genetic pool does not bode well for any fish, with genetic diversity acting like a diverse financial portfolio against downturns from different directions.

"In general, a high degree of genetic diversity in a population allows it to respond to environmental challenges more effectively," said Carter. "If you eliminate that genetic variation, you eliminate the ability of that population to respond to environmental changes."

With repeated introductions of hatchery rainbows, the genetic variations developed across North American trout could get generic in the form of one, ubiquitous, questionably talented fish. Montana geneticists Fred Allendorf and Robb Leary have called it *Salmo ubiquiti*, "a single new mongrel species."

Genetic Pickup Sticks
For years, scientists have theorized about the evolution of fish and their relationships to each other by comparing physical features like colors, spots,

vertebrae, gills, even the numbers of their scales. Starting in the early '70s, Gary Thorgaard set to looking at their genes.

In the days before DNA sequencing, this could be as basic as counting the number of chromosomes a fish had. Rainbow trout can have between 58 and 64 chromosomes, so there was something to work with. Most types of rainbows have 58 chromosomes, but the rainbow from California's McCloud River has 60. It was one of the first hatchery trout, and its 60 chromosomes now show up around the world.

Thorgaard also looked at karyotypes, pictures in which chromosomes are arranged like so many side-by-side squiggles. Looking at them over and over, he started noticing that one Y chromosome in certain male steelhead had shorter arms than the female. He tested himself, looking at nearly two dozen unlabeled karyotypes, and found he could spot the male in every case.

Thorgaard had found the rainbow trout's sex chromosomes. The discovery landed him in *Science,* a prestigious journal that researchers can spend their careers trying to crack. He was still a graduate student.

Thorgaard's research has since been a continuum of genetics innovations in both the study and management of salmonids. As researchers and fisheries managers wrestle with sorting out the genetic and ecological impact of the rainbow, Thorgaard's work will likely play a significant role.

It already does. The trout in Bellinger's speed trap, for example, are clones developed using a technique he refined after seeing his postdoc advisor use it on zebrafish. The technique involves exposing rainbow eggs to gamma radiation, in this case in the College of Veterinary Medicine's linear accelerator. That destroys the egg's chromosomes but leaves the egg cell intact. The egg is then fertilized, producing an animal with only one set of chromosomes. A heat treatment a few hours later inhibits the cell's first division, but the cell's nucleus does divide, leaving an animal with the necessary two sets of chromosomes. Both sets are from the male, so the fish is genetically identical to its one and only parent.

"It's a defined research animal that you can cumulatively build information on rather than having the particular fish gone," Thorgaard said one afternoon as he stands surrounded by tanks of clones in an indoor hatchery on the old Carver Farm. "So we have repeatability in terms of our experiments."

Thorgaard found a number of natural triploid rainbow trout and identified that they were sterile, owing to the rare fertilization malfunction that gives the fish three sets of chromosomes. That means the fish can be put out in the wild without risk of hybridizing with other, native fish.

"I would have to say the development of triploid rainbows is going to be probably one of the most important tools in providing angling opportunities in an area where you have natives," said Jim Uehara, inland fish program manager for the Washington Department of Fish and Wildlife. He calls Thorgaard "a pioneer" in developing the technique to make triploids.

And because the fish's resources never go into reproducing, it can grow to prodigious sizes. The world record rainbow trout, a 48-pound behemoth caught in Saskatchewan, was a triploid.

Last year, Thorgaard was co-author of a paper tracing the genetic differences of nearly five dozen populations of coastal and inland rainbow trout throughout the Pacific Rim. The study added new evidence to theories on why some fish are where they are and how they got there.

For example, the prized rainbows of British Columbia's Blackwater River, a tributary of the Fraser River, are well inland but have genetic markers more similar to coastal fish. However, this makes sense when one considers that the last glacier shifted drainages in the region.

"We can see remnants of things that happened a long time ago," said Thorgaard.

Or more recently. Several types of rainbows in inland eastern Washington shared genetic markers with coastal types—possible evidence of some seven decades of hatchery stocking with west-side fish. The research, which included the use of a new Y chromosome marker, can help future conservation efforts by more clearly identifying non-hybridized inland rainbows.

"This gave us a really good tool for identifying the difference between the native and the hatchery fish," said Thorgaard, "and something that's maybe more crisp and easy to quantify than counting the number of scales."

For the most part, he said, the study showed fish holding on to their unique genetic heritage.

"People talk about all the hatchery fish and mixing everything up, the reality is that some of this evidence shows we still have the imprint of the native fish present."

Tough Fish in Paradise

A century ago, the first of two dams went up on the Olympic Peninsula's Elwha River, blocking migration of all five species of Pacific salmon, cutthroat and bull trout, and steelhead. This fall, work is expected to begin to remove the dams and restore habitat for some of the Northwest's most prolific runs.

The question now is: If you tear the dams down, will the fish come and go?

In the case of the steelhead, said Thorgaard, they never left.

"They're just present in a freshwater form," he said.

In 1995, Carl Ostberg, a Thorgaard graduate student, hiked 17 miles up the Elwha, set up camp, and spent a day fly-fishing. He caught 20 fish, the "hardest fighting rainbow trout for their size, eight to 11 inches, that I've ever caught."

Before releasing them, he drew a milliliter or two of blood from each fish. He had to keep the blood samples cool, but not frozen, so he had brought along a Styrofoam cooler with dry ice and cold packs.

The following day, he hiked out and took his blood samples back to Pullman. There he separated out the white blood cells, analyzed their chromosomes, and concluded that the Elwha still had native rainbow trout stranded upstream by the dams.

Thorgaard suspects there's already a small steelhead population below the dams that can help replenish the run. But he calls the rainbows above the dams "a more abundant genetic reservoir." In time, he said, some of them will answer a deep, ancient call to head to the ocean, streamlining their bodies, increasing their lipid metabolism, altering the biochemistry of their gills and intestines, and synthesizing compounds that will change their color to a radiant, steely silver.

The waters could bubble and the world could burn. But the rainbow would rise, phoenix-like, from the ashes.

A River Rolls On

Brian Charles Clark

After thousands of years of use for food, transportation, and trade, the Columbia River's dynamics have changed, resulting in unforeseen consequences and deeply mixed emotions.

Once there were Five Sisters. Because they loved to eat salmon, the sisters kept a dam at the mouth of Big River to prevent the fish from swimming upstream. Every night they feasted on a wonderful, fat salmon. This didn't suit Coyote, who thought that the salmon need the people and the people need the salmon. Or maybe he was jealous and wanted some of that fat salmon for himself. So Coyote tricked the sisters to get into their camp. He disguised himself as a baby and played to the Sisters' maternal feelings. He saw they had a key that opened the dam. He stole the key, opened the dam, and freed the salmon to run upriver.

Or maybe it was Raven who brought the salmon into the Columbia River watershed. Raven heard a little girl crying. She lived in the eastern desert, and he just knew she wanted fish. But she lived too far upriver, and in those days the salmon stayed downstream. So he went and grabbed one! He flew all the way to the mouth of the river, snagged a fat salmon in his claws, and flew back to the little girl, who smiled. Even so, all the other salmon chased hard after that Raven, and took for a new home a massive watershed that stretched to the Rockies.

Deep in that watershed, Dennis DeHart and his son were visiting the Selway River. "My son was about three," the Washington State University photography professor recalled, "and he scooped up a handful of gelatinous stuff." It took him a moment to register, and then, "I realized, 'Oh! Those are eggs!' And I looked down, and there was a salmon, dying, battered. That salmon came all the way back up through all the dams, all the locks, through a number of rivers, up to the Selway in Idaho, one of the wildest rivers. And that left a profound impression."

DeHart's story is the origin of an ongoing project called "Confluences." Having grown up on the Columbia River, he is fascinated by the layers of history that flow through the Columbia watershed, and how we see those histories. His grandfather was a logger; DeHart counts himself an environmentalist. The development of the Columbia River watershed, he said, is full of unintended consequences. That's something you hear a lot when you start talking to people about the river.

There is a kind of pain or sadness or confusion, even among the most rationalistic economists. To live in the Pacific Northwest with even one eye open is to live with that conflict: between fish and dams, between fishers and farmers, between the wild and the tamed.

Of all the work done by the Columbia River, and all the work people do on the river—fishing, canning, recreation, transportation, power, irrigation, flood control—the work that perhaps needs doing most is emotional.

William Dietrich, the author of *Northwest Passage: The Great Columbia River*, uses tough, direct language to describe our situation: "The Columbia is that cruelest of all stories: a thing changed into exactly what Americans wanted, and, once changed, proving to be a disappointment of an entirely different sort."

It's all Coyote's fault. The trickster is a bricolage of feelings and shape-shifting beings, said scholar and writer Jay Miller: "He was greedy, selfish, stupid, and very, very wise, sometimes." No wonder we feel ambivalent about dams, salmon, irrigation—all the wonders we have wrought have cost us something intrinsic, that cannot be valued by economists because it is priceless.

It's Coyote's fault, too, that we have to do all this work, said another story the First Peoples sometimes tell. It used to be that rivers flowed both ways: downstream on one side, upstream on the other. It was easy to get around back then. But Coyote saw that and said, Nuts, make the young men work, make them push back upstream!

Pushing Upriver

The mouth of the big river, which the Chinook people call Wimahl, is often impossible to enter. It's a cold, stormy mess where the epic outflow of the Columbia wrestles with the ever-flexing muscle of the tides. The weather is wretched with wind and rain, and 200 days of the year the river's mouth is swathed in fog. Waves higher than the old tall sailing ships crack and fume, tearing apart and running aground even modern steel ships.

In 1791, Robert Gray, aboard the *Columbia Rediviva* and sailing north along the Washington coast, tried to investigate the source of a strong outflow. For nine days he tried to gain entry into the soon-to-be-renamed Columbia. He gave up, "not from the current," George Vancouver later recounted, "but from the breakers which extend across it." Gray sailed north to a calm bay, now known as Grays Harbor.

Anyone trying to cross the Columbia Bar, the ever-shifting underwater islands of silt the river gifts the sea, must contend with the breakers, the infolding bombs of water that make kindling out of stout oak beams. Gray eventually gained entry and named the river after his ship.

The mouth of the Columbia, the Graveyard of the Pacific, is the resting place of thousands of ships and nearly as many sailors. Thanks to the U.S. Coast Guard, with their porpoise-like cutters that can power through waves and across the tops of huge swells, many lives have been saved.

The Coast Guard's sister service ran the Quarantine Station a few miles upriver from Columbia Bar. Until 1912, that uniformed branch was called the Marine Hospital Service and since then, the Public Health Service.

Ports needed quarantine stations to fumigate ships that spent weeks and months travelling long distances. Sailing around the Cape from London to Astoria is 18,000 miles. It was a trip of months, sometimes many months. You, too, might welcome a bath in carbolic soap, and having your clothes disinfected with high-pressure steam in a delousing retort. Bubonic plague, yellow fever, cholera, smallpox, and typhus were all dangers exacerbated by close quarters and stowaway rodents.

In 1891, the old Eureka and Epicure Cannery at Knappton Cove had been closed for a few years, a victim of the crash of the commercial fishing industry. The massive, two-storey complex where once skilled Chinese workers sliced and diced salmon all day, before bunking above the packing line for the night, got converted to a quarantine station. Complete with a lazaretto (a pest house), ocean-going steamers anchored in the wide river to be fumigated by sulfur burning in the holds, suffocating rats and killing other disease-bearing critters.

The repurposed cannery, current owner Nancy Bell Anderson said, became a quarantine station for Astoria and Portland in order to compete with the station for Seattle, located at Port Townsend. An October 1921 article in *The Oregonian* dubbed the station "the Ellis Island of the Columbia River." Any passenger who looked "a little green around the gills," said Anderson, was confined to the lazaretto, with deportation waiting in the wings.

Many Scandinavians flowed through the station, WSU history professor Laurie Mercier said, along with people from many other parts of the world. Astoria, just across the river, is still home to a large Finnish community. Excluded by an 1882 anti-immigration law were Asians, and especially Chinese. The derogatorily named "Iron Chink," an automated fish chopper, replaced the Chinese cannery workers. While not nearly as precise as the humans it replaced, the machine reduced labor costs in an industry rapidly contracting due to overfishing.

By 1950, though, the station was no longer needed, and the Bell family bought the place on the federal surplus market. They turned it into a recreational fisher's resort, with camping and docks for canoes and boats. Young Nancy sold bait, tackle, and candy bars from the old pumphouse.

Now, the place is its own museum, the Knappton Cove Heritage Center. Layers of history are presented in the tight quarters of the converted lazaretto: trade beads from the earliest days of contact between Native Americans and Euro-Americans, Chinese porcelain used by cannery workers, glass medicine bottles, canoe paddles. Nancy's older brother, Tom Bell, admits to being an inveterate beachcomber and artifact collector. When the tide is out, he said, all manner of stuff pops up.

Out front, you can still see the massive dolphins in the tidelands just across Highway 401. These heavy beams anchored the big complex where once tall ships docked at the quarantine station.

Celilo Falls

Sunday, March 10, 1957: As the massive floodgates on the new dam at The Dalles are closed, bumper-to-bumper traffic lines Highway 30 as the gathered spectators watch the waters rise behind the dam. Within hours, Celilo Falls is gone, replaced by a slackwater lake.

As many celebrated the new ease of navigation and the forthcoming surge of cheap power, others wept and prayed. In her book *Death of Celilo Falls*, Katrine Barber, who received her master's and doctoral degrees from WSU, wrote that "the region's Indians mourned the loss of fishing sites and a core way of life." One child later recalled that "as the little islands disappeared, I could see my grandmother trembling, like something was hitting her… she just put out her hand and started to cry."

Two and a half years later, as hydropower generation is started, U.S. Senator Richard Neuberger from Oregon tells the gathered crowd that "our Indian friends deserve from us a profound and heartfelt salute of appreciation... They contributed to its erection a great donation—surrender of the only way of life which some of them knew."

Wyam, another name for Celilo Falls, is one of the oldest continuously occupied sites in North America. For the dam builders, the economics were obvious: any value that the fisheries had was negligible compared to that of hydropower and irrigation. But as WSU archaeological anthropologist Shannon Tushingham pointed out, Native Americans "depended on the river not just for food but for spiritual sustenance as well."

Celilo Falls, pockmarked with eddies, chutes, and rapids, wasn't just a great place to fish; it was a gathering place for peoples from many hundreds of miles around. Mercier said that "Celilo Falls was a huge trade mart where people from all over came." Her fellow WSU historian Rob McCoy elaborated, adding that "Yakama, Umatilla, Walla Walla, Cayuse, Warm Springs, Palouse people, Nez Perce" all came to Celilo Falls to fish, to trade, to party and socialize.

McCoy, a local, remembered his father talking about the once free-flowing river, and stopping to buy salmon at the falls. "For the dominant culture, the rivers are seen as economic resources. They move goods, the dams provide power and irrigation. Not that people didn't see beauty in them, but that was secondary to the economic potential. There's been a lot of economic development, but at great cost." When the dams were being built, "we didn't listen to Native people. We're doing a little better now."

McCoy added, "I think there are more and more people in this part of the country who say, 'Yeah, we didn't consider the consequences of these things. Or we just weren't able to comprehend what was going to occur.'"

But as Barber described in her book, *In Defense of Wyam*, some people could foresee the consequences. As the dam at The Dalles was being built, a White woman and a Native woman banded together, not to stop construction, but to prepare for the consequences of the loss of a way of life. Flora Thompson, a member of the Warm Springs Tribe and wife of the Wyam chief, found an ally in Martha McKeown, a member of an affluent farming family. The two became friends and worked together to meet the needs of the people of Celilo Village. But, Barber said, McKeown didn't want to define their work as charity. "She's resistant to charity, she says that [the people there] deserve this."

McKeown was aware of the poverty that would result from the dam and the loss of the falls. "I think there are a lot of people who thought that way," Barber said. The defenders of Wyam worked to establish new fishing sites, to compensate people for their losses, and to find "other avenues to subsistence."

Barber, a professor at Portland State University, recently taught a course on Oregon history and, in finishing the unit on the Columbia River, her students arrived at a place of "ambivalence: what were people supposed to do at this time? We all benefit. It's a series of statements connected by 'and.' This was really awful for people at Celilo. And I have electricity and I'm really enjoying my air conditioning right now. And I'm concerned about the ongoing management of the Columbia River. And I'm really glad it is a transportation corridor through the Pacific Northwest. So it's all these linking, contradictory statements, with no easy resolution."

Layers upon Layers

If you think about it, McCoy said, the Save Our Dams movement is a kind of flip side to what happened to Native peoples. "It's people's livelihoods and ways of life" that are threatened when environmentalists argue that the dams on the Columbia and its tributaries should be removed.

"That's the thing," McCoy said, "there are successive narratives." And, as Barber remembered from her days as a doctoral student at WSU in the late 1990s, "there were some real serious discussions about removing the four lower Snake River dams.

"What's fascinating," Barber continued, "and this is just a matter of living long enough to see the ebbs and flows of some of these discussions, is that [removal] is no longer on the table. Now [there's talk of] privatizing parts of the Bonneville Power Association. And if parts of the BPA are privatized, that raises the question, what is the relationship with those tribal nations? Because their protections are those federal treaties. So it complicates things. Yet again."

McCoy said he doesn't like to think of himself as a historian of Native Americans, "although I write a lot about that. I think more about narratives." As a young man, McCoy read Yellow Wolf's autobiography (as told to Lucullus Virgil McWhorter) and was inspired to think about which stories we remember, and which we forget.

Yellow Wolf, a Nez Perce warrior who fought in the war of 1877, was one of the few Nez Perce to speak to an outsider about the war and its "after hardships." He concludes his telling by saying, "The whites told only one side. Told it to please themselves. Told much that was not true. Only his best deeds, only the worst deeds of the Indians, has the White man told."

The story of the Columbia River watershed, McCoy argued, "doesn't need to be a story of triumph. It is a story about engineering and everything else. We can tell the whole story. It makes us better people, more compassionate." All our stories, like the sedimentary layers of history piling up along the Columbia, are intertwined. When the nation decided it needed plutonium to win a war, McCoy reminded us, "it wasn't just Native people who got kicked out of Hanford."

For WSU landscape architecture professor and poet Jolie Kaytes, the situation is "muddy." She finds her rational responses to the complexity of the watershed colored with emotion—and her emotions colored with rational considerations. Like Columbia Bar, these shift with the exigencies of time, tide, and the news cycle.

Kaytes led her students on a semester-long quest to understand and speak to the situations of particular communities in the watershed. From imagining a vibrant cultural scene along a dam-free Lewiston, Idaho, waterfront to wondering what can possibly be done for the residents of Northport, poisoned by the outflow of mining toxins from north of the border, she and her students made what she calls "offerings."

"That's what I do, too," she said of her poetry, essays, and teaching. "I am unsure what the solution is! I strive to avoid alienating people because I am certainly enmeshed in and benefit from the system."

Reflecting on that fact, Kaytes continued, "We're all part of these stories, whether unwittingly or complicitly." The practice of landscape architecture is one of drawing scenarios, literally envisioning the possible, even if impracticable. By opening doors on new perspectives, reframing ideas and, most of all, getting people to think and talk, consilience, healing, and sustainable development can happen.

DeHart came to a similar conclusion, saying, "Every time I put up 'Confluences,' people see it and maybe a few say, 'Oh, I never thought about it that way.' It generates a conversation. And in a very different way than facts and statistics can. I'm not trivializing, because those are important. But they don't have the emotional impact. Art does."

McCoy said that "very slowly the dominant culture begins to listen" to a range of voices that were once overruled for valuing the intrinsic and the immeasurable. "These shifts in narrative allow us to begin the process of reconciliation, that allows us to begin to move forward with trying to bring the salmon back, trying to perhaps do things that serve multiple purposes. But the only way you can do that is by understanding history, and by listening to those voices, and talking with them."

McCoy gestured at a map of the watershed, "The region is tied up with rivers." We are all bound up together, the people and their equals, the animals, the plants, the soils, the washings away and the depositions of the new. To paraphrase one of the Pacific Northwest's daughters, Ursula K. Le Guin, "the word for world is river."

New Stars on the Market Shelf

Adriana Janovich

It's inherently festive. Crimson in color and flecked with tiny golden starbursts, this attractive apple might just make for the ultimate holiday fruit. And, with its long storage capability, it's also quite possibly the perfect pome for riding out a pandemic.

Cosmic Crisp® apples were bred to maintain their flavor—sweet, tangy, tart but not too sharp—as well as texture—crisp, firm, juicy but not watery—for up to a year in commercial cold storage. Even when cut or cooked, they're naturally slow to brown, retaining their pleasing appearance.

Since their release a year ago, Cosmic Crisps, bred at Washington State University specifically for Washington's climate, have proved to be out-of-this-world.

Good Housekeeping awarded the Cosmic Crisp, a WSU registered trademark, its "Nutritionist Approved" emblem. *America's Test Kitchen* tasters scored it "significantly higher than the other apples," noting the variety sports a thick skin that "snaps when you bite into it." That satisfying crunch was also noted by GeekWire, which declared, "The high crunch and firmness of the flesh are deceptive since the overall impression is light rather than dense, and there is very little softness or grittiness."

Not only is the new apple exceptionally good for eating fresh, it stands up to high temperatures in the oven or on the stovetop. "Cosmic Crisp is truly the most versatile apple on the market," said Kathryn Grandy, chief marketing officer for Proprietary Variety Management, which helps get new fruits to the global marketplace. "I'm totally hooked on Cosmic Crisp. It's amazing to bake with. It holds its texture and shape. But when you put your fork through it, it doesn't fight back."

It is, said Jamie Callison, executive chef of WSU's School of Hospitality Business Management at Carson College, "a beautiful apple." He would regularly buy different apples for particular purposes: Granny Smiths for baking, Honeycrisps for salads and cheeseboards. The Cosmic Crisp's versatility, he said, is "why it's going to be successful. It's durable and ships well and stores well. So it's a win-win for producers and consumers," particularly during the current novel coronavirus pandemic, which has some shoppers limiting trips to the supermarket.

Flavor-wise, Callison said, the Cosmic Crisp is "a perfect balance of sweet and tart. It's a hardy apple, too, so it holds up in galettes and pies. I love cooking with apples. But, sometimes, you get apples that fall apart when you bake them. Not these." And, because of their inherent sweetness, Grandy said, "you don't need to mix them with other apples, and you can significantly reduce the amount of sugar."

Use the Cosmic Crisp in sweet or savory dishes, such as tarts, streusels, cobblers, upside-down cakes, salads, and salsas. The apple also pairs well with chicken, pork, and, Callison said, "of course, Cougar Gold cheese." The sharpness of WSU's signature canned rich white cheddar complements the apple's sweetness. "They balance each other out," Callison said, also noting, "Brie is always good with apples."

Callison featured Cosmic Crisps in a slaw paired with crispy pan-fried Northwest oysters from his 2013 cookbook *The Crimson Spoon*, published by WSU Press, during one of the WSU Alumni Association's Feast of the Arts events last year. "I was able to showcase the Cosmic Crisp the weekend it was going to market, which was an amazing opportunity," said Callison, who's also featured the apples in class. "I gave them to students and challenged them to be creative and come up with their own dish."

Chalk up the apple's appealing attributes to good breeding. Premium-priced and non-GMO, the Cosmic Crisp is the product of 20 years of extensive research and development by WSU's pome fruit breeding program, with support from faculty and staff throughout WSU Tree Fruit Research and Extension as well as the Department of Horticulture in the College of Agricultural, Human, and Natural Resource Sciences. "We have all of these different people who are helping to develop protocols for the best ways to grow them, the best time to harvest them, and how to store them," said Kate Evans, leader of WSU's pome fruit breeding program since 2008, when she succeeded Bruce Barritt.

The retired WSU horticulturalist started lobbying for funding from the university and industry partners in the early 1980s to launch an apple breeding program. Red Delicious had dominated production for decades, and Barritt cautioned against depending too much on a single variety. In 1994, after funding came through, Barritt and his team began producing thousands of hybrid seeds and sampling the results, including WA 38, the 1997 cross that produced the Cosmic Crisp. Two years later, the first Cosmic Crisp seedling was planted. But the first commercial plantings didn't go into the ground until 20 years after hybridization.

"It takes a lot of time to produce a new variety," said Evans, noting work is ongoing. "We have apple selections in every stage all the time. The bad ones are discarded, and the good ones move to the next stage of evaluation."

Nearly 500 Washington growers have so far planted some 15 million Cosmic Crisp trees. Because the state's apple industry helped fund the research, they enjoy the exclusive right to grow the new variety in North America for ten years. That's part of their allure, according to Evans and Grandy.

Consumers in statewide focus groups were also enamored with the little spacey sparkles on the apple's deep ruby-red skin. "Cosmic" became part of the name because of those lenticels, or pores, reminiscent of distant stars. "Crisp" describes its texture while paying homage to one of its parents, the popular Honeycrisp. Its other parent is the Enterprise. Another fun fact: Cosmic Crisp is the first apple variety to be named by consumers.

Cosmic Crisp finally hit supermarkets nationwide in late 2019 with a five-year, $10.7 million marketing campaign. Unless you were living on another planet, you couldn't miss its release. The apple has its own Instagram, Twitter, and Facebook accounts, plus a Pinterest page, YouTube channel, and website. And it's made headlines in the *Los Angeles Times*, *New York Times*, *Seattle Times*, *Wall Street Journal*, *USA Today*, *Popular Science*, *Time*, and more.

Some 1.95 million boxes are slated to ship this season, compared to 346,000 boxes in 2019. The volume will increase each year and by 2026 more than 21 million boxes are expected to ship.

"I call it the billion-dollar apple," Grandy said. "I don't know that that's an accurate number, but to me it feels like our growers have spent hundreds of millions of dollars. They've made just an enormous investment."

That support, she said, has helped the Cosmic Crisp exceed expectations "many times over. It sold out everywhere we sent it."

Washington is America's top apple producer, growing nearly 60 percent of the country's crop of about 135 million boxes that rake in about $3 billion. In all, about 1,300 growers cultivate apples on some 175,000 acres, largely in Central Washington.

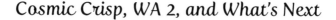

Cosmic Crisp, WA 2, and What's Next

Adriana Janovich

Cosmic Crisp® isn't the first Washington State University apple to go to market. That distinction goes to WA 2, or Sunrise Magic®.

Like Cosmic Crisp, Sunrise Magic was bred at WSU for Washington growers. But it wasn't launched with the same hype. And it still isn't as well-known as its successor. Proprietary Variety Management, which is handling the commercialization of both Cosmic Crisp and Sunrise Magic, is working to change that—just as WSU's pome fruit breeding program continues working on creating new varieties.

"What I can see happening is we'll release a number of different varieties over the next 10 or 20 years, but they may be somewhat smaller production apples," said Kate Evans, the program's leader. "I think we can't expect the amount of infrastructure and investment necessary to put out a big volume apple on a regular basis. That is asking a lot of the industry."

While Washington is the biggest apple-growing state in the country, no apples have been bred and brought to market here until WA 2 and WA 38, better known as Cosmic Crisp. "We've never had our own apple," said Kathryn Grandy, chief marketing officer at Proprietary Variety Management. "It's surprising that we haven't had our own apple. New York has its own apples. Midwest growers have their own apples. But this is a first for us."

Consumers can expect to see more of both of WSU's two apples, each a registered trademark, in the coming years. Cosmic Crisp made national headlines when it debuted in late 2019. And there's another marketing campaign planned for this year's crop. Marketers will also be busy building buzz about Sunrise Magic, particularly on social media, in a brand-specific campaign in 2021.

"WA 2 is a good apple," Grandy said. "It's a very delicious apple. It packs well; it was designed for it. And it grows very well in Washington. The momentum is building. It's starting to pick up. But it doesn't have the volume as Cosmic Crisp. Cosmic Crisp dwarfed everything."

WA 38, the cross that produced Cosmic Crisp, took place in 1997. WA 2, as its numbering suggests, came first. It was developed in 1994, the year WSU's pome fruit breeding program first started. A cross between Splendor and Gala, it was initially released to growers for testing without a name in 2009. The new apple became commercially available in 2011 and was re-launched—this time with a name—five years later. "I do believe with more marketing, more growers will plant it and we'll see it more and more," Grandy said. "It will have its day."

In North America—similar to Cosmic Crisp—Sunrise Magic can only be grown by Washington growers for the time being. They have exclusive rights until 2027. However, growers in New Zealand, Australia, Chile, South Africa, China, and parts of Europe are currently cultivating the crop.

Consumer focus groups in Seattle and Spokane selected "Sunrise" for the apple's pinkish hue and delicate, refreshing flavor. "It offers a different flavor than the Cosmic Crisp," Grandy said, who thinks of it "kind of like a great supporting actress. Not every apple is going to be the center of attention"—especially if they are being bred for niche slots in a boutique portfolio, much like fine wine or cheese.

"Consumers have some really interesting preferences when it comes to different apples," Evans said. "Most can come up with two or three names of apple varieties and will always have their go-to favorite. There are consumers who won't eat anything other than a Fuji. Honeycrisp has incredibly loyal followers. What we need to find is a good range of apple types for consumers. Apple production is a business, so we also need to be producing varieties that work for growers. Growers need to be able to make money from that big investment of planting a new variety.

"When I started in 2008, the question I got from the industry was 'How many apple varieties will you be releasing a year?'" Evans recalled, noting, "More than one a year—even one a year—would be difficult. The cost is not insignificant. It's very difficult to say when exactly we'll put out the next one and if we'll have one at the same level as Cosmic Crisp. The next few apples that come out may be more niche-focused. There are some more elite selections queuing up.

"Not everybody likes every apple. We should have a portfolio of varieties."

Water to the Promised Land

Tim Steury

As an aquifer declines, farmers hope for water promised 80 years ago.

Last summer as we stood in the middle of Brad Bailie's onion fields just north of Connell, the discussion, as discussions seem to do in the Columbia Basin, turned to water.

Bailie pumps irrigation water from a well drilled down 800 feet. Neighbors have pushed wells down to 2,000 feet. At such depths, the water is often laden with salts and minerals. After a while of irrigating with this water, a crust can form over the soil surface. Farmers must use a variety of means to break up the crust, including acid, so the irrigation water can soak in.

Since he farms organically, Bailie, a 1995 Washington State University graduate, is limited in what he can use to break up that mineral crust. He also expressed discomfort with mining the ancient water.

Indeed, after years of continuous pumping throughout what is called the Odessa Aquifer, water levels have dropped precipitously. In some areas of the aquifer, water levels have been dropping about ten feet a year.

Not only is irrigation threatened, so too are the municipal water supplies of 20 towns throughout the region, including Connell, just to the south of Bailie's onion fields.

Bailie nodded toward the horizon. That's the end of the East Low Canal over there, he said. A tantalizing few miles away, the East Low looks to many of the area's farmers the only promise of continuing their irrigated livelihoods.

Short of reverting to dryland farming, farmers across what is termed the Odessa Subarea of the Columbia Basin Project are counting on the federal promise, rooted in FDR's New Deal now 80 years distant, to someday complete the project's full potential.

Now the Bureau of Reclamation, the federal agency responsible for managing water across the western United States, and for building the Grand Coulee Dam and the Columbia Basin Project, has announced its plan to partially expand the project, for a price of $11,800 per irrigated acre and a total cost of more than $800 million.

The Columbia Basin Project is a network of canals, dams, reservoirs, laterals, wasteways, and ditches designed to carry water from the Columbia River to irrigate more than a million acres of the Columbia Basin. Built over a period from before 1946 until after 1966, the project was, as Paul Pitzer points out in his excellent *Grand Coulee: Harnessing a Dream* (WSU Press, 1994), "an accomplishment larger in size, more complicated in engineering, and more costly than Grand Coulee Dam, the project's key feature."

It takes a while to grasp just how big the Columbia Basin Project is. Even presented directly with the evidence, as I am on an April day, with maps and figures and a personal tour of a sizeable fraction of the project, the largest irrigation project in the United States challenges the imagination as much as the vastness of the Columbia Basin landscape itself.

After 18 years as manager of the East Columbia Basin Irrigation District, one of three districts responsible for managing the Columbia Basin Project's water, my guide, 1990 WSU alum Craig Simpson, continues to marvel not only at the geographic scale of the project, but also at the capability and genius of the people who conceived and built it.

"As an engineering geek, when I came here, it was a good job," he said. But as he learned the specifics of a system designed to deliver water to more than a million acres, the marvel of this engineering phenomenon sank in. "Those engineers had their act together," he said.

Crossing the East Low Canal, just outside of Othello, and just north of Brad Bailie's onion fields, where one of the project's main arteries nears the end of its 87-mile delivery of water, gives little hint of the project's magnitude, even if you know that the irrigation sprinklers visible from State Route 26 are pumping water diverted from the Columbia River 50 miles to the north and directed through miles of canal and pipeline. The East Low begins its delivery with a capacity of 4,500 cubic feet per second. By the time it reaches State Route 26, it has already delivered 4,200 acre feet of water to a land rich in soil but poor in rainfall. An acre foot is the amount of water it takes to cover an acre one foot deep, about 326,000 gallons.

Columbia River water becomes Columbia Basin Project water when, with six 65,000-horsepower and six 67,500-horsepower pumps powered by generator turbines in the Grand Coulee Dam, it is pumped 280 feet up from Lake Roosevelt to Banks Lake, the holding, or "equalizing" reservoir. Banks Lake was created by damming both the north and south ends of the 27-mile-long Grand Coulee, which was formed by ancient floods. Banks Lake has a storage capacity of 715,000 acre feet.

From Dry Falls Dam, at the south end of Banks Lake, the water flows into the Main Canal and then into the West and East Low canals. Altogether, Columbia Basin Project water flows through 300 miles of main canals, 2,000 miles of lateral canals, and 3,500 miles of drains and wasteways.

As large as it is, though, the Columbia Basin Project was never finished. A combination of higher than expected costs and the withdrawal of farmers on its eastern edge put its completion on hold for the last 60 years.

Altogether, surface water has been supplied to about half of the intended 1,029,000 acres promised in the original plan. Farmers in the Odessa Subarea, which is included in the project but never received surface water, were eventually given temporary permits to pump from deep wells.

Now, as a proposed antidote to the declining Odessa aquifer caused by that "temporary" deep-well pumping, the Bureau of Reclamation is proposing to extend the project's reach.

The process toward reaching a decision on pursuing such a project is obviously long and tortured. But after numerous studies, reports, and environmental impact statements, in April, the week before my visit with Simpson, the Bureau of Reclamation released its long-anticipated "Record of Decision."

In the 25-page statement, the bureau announced its choice of "Modified Partial-Replacement Action Alternative 4A." If developed, Alternative 4A would provide Columbia Basin Project surface water to 70,000 acres of Odessa Subarea land currently being irrigated from deep-well groundwater. Once water is provided, those wells would be placed on standby status.

The proposal includes enlarging the East Low Canal south of I-90 and adding second barrels to five existing siphons. It would also create a pressurized pipeline system to deliver the water to fields. This would include pumping plants, approximately 150 miles of buried pipeline, various monitoring stations, and 150 miles of electric transmission lines.

Reasons given for selecting Alternative 4A include the most benefits to the area with the least impact on other environmental resources. Also, at the estimated cost of $11,800 per acre irrigated, Alternative 4A is the cheapest.

The Columbia Basin drew waves of settlers in the early 20th century eager to homestead the fertile, but dry, land. Where some had succeeded earlier with cattle, newcomers made an impressive start with dryland wheat. But the climate was fickle. A few years of drought forced many to give up.

Concerned with the depopulation of the area, local businessmen conceived audacious schemes. Rufus Woods, owner of the *Wenatchee World* newspaper, became the champion of a dream to dam the upper Grand Coulee.

A tireless promoter, Woods joined other Columbia Basin dreamers to finally capture the imagination of the other Washington, making a great dam and irrigation project a key part of the New Deal.

"In 1933, when the New Deal assumed the project," writes Pitzer, "it took the vision of the agricultural/industrial empire and added the dimension of planning. President Roosevelt encouraged planning at the federal level and appointed advisors and cabinet members with similar views… In its early stages, the New Deal planners wished to create organized rural communities, and they intended to plan from the top down with guidelines coming directly from leaders at the federal level."

Their goal for the Columbia Basin was what historian Richard Lowitt called "The Planned Promised Land."

This was Progressivism at its boldest. The Grand Coulee Dam would back and divert the Columbia River to irrigate a rich land lacking only water and provide small farms to farmers displaced by the Dust Bowl, populating it with small but vibrant planned communities. The beneficiary of the project would be the small farmer. Indeed, farmers would be limited to 160 acres.

Even though the original idealism had faded, perhaps the culmination of the original idea was realized in "Farm-in-a-Day" in 1952. To mark the first delivery of water to the Columbia Basin Project, promoters determined to build and plant an 80-acre farm near Moses Lake, complete with irrigation, of course, and give it to the most deserving veteran of either World War II or the Korean War. He and his family would be given a fully functional farm, created in a 24-hour period.

Donald Dunn, a veteran of World War II and a dryland farmer from Kansas, was chosen through a search by the Veterans of Foreign Wars. In the spring of

1952, 70 pieces of heavy equipment and 34 tractors leveled, tilled, and planted the land. Crews began building the house and outbuildings.

At 4:30 that afternoon, Bureau of Reclamation commissioner Michael Straus opened a valve to begin irrigating one of the farm's fields. "Here this afternoon we celebrate the addition of the equivalent of a new state to the union," he told the gathered crowd, alluding to the fact that the Columbia Basin Project was comparable in size to Connecticut or Rhode Island.

Within two years, however, Dunn, unable to secure loans or otherwise make a living on 80 acres, sold the farm and moved back to the Midwest.

As Paul Pitzer pointed out in an article for the *Pacific Northwest Quarterly* (January 1991), Dunn was not alone in his failure. "Of 725 units sold by the government from 1952 through 1956, 16 percent changed ownership during that period; another 106 parcels went unsold."

Increasingly, farmers rented additional land or consolidated land by registering it under the names of other family members. In 1982, the Reclamation Reform Act legalized that consolidation by allowing each project owner 960 acres.

About the same time as the Farm-in-a-Day was being built, Orman Johnson's father started growing potatoes near Othello, though his Washington roots are much older. His grandfather Reaugh graduated from Washington State Agricultural College in 1906 and wrote his senior paper on irrigation, then helped develop irrigation around Chelan.

His father's family, originally from Sweden, moved to Washington from California the same year Reaugh graduated from Washington State.

With his brother Gavin and nephew Nick, Johnson farms 6,000 acres, irrigating from deep wells, just outside of Othello. The big "Go Cougs" potato storage shed east of Othello belongs to the Johnsons.

"We got our first well permit in 1964," said Johnson, a 1969 WSU graduate. "The assumption was that the Columbia Basin Project would be finished in a few years."

Under that assumption, that the wells would be temporary until the project was completed, many wells were drilled in the 1970s.

And the water level started dropping, he said.

In the 1980s, the Johnson wells could pump 10,000 gallons a minute at the beginning of the growing season and 8,500 by the end of the season.

"Now," he said, "they start out at 6,000 gallons a minute and end with some wells not producing in August or September."

The Johnsons plant late-season crops like onions and potatoes according to how much water they think they will have left in August and September. Over the last decade, they have reduced the amount of onions and potatoes they grow simply because they don't have enough water left by the end of the season.

In addition, said Johnson, echoing Bailie, "The deeper you go, the poorer quality the water is."

The Johnsons' wells are 2,200 feet deep, and they are pumping from 900 feet. In spite of the shortage, "We've decided not to drill deeper."

"My dad was on the irrigation board in the '60s and '70s," said Johnson, who himself is currently on the board of the East Columbia Basin Irrigation District. "He thought we were going to have expansion back then.

"The situation is getting scary," he continued. "We're losing production every year, which affects all the industries. If a number of these farms went dry, processors would have to find their crops from some other acres."

Not only are communities such as Connell and Othello concerned about their water supplies, they are also nervous about losing their businesses and livelihood.

Like others in the Basin, Johnson does not see expansion of surface irrigation as optional.

"Look at what we can grow here," he said. "There is no place in the world that can grow as many tons of potatoes per acre."

Besides its rich soil, the Basin has a long growing season, far enough north that it has more hours of daylight than, for example, southern Idaho. Other potato growing areas, Maine and Michigan, have the same hours of sunlight as Washington, but have a shorter growing season because they cannot get into their fields as early.

"So this is the place to have water," he said.

Among the alternative scenarios offered by the Bureau of Reclamation to offset the decline of the Odessa aquifer was one that is required of such reports: that of no action.

In typical projects, said irrigation district manager Simpson, a "No Action" alternative would simply mean that the situation does not get better, that somebody does not get something they want. But in this case, he argued, it's pretty easy to document how bad things can get if there is no action.

No action would have a huge cost, he said. If the expansion of surface water irrigation were put off, landowners would go out of business and the local economy would take a huge hit.

"If you go talk to the processing plants, they're concerned," he said. "They're not doing expansions because of the uncertainty of what's going to happen."

Regarding the bureau's proposal, Simpson said, "Maybe I drank from the goblet too long, but it just seems common sense to me."

Agricultural revenues in the Columbia Basin, largely made possible by irrigation, totaled $1.44 billion in 2008, according to the Columbia Basin Development League. Even so, critics have argued that the balance sheet simply doesn't balance. Revenues will never match expenditures in a project so grand, say some economists, who narrow the difference to a benefit/cost ratio.

Critics of expansion note two main problems. One is whether the benefits of the projects will outweigh the costs. The other is the matter of who pays.

Jonathan Yoder, WSU professor of economics, has reviewed economic analysis by the Bureau of Reclamation and questioned the very basis of their results. "Their *modus operandi* seems to be to start with that cost and figure out ways to get the benefit estimates up."

He also questioned how water is valued in the bureau's analyses. In an earlier review, bureau economists valued water at $21,000 an acre. "The average difference in eastern Washington between irrigated land and dry land value is around $4,000," said Yoder. "The value of ag land rental rates and market prices reflect the value of water for production, so [the bureau analysis] is overstating the value by about $17,000."

Norm Whittlesey and Walt Butcher, professors emeriti of agricultural economics, have a long history of questioning the value of expanding the Columbia Basin Project. In general they base their criticism on the fact that in order for a project to be justified, bureau rules dictate that it must show a benefit/cost ratio of at least 1.0.

Although the Columbia Basin Project was officially authorized in 1935, its development was interrupted by World War II. The Grand Coulee Dam provided an opportune source of the massive amounts of electricity necessary for two key parts of the war effort: the aluminum industry, essential for production of airplanes, and Hanford, where plutonium was produced for one of the two bombs dropped on Japan.

So it was not until the late 1940s that the dam's original purpose, irrigation, was revisited. By the mid-1960s, the first half of the project, the funded half, was essentially finished.

Toward the late 1970s, Washington's powerful senators, Henry "Scoop" Jackson and Warren Magnuson, "greased the skids" for federal funding for the second half of the project. However, both the Carter and Reagan administrations insisted on the state's contributing to the project, and Carter actually tried to kill the project altogether.

In the early 1980s, the Washington legislature gave Whittlesey a grant to study the benefits and costs, assuming that the results would come out heavily in favor of more irrigation. With no reason himself to think otherwise, Whittlesey designed a study, involving a number of colleagues both at WSU and the University of Idaho.

"By the time we finished," said Whittlesey, "it became apparent that costs, even that the state was asked to contribute, far exceeded the potential benefits."

In 1984, the state Senate published a budget to provide state money that would allow the federal money to be spent on expanding the project.

Approval depended only on the passing of the House version.

"To make a long story short," said Whittlesey, "I presented my side of the story to the House budget committee."

Whittlesey finished his testimony about 8:00 that evening and rushed to catch a plane, fully believing that his testimony had been ignored. After all, the House already had the funding written into its budget.

Much to his surprise, however, the chair of the House budget committee called him the next morning to tell him that the House had pulled the funding out of its budget.

The uproar was immediate. The federal government announced it could not fund the project without state participation, and proponents of the project leveled their anger at Whittlesey, to the point of trying to have him fired.

"It wasn't just me," he said. "I always made sure we had peer review… Fortunately, I had tenure.

"Most of what I did around here," he insisted, "was favorable to agriculture."

Indeed, Whittlesey, who retired in 1996, enjoyed a long productive career in agricultural economics, with many accolades.

It just happened that his concentration was water, a most troublesome subject indeed.

Whittlesey's critique of the current proposal is no less withering than his testimony in 1984. But this time, it's been effectively ignored. Which has him exasperated.

"They're not going to get federal money," he said, "the state doesn't really have the money and shouldn't be funding it, and the farmers can't afford it."

Regarding Whittlesey's first point, federal funding would require a GAO benefit/cost analysis that would figure in lost hydropower involved in pumping the water to Banks Lake.

Lost hydropower will, said Whittlesey, amount to $300 worth of energy cost per year per acre.

"That's more than the net revenue coming off land," he said. "That's another tax on you and me through utility rates. Nobody talks about that."

The question of who would actually pay for the Columbia Basin Project was a problem from the beginning, argued Pitzer in *Grand Coulee: Harnessing a Dream*.

"Without the link to power and its direct subsidy," he wrote in 1994, "plus additional subsidies from the government, such as its assumption of interest charges, the project could not exist."

In short, whereas the Bureau of Reclamation figures the benefit/cost ratio at just over 1.0, Whittlesey and Butcher, once they corrected what they perceived as erroneous figures, estimate the ratio at 0.1.

Supporters of the project's expansion, however, insist that benefits far outweigh the costs, because the costs have been overstated.

"The Bureau puts in things way too high," argued Orman Johnson, "which is why it is difficult to get the benefit/cost ratio."

As an example, he pointed to the Weber Siphon project a couple of years ago. A siphon is simply a pipe that will enable a canal to cross a lower level of land without diverting from as straight a course as possible. Although expensive, they are much less so than building a canal according to the landscape.

The Bureau's estimate for building the siphon under Interstate 90 as $57 million, said Johnson. The bid was actually $22 million, and the cost ended up in the low 30s.

Farmers will also have the option of taking the new surface water or continuing to pump, he said. Not including all lands on the pipeline makes the ratio higher.

Simpson agreed that the costs have been overstated. Also, he strongly disagreed with Whittlesey and Butcher's inclusion of lost power generation.

"How do you figure lost power generation when they [Bonneville Power Administration] don't have a right to it?" he asked.

"I think this is a fairly balanced approach."

"The economics of the Columbia Basin Project involve an intricate mix of hydroelectric power, irrigation, recreation, wildlife, navigation, conservation, agricultural surpluses, and Native American rights," wrote Pitzer in 1994. "Furthermore, these aspects of the project do not exist in a vacuum." Indeed, these interactions and needs have become even more complex over the last 20 years and will only increase in complexity with growing power needs, agricultural needs, and so forth. Add to this the approaching reassessment of the Columbia River Treaty between the United States and Canada, which will surely lead to changing flows and power needs. And then there is climate change and the possible effects on river flow and agriculture and many other factors.

The Water Research Center at WSU produced a report in conjunction with the Washington Department of Ecology in 2011 that assesses projected water needs in the coming decades, including effects on agriculture. One of the most interesting projections, based on computer modeling, is that the Columbia Basin will become a little wetter. As a result, director Michael Barber argued that the return of some areas, particularly in the Odessa Subarea, to dryland wheat will be far more cost-effective than the $11,800 an acre price tag attached to Alternative 4A.

On the other hand, said Barber, even if we accept the high cost of taking water to the Odessa Subarea, he worried the approach is self-perpetuating, that fluctuations in Banks Lake will lead to outcries from recreational users, leading to a proposal to build another reservoir, with a price tag in the billions. Indeed, that reservoir has already appeared in alternative proposals, with no suggestion of how it might be paid for.

John Sirois, chair of the Colville Business Council in Nespelem, 20 miles north of Grand Coulee Dam, condensed tribal concerns over the project's expansion to possible fluctuations on Lake Roosevelt and effects on cultural resources, the effect of changing flows on the tribe's new salmon facility at Chief Joseph Dam, and the general effect on what he calls the Columbia's "integrity." Besides, he said with a wry smile, wouldn't it be nice if we got some irrigation up here?

The extent of the controversy over the project's expansion and the accompanying complexities exemplify issues regarding the future of water use and availability in Washington and throughout the West and raise many questions: What is the best use of this extraordinary resource? What is the greater good? How shall public expenditure be allocated? *And who*, exactly, pays?

Vancouver Lake: A Search for Solutions Great and Small

Hannelore Sudermann

One day this winter Ron Wierenga and I drive out to Vancouver Lake. The road from downtown bends north and west, paralleling the Columbia River for several miles through an industrial district and past the port. Wierenga, who manages the clean water program for Clark County, points to a gray structure a few hundred yards to our left. "That's a barge right there," he said. "The Columbia River is just on the other side of that dike." As we ease out of the city, the landscape flattens and opens up. A gaggle of cackling geese in a field ignores us as we drive by. As we get out to look over the lake, a man with a small black cockapoo climbs down from his pickup for a lunchtime walk.

There was a time when this spot would routinely go underwater. The Columbia would rise and flood its banks and pour into this area, said Wierenga, a 1993 graduate of Washington State University. It would recharge the lake with fresh water, which would later flow back out to the Columbia through Lake River to the north.

But that was more than a century ago. The area was settled, the land was deeded to the port, and dikes were built. Then in the 1930s construction of the Bonneville Dam 40 miles upriver changed the way the Columbia behaved. For the lake, that meant an end to the regular flooding and cleansing.

Late last summer, Vancouver Lake was closed by the Clark County Health Department.

The lake may be picturesque, but at the time its waters had dangerous levels of *E. coli* and cyanobacteria (blue-green algae). Swimmers, waders, and wind surfers were banned for 30 days from the quiet, shallow water.

Other users—including walkers and birdwatchers—shied away as well.

The bell-shaped lake covers about 2,300 acres. It is about two miles wide, but only 15 feet in its deepest spots. The middle of the lake is less than four feet deep most of the time. Still, it has seven miles of shoreline as well as views of Mount Hood, Mount St. Helens, and Mount Adams.

On one side it is surrounded by fields, farms, and the Shillapoo Wildlife Recreation Area. That landscape has barely changed from the time of the city's settlement. The other side is flanked by Fruit Valley, a neighborhood that sprouted during the ship building boom of World War II and today holds about 1,000 households.

The lake is home to several rowing teams and a 93-member sailing club. It is where beginning kayakers first hit the water, and children can learn to sail in little O'pen Bic boats.

For the resource that it is, though, the lake is pretty quiet. "From my perspective, it is underutilized considering its proximity to Vancouver and the size of the lake," said Wierenga, who has a master's in environmental science. "I think people are intimidated by the water quality problems. They really love the lake; they're just afraid of the water."

Troubled Waters

About five years ago, the community grew concerned over algal blooms and the levels of possible toxins in the lake. They were worried about public health, and that their pets might become sick from drinking and playing in the water. The lake became a high-profile public issue and in 2004 a community partnership was formed to bring together the port, the city, and the county to manage activities around the lake, including guiding research and involving the public. As well, the U.S. Army Corps of Engineers, the state departments of Ecology, Fish & Wildlife, and Natural Resources, and nine citizens joined the group.

It wasn't the first time someone tried to fix the lake. In the 1960s, a team led by WSU engineer William Funk studied it to see if changing the way water flowed through would clear up some of the blue-green algae problems. Vancouver Lake was one of Funk's first projects in Washington, where he had been hired as a limnologist—"sort of a fresh water oceanographer."

At the time the lake was extremely shallow and very stagnant, said Funk. "You couldn't take a boat in." The mud was so deep and viscous that one day when he waded in, his team had to pry him back out with a pair of oars.

To better understand the lake's history, Funk visited with longtime locals, who told him they remembered when the lake had been at least 30 feet deep. "But it was pretty well down the tubes when we saw it," he said. With massive "blue-greens," it was perhaps the worst lake that he had ever seen. Much if its water was coming in from Salmon Creek where there was septic tank drainage. The high level of nutrients, shallow depth, and stagnant water made it an ideal home for algae blooms.

Funk's crew, which included colleague Surinder Bhagat and several graduate students, spent July of 1967 on the lake in a boat they called "Big Red." Their assignment was to take samples to assess water pollution and see if the lake could serve the community as a large water-based recreational site. Funk's team also researched plans for dredging and flushing the water body. But the proposal made elected officials nervous. In addition to being intensive and expensive, "I thought there was a 70 percent chance it would work and a small percent chance there would be a disaster," said Funk.

His study and recommendations eventually succeeded, though it took close to 20 years to complete. In the 1980s, the U.S. Army Corps of Engineers dredged the lake and massed up the sediment in the middle to form what is now called Turtle Island. Then, at the spot where the lake is closest to the Columbia River, the Corps dug a canal about 4,000 meters long and installed tidal gates at one end. The nearly $20 million effort linked the Columbia to the lake. When the ocean tide is high and the river is up, water flushes down the canal and into the lake. Then it flows around the lake and then out to Lake River, which feeds back into the Columbia downriver as it heads toward the Pacific Ocean.

Funk went on to help clean up of a number of other Washington waterways, including Liberty Lake, Newman Lake, and Lake Roosevelt. He was also director of the State of Washington Water Resource Center housed at WSU in Pullman. As for Vancouver Lake, the project was right for the time, said Funk. But in the ensuing years the population of Vancouver has nearly quadrupled to 160,000, farming has faded, and the lake may be facing a whole new source of problems. The dredging and digging of a flushing canal "did improve it some, but it definitely didn't solve the issue," said Wierenga.

Small Solutions

Recently, the local agencies turned again to Washington State University for help. This time it came through two newly arrived scientists at WSU Vancouver: ocean biologist Steve Bollens and his wife, biologist Gretchen Rollwagen-Bollens.

While Funk had urged a large-scale solution of dredging and flushing the lake, Bollens and Rollwagen-Bollens work on the much smaller scale of microorganisms. These single-celled and multi-cellular invertebrates are another piece of the mystery of why the water clouds over with cyanobacteria each summer. Normally they eat the blue-greens, but for a time each year they're not able to keep them in check.

Local volunteers had already started sampling the water for algae and toxins, but no one to that point had looked at the zooplankton, the microscopic underwater "grazers" (as Rollwagen-Bollens calls them) who eat algae and bacteria and in turn become food for fish.

Blue-green algae is a particularly tricky problem, she said. It's not really an algae, but a bacteria. While it is an aquatic organism and it does photosynthesize, it lacks a nucleus. And it can be toxic to people and animals, particularly when a number of them get together and form colonies that become strands and tangles of the bacteria linked together. Given the right amount of warmth and nutrients, these colonies bloom and form a thick mat on the lake's surface, blocking the sun for other organisms. And as they die and decay, they leech the oxygen from the water.

"The county was really interested in knowing what causes these blooms," said Rollwagen-Bollens. "One, there are lots of nutrients in the water. That's no mystery." But there are also the predators to consider. "We need to know what's going on with the grazers."

Now in their third year of sampling, the WSU scientists have found that different kinds of cyanobacteria have dominated the lake in different years. There's *Anabaena*, *Aphanizomenon*, and *Microcystis*, "or Annie, Fannie, and Mike," as the aquatic biologists like to call them, said Rollwagen-Bollens. They may sound cute, but they're nasty. "Mike is probably the most toxic," she said. This particular bacteria can form a toxin that triggers liver failure.

So the scientists and their graduate students have been sampling from the lake and watching the movement, behavior, and diets of the plankton that normally feast on the algae and bacteria. "It turns out, at least in Vancouver Lake, a couple weeks prior to the bloom, the microzooplankton seem to be almost exclusively grazing on taxa other than cyanobacteria," said Rollwagen-Bollens. That leaves the door open for the blue-greens to colonize. Once they're in strand form, they're more difficult for the small plankton to eat.

"We're still analyzing the larger grazers, but they seem to be playing a role here as well," said Rollwagen-Bollens. It's important to know the biological interactions in the lake so that perhaps something can be done to encourage or discourage certain behaviors.

"The sad fact is Vancouver Lake is not unique," said Rollwagen-Bollens. "But what we learn in Vancouver Lake is going to help us understand shallow, warm-temperature lakes even more."

"Having a research site in one's own back yard is a good way to put it," said Steve Bollens. "It's really valuable for training graduate students as well as undergraduates." They're regularly at the lake collecting samples. They're also running well-controlled experiments back on campus with types of grazer populations in the laboratories. While the case is very local, and a good example of how WSU is fulfilling its land grant mission by serving a Washington community, the problems of this lake are concerns in lakes throughout the Northwest, said Bollens, "and even more significantly, really occurring in temperate or mid-latitude regions around the globe."

Rainier Cherries

Adriana Janovich

Their skin is thin and sensitive. They're easily bruised. And their season—six to seven weeks, if we're lucky—is more fleeting than summer itself. That short harvest time and extreme susceptibility to wind and rain and temperatures either too hot or too cold are just a couple of reasons why Rainier cherries are so special.

These spectacular stone fruits are prized for their sweetness and color. Distinctive and delicate, Rainiers—the color of a buttercup tinged with a pleasing pink to bright red blush—are little gems.

"The appeal of those contrasting colors is what makes them stand out on the tree and in the retail market. It's just a good combination," said Washington State University horticulturist and cherry expert Matthew Whiting. He calls Rainiers "tree candy."

Their flesh—creamy, yellow, firm, gently floral, exceptionally sweet—is made up of nearly one-fifth sugar, or anywhere from 17 to 23 percent. "The Rainier is a wonderful-tasting fruit," Whiting said. "With such high sugars and typically very low acidity, it truly is like eating a piece of candy, except it's much better for you."

Customers have been willing to pay more for this two-toned premium cherry than for other sweet cherries. And, over the years, they've become increasingly popular. The 2018 crop was the largest ever for Rainiers, according to an annual review by the Northwest Cherry Growers, a Yakima-based organization that markets cherries for growers in Washington, Oregon, Idaho, Montana, and Utah. Packers moved 2.52 million boxes of Rainier cherries last year, breaking the previous record of 2.36 million in 2014.

Named for Mount Rainier and developed at WSU, Rainier cherries are a cross between two cultivars: the Bing, which originated in Oregon in 1875, and the Van, which originated in British Columbia in 1936. "I was just as surprised as anyone that 'white' ones showed up," Harold Fogle told the *Seattle Times* in 2004. The late USDA breeder developed Rainier cherries at WSU's research station in Prosser in 1952. Back then, Fogle told the *Times*, "we didn't really understand the genetics of cherries."

Fogle had been looking to create a new Bing variety to help extend cherry season. The richly red Bings and Vans he crossbred carried a recessive gene, and the result was P 1-680. It stood out, Fogle told the *Times*, "from the moment I first saw it ripen."

Golden-hued Rainier cherries were first released in 1960. Despite their unusual good looks and natural sweetness, Whiting said, they were "initially sold out as a pollinizer. The Bing itself is sterile and needs a compatible pollinizer tree to fertilize its flowers." Rainiers were largely planted to support Bing crops until the early 1980s, when growers really began to realize their potential on the fresh market. "Now," Whiting said, "it is the premier cherry around the world."

Sweet cherries are thought to have come from the region between the Black and Caspian Seas, and cultivation is believed to have begun with the Greeks. Colonists brought sweet cherries to the New World, and they arrived in the Pacific Northwest in 1847 when Henderson Luelling traveled from Iowa to Oregon with nearly 1,000 trees and shrubs. His younger brother, Seth, later developed the Bing, named for his Chinese workers' foreman, Ah Bing.

Today, Washington state is the top producer of sweet cherries in the country. According to the Washington State Department of Agriculture, sweet cherries are the state's number six cash crop with a value of about a half billion dollars.

Growing cherries of any variety is a fickle business. Birds love them. And there's that thin skin. A summer rainstorm can split it. Rainiers are super sensitive—not just on the tree but also during the process of picking and packing. "They're not easy to grow," Whiting said. "The number one issue is bruising, and when they're damaged it shows up. With most cherries, the color of the skin can mask the bruising." Rainiers, he said, need "to be handled with care and patience."

Growers pay more for that special attention. "They typically have their best pickers handle their Rainiers," Whiting said. "They pay them at a higher rate to go slow." The idea is to encourage workers to exercise caution, select fruit for optimal color and size, and gently lay—not drop—the tender fruit into a bucket worn around the neck. In Prosser, at WSU's Irrigated Agriculture Research and Extension Center, Whiting does research to support the entire sweet cherry industry. He works with growers to improve yields, production efficiencies, and labor-saving techniques as part of WSU's Pacific Northwest Sweet Cherry Breeding Program.

WSU re-established the cherry program in 2004, after a hiatus of two dozen years, to develop superior new cultivars for the Pacific Northwest sweet cherry industry. One area of research is breeding resistance to diseases, particularly powdery mildew, which attacks both the foliage and fruit. "It's primarily a Pacific Northwest problem," said Per McCord, WSU's new cherry breeder and associate professor of stone fruit breeding and genetics. "It won't kill the tree, but it will certainly make the fruit unmarketable and that's why it's such a challenge. There's also a risk of losing the ability to control it via chemicals, so that makes breeding an attractive option."

Rainiers could still be improved. They, too, are susceptible to powdery mildew. And, like both of its parent varieties, Rainiers require a compatible pollinizer. "That's one area you could improve upon for the grower: to produce a Rainier cherry that's self-fertile and doesn't require another cherry to pollinate it," McCord said. "If we could develop a blush variety that was earlier or later than the Rainier, we could increase the market window for that class of cherry."

Meantime, these blushing beauties—plump, juicy, and a good source of Vitamin C—are best enjoyed fresh, according to *Cook's Illustrated*. Use raw Rainiers to top desserts or add a pop of color to a green salad. Chop them up for salsa. Muddle them into a cocktail. Eat them straight from the bowl. They're simply too pretty to tuck into a pie. But, if you want to bake with them, consider WSU executive chef Jamie Callison's Rainier Cherry Clafoutis. His take on the firm French custard—traditionally made with whole dark sour cherries from the Limousin region—is completed by orange zest and a splash of orange liqueur.

McCord personally likes fruit with a bit more acidity. But, no matter how Rainiers and other sweet cherries evolve, McCord said, they're "always going to be a premium fruit. I don't think we're going to see bargain sweet cherries. It'd be like saying a bargain BMW."

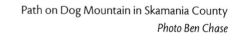
Path on Dog Mountain in Skamania County
Photo Ben Chase

In the Mountains

Near Cascade Pass in the North Cascades
Photo Zach Mazur

A New Land

Eric Sorensen

John Bishop was late getting to Mount St. Helens.

He was only 16 years old when it blew in 1980, and it would be another decade before he began crawling around the mountain as part of his doctoral studies.

"I was worried I missed all the action—'Ten years, it's all been studied,'" he recalled.

It turns out the dust, pumice, and other ejecta were only beginning to settle, and the mountain would continue to rumble, spit, and recover. In 1994, he found himself running from a mudflow, then watched as it moved fridge-sized boulders and shook the earth beneath his feet. Arriving at Washington State University Vancouver in 1998, he could make work on the mountain a weekly commute, a rare convenience for those eager to study the earth's volcanic hotspots. In 2006, after a period of activity in which the mountain was closed to the public, he was one of the first to climb to the summit and watch whalebacks of solidified magma ooze out and break off 2,000 feet below.

More important, Bishop, now an associate professor in WSU Vancouver's School of Biological Sciences, bore witness as various life forms struggled to get a toehold among the rocks left virtually sterile by the blast 30 years ago. He's seeing a biological Wild West where certain characters arrive on the scene and wreak havoc in the absence of established community forces or the usual ecological rules. The process is so tumultuous that Bishop and his colleagues are starting to rethink the process of succession in a heavily impacted biological system.

"It gets to how science occurs," he said one crystal-blue summer day, with grasshoppers sounding like golf course sprinklers and the sun beating down on the white-gray rock of the Pumice Plain. "You work here for a decade or two and then you step back and say, 'Wait, this is actually telling me something about the entire process of going from nothing, no biological organisms, to a forest that stood here before and will someday stand here again.' We're getting at really fundamental processes that determine how that happens."

Biologists divide the blast zone around the mountain into various zones of disturbance. The outer edges were layered in ash and pumice. Areas closer in had singed but standing dead trees. Even closer to the volcano, forests were flattened.

"One-hundred-foot matchsticks," said Bishop.

The Pumice Plain was Ground Zero for the blast's debris avalanche and 800-degree pyroclastic flow. That life has returned at all is somewhat miraculous, but it's also had a tough go of it.

The central player on the plain has been the lupine, a robust purple flower that in effect brings its own lunch by synthesizing nitrogen in the barren volcanic soil. Along with a few grasses, it's the most obvious vegetation as we start walking on to the plain after a hair-raising drive from Windy Ridge on the mountain's eastern flank.

"It's a very two-dimensional plant community," said Bishop, which is to say the plants are so low they offer little shade or protection for other plants and animals. "But you also see at the same time we have willows colonizing here. It's easy to overlook them, but actually there are a lot of them. They're everywhere, but at low density, and they're quite small. And you have conifers colonizing. You have the beginnings of your next coniferous forest."

In the two-dimensional world, the main animals are deer mice, killdeer, and horned lark. But the 3D world has voles, shrews, porcupine and weasels, yellow warbler and orange-crowned warbler, willow flycatchers, and sparrows. Elk come through pretty regularly.

"The willow," said Bishop, "changes everything."

Still, it's a largely unsettled place. It lacks the diversity that can give an ecosystem both resilience—the ability to spring back from a disturbance—and stability—the ability to resist change in the face of a disturbance. As a result, the community is easily devastated by two insects—the willow stem-boring weevil and the poplar clear-winged moth.

Bishop pointed to a small willow with dead branches and a tell-tale dusting of what looks like sawdust. It's frass—larvae dung—and evidence of the willow getting hammered. In an established ecosystem, the larvae might have predators to keep them in check. Not here. As Bishop and his students walked transects across the plain and document birds, mammals, and vegetation along the way, they noticed that 85 percent of the willow stems over a certain size are being attacked.

"This plant is not that young," said Bishop pointing to a battered willow. "It's been here a while but its stems keep getting killed. It could easily be ten years old."

Further down are willows that researchers sprayed to keep insects off. They sport tags—blue for male willows and pink for females—but they're instantly recognizable without them.

"They're the big ones," said Bishop. Without the outsized impact of the insects, these willows flourished.

In the past, ecologists haven't given much thought to the roles of insects in succession. Now Bishop is wondering if succession itself might be rethought to give greater weight to such high-impact species.

"What it's made us realize more generally is that, as the species here sort out into a more stable community, you probably have a very unusual distribution of interactions among those species, where you have a lot of fairly extreme impacts of one species on another, more extreme than we see in more developed systems."

He's noticed something else as well. There are a lot of lupine and a lot of insects, in fact, millions of lupine and tens of thousands of herbivores that only eat lupine. Some are being described by scientists for the first time. Elsewhere on the mountain and surrounding Mount St. Helens National Monument are species like the western toad, which has its largest populations here. There's the tailed frog, and large, diverse communities of huckleberry, mountain ash, salmonberry, often with animal-dispersed fruits. Bishop is seeing birds and mixed communities here that one doesn't see elsewhere.

"I think that leads to a need to rethink the value of a place like this," Bishop said, "that it may actually be extremely important for the long-term health of those species, that they can find a disturbed place and become very common."

His thoughts on this are still forming, but they echo recent observations by WSU ecologist Mark Swanson and others in the journal *Frontiers in Ecology and the Environment*. It's the kind of thinking that might alter how we, say, go into a burned forest and start replanting it, or how we take a clearcut and try to rush it back to an old-growth condition.

Indeed, if you want to make a case for natural disturbance, you might do well to start with this: Bishop, Swanson, and the platoon of researchers working here over the past few decades are coming to think that battered, burned, and blown-down Mount St. Helens now has the greatest biological diversity in the Cascades' vast, forested terrain.

Remains of the Day

Adriana Janovich

J. Lewis Payne popped the lid on one of the vintage barrels—a mix of surplus military metal and heavy-duty cardboard—stacked in a WSU barn that once housed moose, elk, and woodland caribou. The drums look rather dusty and nondescript, but they hold an unusual treasure: ash from the May 18, 1980, eruption of Mount St. Helens—and left largely untouched for the past 40 years.

The ash is quadruple-bagged and tagged with hand-written labels noting collection sites. Most came from the rooftops of Eastlick and Heald Halls. But there's some from Pullman's Lincoln Middle School, too, as well as at least one bin simply described as coming from "Yakima."

Payne—the caretaker of the ash as well as the 800-acre Hudson Biological Reserve at Smoot Hill, where the cache is stored—reached down into one of the drums and scooped up a handful. "It's like there's no weight in my hand," he marveled. The ash feels powdery and fine, like pastry flour or powdered sugar, but is very light gray in color. It's soft, cool, and dry, and smells faintly of wet cement and—oddly—dried mushrooms.

Today, nearly 100 barrels of Mount St. Helens ash are stacked in two kennels of the barn, which—Payne pointed out—used to be home to Morty, the moose featured in the opening credits of the CBS series *Northern Exposure*.

Payne's lived at Smoot Hill since 1994, when he was a research assistant at WSU. He came to Pullman as a doctoral student, studying under Richard "Dick" Mack, now a professor emeritus of ecology in the School of Biological Sciences. Shortly after the eruption, Mack and his graduate students worked quickly to gather ash for future research projects. "There was a prediction of rain," Mack said. "And I knew we needed unadulterated ash."

One of his students, Stewart Higgins, a now-retired senior scientific assistant with WSU's Center for Sustaining Agriculture and Natural Resources and WSU alum, collected samples in Yakima. Mack used some of the ash for research through the mid-1980s, particularly studying its effects on vegetation. The rest has been stored, tightly sealed, for safekeeping—and largely without much interest. The fact that it's here and available is "not widely known," Mack said.

In fact, "To the best of my knowledge, only two people in the last 20 years have come to look at the ash," Payne said, noting both were from the United States Geological Survey. "It's a resource that needs the right project."

■

Journalism's Grandest Prize

Eric Apalagetui

On the morning of Tuesday, May 20, 1980, journalists arrived at *The Daily News*, turned on their computers, and were greeted with the daily message from managing editor Bob Gaston. That day's message was far from typical.

This was two days after the devastating eruption of Mount St. Helens and less than 24 hours after the Longview newspaper staff published an astounding 45 of its own stories and numerous jaw-dropping photographs of the deadly blast.

Although his exact words are lost to time, the gist of Gaston's message to the newsroom was this: After just one issue, there was a tremendous buzz in the community about their coverage. If they kept it up, Gaston said, they might just win a Pulitzer Prize. His staff was even greener than it was small, but they knew that few journalists ever get a shot at the most coveted award in the profession.

Andre Stepankowsky, then a young reporter and now the newspaper's city editor, said Gaston's message further motivated them to charge after the mammoth story. "I'd be lying through my teeth if I said no," he said.

"We knew this [eruption] was going to make a huge impact on our community," Gaston said earlier this year. "I didn't want anybody else to do a better job than we did."

In April 1981, 25 years ago this spring, the Pulitzer Prize Board decided that *The Daily News* accomplished Gaston's goal and honored the staff for best local reporting. Despite fierce competition, including other Mount St. Helens entries from larger newspapers, the chairman of the jury that evaluated submissions rated *The Daily News*'s coverage "far superior."

That accomplishment is proof that "a small staff can perform excellent journalism as well as a large staff," said retired Washington State University journalism professor Tom Heuterman, who earned an English degree in 1956 and a doctorate in American Studies in 1973 from WSU.

Gaston arrived at WSU as a junior in 1965, the same year Heuterman left newspaper reporting to teach journalism. The professor remembered Gaston, who graduated in 1967, as sharp and unflappable. "His subsequent performance never surprised me," Heuterman said.

After a year at WSU, Gaston landed a summer internship at the Longview paper, then owned by the McClelland family.

After graduation, Gaston returned to Longview. But this was the Vietnam era, and he soon left for the U.S. Air Force's officer training school. After serving stateside, Gaston was an editor at two Oregon newspapers before the McClellands lured him back.

Still in his early 30s, Gaston became managing editor in 1976 and took over newsroom hiring from Ted Natt, a member of the McClelland family who rose to editor and publisher. Gaston lobbied his bosses to replace typesetter jobs—being phased out with the arrival of computer technology—with reporters and photographers. By the time Mount St. Helens erupted, Gaston had increased his staff by a third and had a newsroom stocked with hungry journalists.

Gaston was quick to turn the spotlight toward newspaper staffers and owners, who busted their buns and their budgets to cover the eruption. Others credit Gaston's steady leadership and his guidance in keeping them on top of the ever-changing story as critical to their success.

"I doubt whether we would have won [the Pulitzer] or done the job that we did if it hadn't been for Bob," said Rick Seifert of Portland, a semi-retired writer and journalism instructor who was on *The Daily News*'s volcano team.

"One of his great talents was to spot talent," said Roger Werth, photo editor then and now. Better yet, Werth and coworkers agree, Gaston entrusted employees with enough freedom to find untold stories.

Gaston retired from *The Daily News* in 1999, when a chain bought the newspaper. Leaving daily deadlines behind "was a real gift of time," said Gaston, who is on the boards of his church and a local social service agency. He and wife Georgeann ('67 Ed.) also help watch two of their grandchildren. "I feel like I'm making a contribution to the community and my family."

For five years, ending last December, Gaston was the volunteer editor of the *Cowlitz Historical Quarterly*. He resigned partly to pursue two book projects—one a family history and the other the story of a local character.

It is often repeated that journalists write history's first draft. Gaston devoted one of his final *Quarterly* issues to a second draft of *The Daily News*'s Pulitzer-Prize-winning history and convinced many of his former staffers to write one last volcano story. The task stirred old memories and new pride in winning journalism's grandest prize.

The Making of Mountaineers

Hannelore Sudermann

When she was just 15, Danielle Fisher discovered her alpine addiction on Mount Rainier.

That trip wasn't the first climb for Fisher. She ascended Mount Baker a few weeks before, and she hated it.

"I was tagging along with my dad," she said. "He liked being in the mountains, and so did I." But the climb was scary and challenging. At one point Danielle lost her footing and fell, posing a threat to the team to which she was roped.

A couple of weeks later, she went along on an ascent of Mount Adams, the second-highest peak in the state and a popular mountain for beginners. "It was harder," she said. "I didn't enjoy it at all." Still, when her father offered to turn around, she refused.

"Two weeks later, we did Mount Rainier," said Jerome Fisher. To their surprise, "that's when it clicked." Even though Danielle had injured her leg, was carrying more weight in her pack, and had to spend the night on the mountain, Rainier did the trick. Neither of the Fishers could account for the change.

Last summer, the slender 20-year-old from rural Bow, Washington, became the youngest person in the world to summit the highest mountains on all seven continents.

Since Danielle was a baby, her parents, Jerome, a former Washington State University student, and Karen, a 1975 agriculture graduate from WSU, would take her and her sister, Bobbi, on outdoor trips, day hikes, and horse camping. The Cascades were familiar territory for the Fishers, who could see Mount Baker from their backyard.

After the Rainier climb six years ago, Danielle was eager for whatever the Cascades could offer. That summer, between her freshman and sophomore years of high school, she summited 12 mountains.

When Fisher took on Mount Baker again during her second summer of climbing, she tackled the north ridge, a more technical climb than her previous one. Her guide was Christine Boskott of Mountain Madness, one of the leading woman alpinists in America. "She is a strong and driven climber," said Boskott of her young client, adding that Fisher was a good team member who took the initiative to help another climber out of a jam.

That strength showed again in her uncomplicated ascent of Everest last summer. Fisher was one of the few on her team to reach the top. "Danielle … seems genetically designed for high altitude, and nothing slows her down," noted Tony Van Marken, a fellow climber who struggled to follow her up the mountain.

"She has the gift to go climb high," said her father. Jerome Fisher realized that a few years ago on a peak in South America. Though he and Danielle at first lagged behind the other climbers, having stopped for about an hour to warm Danielle's feet and ward off the early stages of frostbite, she caught up to and passed everyone who had gone ahead, showing no effect from the thin air.

Fisher asked his daughter if she would like to try climbing the Seven Summits—the highest points on each continent—since she had a shot at being the youngest person to reach all seven peaks. The record holder at the time was a 23-year-old man, and the youngest woman to have climbed all seven was 33.

"I said yes," said Fisher. "At that point, I figured I had five years to do it."

She did it in two, joining the ranks in 2005 of an elite fellowship of world-famous climbers who got their start on Washington's peaks—climbers like Ed Viesturs, known around the world for his high-altitude abilities.

Viesturs first got hooked back in the 1970s on the pre-eruption Mount St. Helens. The climb's stunning views and technical demands were thrilling enough to send the raw college freshman from Illinois back for more.

If you look around the world for alpinists, you'll find one of the highest concentrations right here in Washington. Whether they're born here like Fisher or drawn to the state like Viesturs, they all develop their mountain habits and hone their skills on the sharp teeth of the Cascades.

One of the most widely read adventure stories of recent history, *Into Thin Air*, the account of a deadly season on Mt. Everest, was written by Jon Krakauer, who lives in Seattle. Many of the book's characters were Washington based, including a member of Krakauer's climbing team and a guide on another team. Viesturs was there, too.

Then consider Jim Whittaker of Seattle, who in 1963 was the first American to climb to the summit of Everest, and his brother, Lou, founder of Rainier Mountaineering, Inc.

Washington was also home to writer and teacher Willi Unsoeld, one of the most famous of American climbers of the 1960s and 70s.

A Mountain Legacy

So why is there such a Washington presence on the world's highest and most dangerous peaks? Simply put, "Washington breeds climbers," said Jerome Fisher.

August Valentine Kautz, a lieutenant stationed at Fort Steilacoom, tried to climb Rainier in the summer of 1857. The German-born soldier prepared himself by reading the accounts of European alpinists who had climbed Mont Blanc. He and a few soldiers who volunteered for the expedition took along shoes with nails pushed through the soles for the ice-covered portion of the climb of the highest peak of the Cascades. The group made it across a glacier and to a high point, but could see that it was still farther to the top. As it was freezing cold and night was imminent, they decided to turn and head for camp, considering their near-summit a success.

While the earliest explorers extolled the stunning views of all the mountains in the range, Rainier remained an obsession. Thirteen years after that first attempt, General Hazard Stevens, son of the first governor of Washington Territory, and his acquaintance, P. B. Van Trump, reached the summit. According to Stevens's account, published in the *Atlantic Monthly* magazine, they were helped by a farmer named James Longmire and an Indian named Sluiskin.

Stevens and Van Trump reached the top of Rainier on August 17, 1870. It was after 5 p.m., and a storm was blowing in. They had to spend the night on the glacier. What saved them was a steam vent that exhaled warm sulfur breaths into a snow cavern. There they huddled through the night and then raced back to camp during a break in the weather the next morning. They celebrated their return with hot coffee and morsels of marmot, the only creature their Indian guide had managed to trap.

The first Rainier fatality came in July 1897, when Edgar McClure, a professor at the University of Oregon, was on an expedition to measure the exact height of the mountain. Standing on a precarious ledge, a large barometer strapped to his back, he turned to his companions and said, "Don't come down here; it is too steep." Those were his last words, according to an article published that year in the *Seattle Post-Intelligencer*, before he lost his balance and fell into a deep ravine.

Still, the popularity of the 14,400-foot mountain grew. A 1911 article in the *Chicago Evening Post* observed, "The public is just beginning to realize that one of the wonderlands of the world is within the confines of Mount Rainier National Park." The story noted that in 1906 the park had only 1,786 patrons, but in 1911 was expecting 12,000. Today the park sees about two million visitors annually, about 11,000 of whom try to climb the mountain. Usually only half succeed.

Nowadays, the summer crowds at Rainier tend to drive away the most serious climbers. Consider John Roskelley, a 1971 WSU graduate who first climbed Rainier when he was a teen. His father was the outdoors editor at the *Spokesman-Review* and often brought home books about climbing to review. Roskelley devoured the books and was eager to have his own adventures. So his father signed him up with the Mountaineer club in Spokane. He remembered the day they tackled Rainier. The weather was poor in the morning, and his equipment included his old Boy Scout pack, his dad's Army sleeping bag, jeans, and a pair of rubber boots. "It took me a few years before I got some decent equipment."

Roskelley didn't let a little thing like college get in the way of his mountaineering. His first weekend at WSU, he stayed on campus to study for a test, which he then flunked. "When I got that F, I said to myself, either I'm not supposed to be here over the weekend, or I'm not supposed to be here at all." From then on, as soon as his classes were over, Roskelley and his climbing buddy, 1971 WSU alum Chris Kopczynski, would head for the mountains. "The whole Northwest was our playground," he said.

Today, Roskelley makes climbs around the world. In 2003, he climbed Everest with his 20-year-old son, Jess, who set the record as the youngest American to summit the mountain. And when he's home, Roskelley climbs everywhere but Rainier. It's the perfect situation. Thanks to the mountain's popularity, "everyone neglects the other peaks," he said.

There's Mount Baker, all glaciers and views, the massive Mount Adams to the south, and the pyramid-topped Mount Shuksan to the north. Out toward the coast through old-growth forest rest Mount Olympus and the steep slopes of Mount Deception.

The state is covered with mountains and ranges, from the Olympics, east to the Cascades, north to the Selkirks, and south to the Blues. Hiking, climbing, bouldering, snow camping, rock scrambling, back country skiing, or just walking in the woods—-there are dozens of parks and thousands of acres to do all of these things in Washington.

"You can spend your whole life here and be happy," said Viesturs.

Drawn to the Peaks

Growing up in Illinois, Ed Viesturs could only read about mountain climbing, and he developed quite an appetite for the adventure tales. Then one day during his senior year of high school, a friend's mother mentioned someone at college in Washington, and "a light bulb went off," he said. He enrolled at the University of Washington sight unseen. He saw campus for first time on the fall day in 1977 when his parents dropped him off. It was a step into the unknown. But if he ever needed reminding of why he chose the school, he had only to look out his dorm window to see Mount Rainier. "It was like my Everest," he said.

Viesturs didn't know anyone in Seattle. But he was quick to find the sporting goods stores. He'd pore over their reader boards, hunting for announcements from people looking for climbing partners or carpools. He'd call the numbers and say, "Hey I don't know much about climbing, but I'd like to learn. And I hope you have a car."

He experienced his first big climb that fall: Mount St. Helens, one of the most popular peaks in the Cascades prior to its 1980 eruption. Its gentle slopes and 9,000-foot stature made it an easy target, but it locked Viesturs into climbing for good.

"To have read about all these mountaineering expeditions and not to have done one was so frustrating," he said. The glaciated St. Helens, which required crampons and ropes, was everything he had hoped. "When I got to the summit, I thought, 'This is it. This is what I've been seeking.'"

After St. Helens, Viesturs couldn't wait to climb Rainier. So in the winter of 1978, he and some friends decided to avoid the warm-weather crowds and made several attempts at the mountain, finally succeeding. The park rangers advised them to be prepared, but in a manner that has served Viesturs throughout his climbing career, the group was willing to turn around when things weren't going well. "I decided long ago that this has to be fun, but I want it to be safe," said Viesturs. "I do not want to die on a climb.

"The art of mountaineering is managing the risk," said the climber, who has walked in the footsteps of friends who had died on a climb a few days earlier. "You are either allowed to go up, or the mountain just says, 'Uh, uh, you've got to go home.'"

What makes mountaineering interesting for him is the uncertainty. "If you knew you'd get to the summit, why bother?" he said. What brings him the most respect from other climbers is his willingness to turn around, even with the summit in sight.

The mountains of Washington are the perfect training ground for mountaineers, said Viesturs. "They're glaciated, they're steep. The weather sucks."

"Climbing here makes you tough, strong, and capable," he said. "You can take that experience all over the world. You are used to the hardship."

After college, Viesturs enrolled at WSU, following through on his plan to become a veterinarian. The challenge of the program and the distance from the mountains really ate into his climbing time. "I was so bummed," he said. He consoled himself by spending summers as a guide on Rainier. At the time, he didn't have an inkling of becoming a professional climber. He finished vet school—and made his first Everest expedition—in 1987 and joined a practice, taking time off to go on climbs. But that arrangement didn't last beyond 1989. He had to choose between climbing and a veterinary career. Climbing, of course, won. Still, Viesturs manages to use his training in biology, medicine, and physiology when he's in the mountains, sometimes serving as medic for his team.

Viesturs attracts climbers and fans who are more interested in his accomplishments and his lungs than his durable good looks and affable personality. He is one of those rare climbers with both the mental acuity to safely and efficiently climb a mountain and a natural ability to thrive at high altitudes. In 1997 pulmonary experts looked at Viesturs and determined he had a greater-than-normal lung capacity, above-average endurance, and the ability to manage on low oxygen. Simply put, "at high altitude, I'm not as debilitated as most people," he said.

In 1996, the season of the events described in *Into Thin Air*, he came to climb Everest without supplemental oxygen in pursuit of his goal to scale all 14 of the world's peaks higher than 8,000 meters. He became a hero on that expedition, helping to save lives on the mountain, and gaining the summit as he had hoped.

Last May, completing a successful assault on Annapurna, he climbed into the record books as the first American to summit all 14 peaks without the aid of oxygen.

Today Viesturs and his wife, Paula, live with their two children in the Seattle area, just a quick drive from the mountains. Twice every summer the elite climber is the star attraction in a guided climb up Rainier, an exercise he modestly calls "a good workout." It's one he's done nearly 200 times.

At Home in the Hills

Since her first difficult climb of Rainier, Danielle Fisher has quickly become a seasoned mountaineer. In fact, she's somewhat embarrassed to tell people just how quickly. In January 2003, she and her father climbed Aconcaqua, the highest peak in South America. That summer, while her friends were headed for the beach to celebrate the end of high school, Fisher boarded a plane bound for Africa and Mount Kilimanjaro. She climbed that mountain, got on the next plane to Russia, and in the same month ascended Elbrus. In January 2004, she climbed Kosciusko in Australia, and that spring went on to Mount McKinley. The following January, she climbed Vinson in Antarctica, and in June 2005, with a team from Seattle-based Alpine Ascents, topped off the seven summits with Everest.

It wasn't the best season for the world's highest mountain. In 2005 there were only three days when climbers could even attempt to summit Everest. Part of it was a waiting game: weeks of waiting for a break in the weather, waiting for her teammates, and waiting for her body to adjust to the altitude. Fisher found she was better at it than many of her fellow climbers. In fact, most of her 12 teammates didn't make it above Camp Two, the second of four stations on the way up the mountain. Some left because they were scared. Some were physically unable to continue because their bodies wouldn't function in the oxygen-deprived atmosphere. "And then there were people who just lost the heart to go further," she said.

"I was never going to lose heart and turn around," said Fisher. "I thought, 'If I'm sick and throwing up, I'll turn around, but not right now.'"

But then she got to the South Summit and realized she had the energy to make it to the top and back. "I started crying," she said. She cried, as she trudged up the steep glacier, all the way to the top, where she sat down, buried some pictures for a teammate who couldn't do the climb, said a prayer, took a picture, and worked with a Sherpa to change her oxygen bottle. Yes, her body was surviving the altitude, but "It was still incredibly hard for me," she said.

There was some excitement at her setting new records, bringing TV interviews and newspaper articles, but Fisher went into the limelight with reluctance. "It's not about the record for me, really," she said. "I got to see the world and make some of my best friends."

Today Fisher, like Viesturs and Roskelley before her, lives in two worlds. In Pullman, she's a student majoring in materials science and planning for a career. None of her college friends climb, and none of her climbing friends come here to visit. And most who see her at WSU don't know about her other life, the one she lives in the record books and on the world's highest peaks.

Still, her heart often strays to places like the Himalayas. She still wears the orange prayer strings placed around her neck by the lamas she has met on her journeys.

"They're for protection," she said, as she untangles them from the silver cross she also wears. "You don't take them off while you're climbing. You're supposed to wear them until they fall off." She has already planned her summer 2006 trip to Pakistan to climb Gasherbrum 1 and Gasherbrum 2, the 11th- and 13th-highest peaks in the world.

And now that she can climb anywhere, is she ready to quit the Cascades?

"Never," said Fisher. "That's where I think you can find the best climbing in the world. There's rock, there's ice, there's mountaineering. It's clean. And it's beautiful.

"You just don't get that in many places in the world," she said. "And that's my back yard.".

The Man Who Gave Away Mountains

Andrea Vogt

The pool is shaded by maidenhair ferns and thirsty red cedars, but his initials, "VTM 1964," are still visible, etched in shaky script at the bottom of the concrete basin that captures spring water off the mountainside.

Virgil Talmadge McCroskey, a Colfax pharmacist from one of eastern Washington's most prominent pioneering families, carved his initials into the bottom of this concrete basin at age 88.

Though he passed away a quarter of a century ago, the spring and the forested ridge from which it bubbles up are part of the legacy of land left by a man ahead his time: The wheeling, dealing Whitman County bachelor—one the first graduates of Washington State University—spent his life and fortune amassing thousands of acres for the rest of us to enjoy.

In the beginning, the odds were overwhelmingly against him—state legislators repeatedly refused his gifts, locals gossiped about his eccentric ways, family members were convinced he was squandering their wealth, and there was no end to the red tape and backbreaking labor the parks would require. But by the time he died in 1970, McCroskey's visionary conservation efforts had made headlines in *Life* magazine, which heralded him by the nickname locals had been calling him for years: The Man Who Gave Away Mountains.

Today, most residents of the Palouse have benefited at least once from McCroskey's gift of Steptoe Butte. A narrow road winds several times around the naked peak, which rises abruptly from the soft folds of farmland between Colfax and Spokane. The view from the top spans 360 degrees—from the Palouse Country's gentle hills, quilted in a colorful patchwork, to the mountains beyond. The requisite scenic drive up to the top of the butte is a ritual for students and their families arriving for the start of school or football games, for foreign students eager for a bird's-eye view of their new home, for couples searching for the most romantic sunset, for paragliders learning to take flight, for professional photographers from all over the world.

"Steptoe Butte could be developed. There could be houses on top and at the base of it, said heir Lauren McCroskey, who works as an architectural historian for U.S. Army Corps of Engineers, Center for Expertise for the Preservation of Historic Buildings and Structures. "Instead it is something for everybody to enjoy."

Like water, open space is an increasingly precious commodity in the West. The yarn goes that Daniel Boone would always move westward whenever he saw smoke from another man's cabin. McCroskey heard that "me first" attitude knocking at the door of the nation's most treasured places long before the region's salmon runs became threatened and clearcutting left scabs of barren land visible to every jet passenger crossing the West. He had plenty of his own property to preserve and improve, but he knew such efforts wouldn't endure.

"Some folks spend their whole lifetime beautifying an estate," he once said. "They spend a lot of money, but sometimes all that beauty disappears after they are gone, particularly if the property falls into the hands of someone who has no similar interests." McCroskey envisioned what he called "enduring projects," and as the conservation fervor of the early 1900s began to spark state movements across the nation, he wasn't alone. Like Gifford Pinchot, Aldo Leopold, John Muir, Bob Marshall, and other key conservationists who gained prominence in the 1930s, Virgil McCroskey had not only affection for nature, but a utilitarian vision of access for "everyman" and a steadfast determination to save it through his own personal efforts.

Born in 1876, McCroskey traveled west from Tennessee as a toddler with his parents and nine siblings on an immigrant train. The family stopped in Hollister, California, while McCroskey's father went ahead by boat from San Francisco to Portland, Oregon, then by river steamer to Almota, Washington, and finally by stage to Colfax. After locating a 640-acre homestead near Steptoe, he sent for the 11 members of his family. When they arrived at the base of Steptoe Butte, they found their father had already begun constructing a crude, one-room cabin with an attached kitchen and a leaky roof.

They spent the first difficult summers on the Palouse busting sod, plowing under bunchgrass, and preparing the fields for crops. The winters were severe and accompanied by deprivation and illness. Virgil worked the farm until he was college age. In 1892, he joined the first preparatory class at the newly created Washington Agricultural College and School of Science, now WSU. He graduated in pharmacy in 1899, and, after personal encouragement from "Dr. Bryan," as he called the college's third president, he went on to complete two other degrees, in history and economics, one year later. He was one of the first editors of the student newspaper, the *Evergreen*, and "can tell you all about the early history of the college, especially the potato patch and the rotten egging," recalled the 1899 *Chinook* yearbook. He went to work as a pharmacist in drugstores in Walla Walla, Waitsburg, and Olympia for the next five years. In 1903, he bought the Elk Drug

Store in Colfax, which he operated for another 20 years, a period in which "it wasn't too hard to get a prescription for alcohol during prohibition," recalled one Whitman County resident.

That same year, 1903, McCroskey became a charter member of the Washington Outing Club, qualifying by a successful ascent of Mount Rainier, which had only recently been preserved as one of the first national parks. A series of other inspirational outings to Mt. Hood and other Northwest peaks would follow.

In 1938, he embarked on a formative automobile road trip to Tennessee to see his birthplace. On his way home, he drove across the southwestern U.S. and toured Grand Canyon, Zion National Park, Bryce Canyon, Painted Desert, Yosemite, Sequoia National Forest, and Crater Lake. The next year he visited Yellowstone National Park and the Grand Tetons, also by car.

Energized by his visits to America's new national parks, as well as his world travels—he eventually toured Asia, the South Pacific, and New Zealand—McCroskey felt increasingly called to promote a similar park preservation concept on the Palouse, with hopes of designating the region's natural wonders as state parks. And unlike today's conservationists, who cringe at road building, McCroskey placed particular importance on creating access for motorized vehicles to the sites, convinced, as Roosevelt was, that the automobile would revolutionize Americans' appreciation for nature—simply by getting them there.

Over a 30-year span between the mid-1920s and 1955, McCroskey made a series of shrewd, strategic land deals to patch together parcels of land he was convinced were worthy of perpetual protection.

The large McCroskey family had great influence. Virgil's father, who was once county sheriff, was credited with drawing thousands of Tennesseans to Whitman County. Virgil's uncle was a prominent farmer, banker, and state senator and one of WSU's first regents. One brother became a Superior Court judge, another the mayor of Colfax. Family affairs—weddings, deaths, land deals—made headlines in Spokane.

The family eventually grew so big the joke was that you couldn't go bird hunting near Steptoe without hitting a McCroskey.

In 1927, Virgil and his brother, George, began lobbying to preserve Steptoe Butte as a historical landmark, a desire shared by the Washington State parks commission, which placed it on its list of proposed parks in 1927. More than a decade later, in 1936, Spokane conservationist Aubrey White traveled to Colfax to pitch McCroskey's cause to the skeptical Colfax Chamber of Commerce.

"He had a heck of a time," recalled Lavelle Gardner, an Oakesdale history buff who remembers McCroskey's battle.

Slowly, McCroskey won over or out-negotiated each and every recalcitrant landowner on the butte. The process spanned nearly 20 years.

Yet McCroskey's fight was only beginning, for one park was not enough.

In 1939, while he was waiting out one Whitman County farmer foe—it was still seven years before Steptoe Butte would become a park—McCroskey, then 63, purchased the first right of way for his next project—a state park in neighboring Idaho, which extended into Washington's Whitman County. Commonly called Skyline Drive, Mary Minerva McCroskey State Park is today Idaho's second largest state park, at 5,400 acres. Named after McCroskey's mother, and dedicated to all pioneer women in the inland Northwest, the forested spine stretches across Idaho's Latah-Benewah county line and into eastern Washington. As a boy, McCroskey often picked huckleberries and picnicked under the trees there with his family. The views from the top encompass four states.

For the next 15 years, he battled scornful legislators, he worried family members who feared he was squandering their fortune, and he puzzled local townspeople, who remember him as an eccentric playboy driving into Oakesdale in a white Buick convertible upholstered with red leather, his white hair flying wildly in the wind.

Youngsters were fascinated by the tall, weathered adventurer's exotic travels to Asia and the South Pacific, but wary of his affection for cheap park labor. He often rounded up groups of Boy Scouts and other local youths and hauled them up to the ridge in the back of a pickup truck to help build trails, tables, and roads.

McCroskey was not a strict preservationist. He used chemicals to stop a moth infestation and allowed many non-native flowers, shrubs, and trees to be planted. He logged some of his lands for revenue and labored tirelessly to punch a 26-mile road across the future park's ridge. He made calculated land deals, even waiting out unwilling landowners and then buying their land at a discount after their deaths, recalled logger and retired shop teacher Terry Doupe of Tensed, Idaho, who knew McCroskey personally. A Benewah County commissioner, Doupe helped found the Friends of McCroskey group and is its acting president. As a teenager, he and his father logged at McCroskey's request. He once asked McCroskey why he worked so hard on land to give away.

"He said, 'I have traveled all over the world. I have seen what happened to the land. There will be clearcuts done,'" Doupe recalled. "The joke has always been that we're 20 years behind around here. But he was looking that far ahead."

But while McCroskey wanted to give willingly, the myopic bureaucrats working in the state house did not readily accept his gift. He requested two stipulations: that cattle and sheep be prohibited from grazing in the park and that it be named after his pioneering mother. Two north Idaho legislators in particular lobbied fiercely against accepting the land, because they didn't want it taken off of the tax rolls ($178 a year to Benewah County). They argued it would be costly to maintain and would create a road to "lure tourists away from Idaho into Washington." They even balked at naming the park after the McCroskey family, grumbling that there must be Idahoans it could be named after.

In 1955, after a series of rejections and fierce lobbying on his behalf by Latah County supporters, McCroskey persuaded Idaho legislators to take the land, but they did so only grudgingly, insisting on a clause requiring him to care for the park himself for 15 years—he was 79 at the time—and give an additional $40,000 endowment for its continued maintenance.

"They thought he would die before the 15 years was up, but he didn't," recalled Doupe. "He outlived the contract, so they had to take it."

McCroskey died just a few weeks short of his 94th birthday, in September 1970, 15 years and three months after Idaho accepted his gift. He managed to expand, improve, and maintain the park well into his 90s.

Unfortunately, the state hasn't always acted with McCroskey's interests in mind. From his death until the 1980s, the park gradually fell into serious disarray, its signs rotting, its trails and picnic areas overgrown. Relatives and friends joined together to lobby the state to quit claiming interest off McCroskey's gift and start keeping up their end of the deal. Since then, the state has erected highway signs and historical markers and has begun clearing roads and trails.

"I wish his work had been better recognized while he was still alive," said historian and 1973 WSU graduate Keith Petersen, author of *Company Town* and several other noted regional histories. Petersen wrote the first official history of McCroskey back in 1983 as part of his WSU graduate studies. The account, co-written and researched with his wife, local historian Mary Reed, was eventually published as a booklet to supplement a traveling exhibit on McCroskey that Petersen and Reed organized between 1983 and 1985.

"He is one of my favorite local characters," said Petersen. "He seemed to be a person who was unafraid of hard work, not overly interested in flattery, whose heart was in the right place and was determined to do the right thing—even if many people refused to recognize at the time that what he was doing was the right thing. He was, in many ways, ahead of his time. The times eventually caught up with his vision, and the Palouse is a better place for having had him live here.".

North Cascades Highway near Washington Pass
Photo Zach Mazur

On the Plateau

How Cougar Gold Made the World a Better Place

Tim Steury

The Cheese Evangelist

Kurt Dammeier is a cheese evangelist. He traces the roots of his passion and faith to discovering Cougar Gold during his days at Washington State University. In November, his Beecher's Handmade Cheese celebrates a year of business at Seattle's Pike Place Market with the release of its aged Flagship cheese, which is inspired by Cougar Gold.

Even though it is only seven months old, Dammeier gives me a slice and waits expectantly as I taste it. And yes, it reminds me of Cougar Gold. A cheddar style, but with a creamy finish rather than the normal sharp finish of a cheddar. But it is different. A little denser. A little creamier. It is fabulous.

Dammeier is pleased by my response, but not surprised. He knows how good it is.

The butterfat is higher than in Cougar Gold, he explained. The milk Beecher's uses contains 3.9 percent butterfat. "We'd like to get to 4.2 percent." Cougar Gold uses milk that contains 3.8 percent butterfat. This translates to about 35 percent butterfat in the cheese.

The milk that makes Cougar Gold comes from the university's 135 Holstein cows. Beecher's buys its milk exclusively from Cherry Valley, a small dairy farm outside of Duvall. Their cows are primarily Jersey and Brown Swiss, lovely breeds that have largely disappeared from American dairies, because even though they produce a higher-fat milk, they are not so prolific as the Holsteins. In order to boost the fat, Beecher's itself bought an additional 40 Jerseys to add to the herd.

When he noticed one morning that Molbak's garden store at Pike Place was closing, Dammeier suddenly realized what route his cheese quest would take. His initial foray had reached an apparent dead end. He recalled consulting with former WSU Creamery manager Marc Bates, a 1970 and 1976 graduate and an agricultural economist, when he was still contemplating making a farmstead cheese.

"They thought I was really naïve," said Dammeier. "They tried to talk me out of it."

What Bates and the economist had not considered was that Dammeier is, as he calls himself, a marketing guy.

Dammeier's Sugar Mountain Capital owns Pasta & Co. and holds a major share of Pyramid Breweries.

"The usual problem," he said, "is you know what you want to make, but don't know how to sell it."

"I knew how to sell it. I didn't know how to make it."

So he hired Brad Sinko as his cheese maker. Sinko had been creating artisan cheeses for his family's Bandon Cheese Company in Oregon until Tillamook bought it. Now at Beecher's, Sinko makes the cheese. Dammeier sells it. They're a great pair.

Beecher's cheese is made on site, the production area enclosed by glass. "You can always tell when little kids have been here," said Sinko, "because there's lip and nose marks everywhere."

Beecher's makes and sells a number of cheeses other than the forthcoming Flagship and also features a small café, serving assorted cheese-based dishes, including what Dammeier calls the world's best macaroni and cheese.

The store also sells cheese by a number of cheese makers throughout the Northwest. And it's here, when talking about other people's cheese, that Dammeier's true evangelism shines.

Dammeier wants Beecher's to be Seattle's first cheese—but not its only cheese.

"I'll bet you on an average day there's a hundred people enter our store who've never thought of cheese beyond the yellow Kroger-variety cheddar," he said. However, you don't convert people to premium cheese by providing them with something fuzzy and blue that stinks of a barnyard, no matter how exquisite that cheese might be to the gourmand.

Rather, you make it familiar. But better. People are comfortable with cheddar and jack and even the frenchy-sounding fromage blanc—which Beecher's calls "blank slate."

But give the people a familiar cheese that tastes like cheese should, and before you know it, they're trying that fuzzy blue stuff. In other words, they're buying more cheese. They're buying more not only of Beecher's cheese, but of the many regional farmstead and artisan cheeses that Beecher's also sells. Dammeier sees his store as a way to both market small production cheeses and also build a market.

"The same thing happened in the early days of craft brewing," he said. "It took a while for consumers to understand the value of a $7.99 six-pack versus a $4.99 six-pack and why it's more flavorful, more authentic, more interesting.

"When you're making things in small batches, it costs more."

Dammeier ticked off the three tenets that underlie his approach to business. Full-flavored, great-tasting food. Fun and theatrical. Finally, he said, "Not a single thing produced by us has any additives, any preservatives. It's pure, simple food."

Along those lines, Dammeier announced in August that 1 percent of Beecher's sales will go to a foundation dedicated to educating the public, especially children, about food production, how it is grown, processed, and transported, as well as what's in it and what those ingredients mean to the health of the consumer and of the planet.

Not Your Average Cheddar

In the 1930s, Washington State College food scientists started research on packaging hard cheese in cans. Responding to a need for more canned foods during World War II, the U.S. government and American Can Company invested in the research in the 1940s. Cheese at the time was sealed in wax, as much still is. Wax can crack, allowing spoilage.

The main obstacle toward putting cheese in a can was the production of carbon dioxide by bacteria in the cheese, which caused the cans to bulge and even burst. Finally, N. S. Golding, a professor of dairy husbandry, discovered that adding a second starter culture to the cheese greatly reduced the carbon dioxide production. This second culture, known to us non-initiates simply as "WSU 19," is what sets Cougar Gold apart.

This "adjunct culture" transforms a cheese that starts with a standard cheddar culture into the unique flavor and finish of Cougar Gold. Whereas cheddars generally have some bitter notes and finish on the palate with a sour milk sharpness, Cougar Gold finishes softer and creamier.

The texture is also different from most cheddars, more crumbly, largely due to its being aged for a year.

This uniqueness presents a certain difficulty in cheese competitions. Even though Cougar Gold is basically a cheddar in its youth, the texture, as well as its extra flavors, prohibits its entry in cheddar categories, which are quite specific in their criteria. Despite the categorical difficulty, though, Cougar Gold won the top of its class (hard pressed non-cheddar cheeses) in the World Cheese Awards in England in 2000.

Cougar Gold today is much the same cheese as it was when first produced in 1948. Of course the cows that produce the milk come and go, and their feed will vary over the years in nutritional makeup. A few years ago, the salt was reduced slightly. But the starters and recipe remain the same.

"We just try not to break it," said Marc Bates, who was Creamery manager for 27 years and is now a consultant.

Other cheese makers are now experimenting with using a second culture to achieve the same effect as Cougar Gold, said current Creamery manager Russ Salvadalena, a 1977 alumnus. Indeed, Beecher's uses an adjunct culture with its

Flagship, their homage to Cougar Gold. Close as it may be, however, it is not the same culture. The actual identity of WSU 19 is closely guarded.

Although the Creamery also makes a traditional cheddar, a jack, and several flavored cheeses, Cougar Gold accounts for 75 percent of its sales. In fact, because of steadily increasing demand, the Creamery recently dropped a couple of its less popular varieties in order to increase Cougar Gold production. It has also started buying milk from a herd managed by the WSU student dairy club, CUDS (Cooperative University Dairy Students). In all, the Creamery produced last year 375,000 pounds of cheese, in 200,000 cans. Sixty percent of their cheese sells between October and Christmas. The campus store accounts for 20 to 25 percent of revenue. Most sales are by mail. The newest outlet is the Washington State Connections store in Seattle.

All that cheese requires someone to make it, of course. Including Salvadalena, the Creamery supports seven staff positions, a full-time faculty member and a staff member in Food Sciences and Human Nutrition, two research graduate assistants, and part-time work for 50 students. Many people working in the dairy and cheese industry today got their cheese education at the Creamery.

The Creamery's cheese-making education is not restricted to undergraduates. For the past 20 years, WSU has offered an annual four-day cheese-making course. The bulk of the class entails lectures by cheese experts from around the country. But one day is devoted to hands-on cheese making. This year, the class made gouda, havarti, mozzarella, cheddar, feta, cottage cheese, queso fresco, and ricotta.

Beecher's Sinko, who took the class in 1993 (Dammeier has also taken it), calls the course "way, way, way better" than any of the others offered around the country. Class size is limited to 27 students. This year, said Salvadalena, they didn't even have to advertise. They simply called up everyone on the waiting list and filled the class.

The makeup of the class has changed significantly over the years, said Salvadalena. Originally, students were primarily from big cheese making plants such as Tillamook and Darigold. "Now more than half are farmstead."

"Farmstead" describes small-scale cheese makers who make cheese from their own animals rather than buying their milk.

After 20 years, the influence of the cheese-making class has spread around the country. Students this year came from Vermont, British Columbia, and Louisiana, as well as Oregon, Washington, and Montana. Bates knows of four cheese makers in California in business today who date back to the third or fourth class. Here in Washington, a number of successful cheese makers list the course on their cheese-making resume. Sandra Aguilar, Quesaria Bendita, in Yakima. Roger and Suzanne Wechsler, Samish Bay Cheese, in Bow. Lora Lea Misterly, Quillasacut Cheese Company, in Rice.

And not all of the students are neophytes. Joyce Snook has been making cheese for 20 years, she said. She took a week off from her role as cheese maker at Pleasant Valley Farm in Ferndale.

"I didn't know the science," she said. Fortunately, she said, smiling, the course was confirming her practices.

Older and Sharper

"The older I get, the sharper I like it," said Snook, in the cheese house at Pleasant Valley Farm near Ferndale. "At my house, I'm eating a 15-month-old Mutschli."

As she packs curd into molds, Snook talks about the cheese that she's made for the last 20 years. Today she is making gouda, which will be five months old by Christmas. On other days she makes a farmstead cheese from a French culture, or a Mutschli, using a Swiss culture and recipe. She also makes flavored goudas and a Norwegian holiday cheese with cloves, cumin, and caraway. (This cheese, Snook instructs, should be eaten as dessert, with ginger cookies or dark beer.)

Because she makes her cheese from unpasteurized milk, it must be aged at least 60 days before sale. That is fortunate for us. Her aged gouda is divine—rich, complex, and tangy.

Snook is adamant about her milk. "You can make a good cheese with pasteurized milk," she said, quoting another cheese maker. "You can make a better cheese with unpasteurized."

Cheese from unpasteurized milk is a living product, she said. "It leaves you satisfied. When you pasteurize, you kill all the good stuff, too."

Although Snook's observation echoes one of the principal controversies in cheese making, the fact that WSU and Beecher's use pasteurized milk complicates the argument.

Snook's father, George Train, who milks the farm's 70 cows, attended WSU in the 1950s and was a member of CUDS. Train and his wife Dolores bought the farm in 1963 and started building a herd, which now numbers about 70, a mix of Jersey, Guernsey, Brown Swiss, Holstein, and Milking Shorthorn. Originally, the Trains bottled and delivered milk. But Train figured there had to be a way to get more value from his milk. He decided to make cheese. In spite of the skepticism of the Creamery manager at the time, whom Train consulted, he forged ahead, experimenting with different cultures and working toward the fine cheese made by his daughter today.

Snook packs the curds into rounded molds and stacks them nine high, then places a metal weight on top and leaves them for two hours. Tomorrow she will soak them in brine for 24 to 48 hours, then coat them in wax and place them in the aging room.

Aging is what turns the bland, rubbery curds into anything from simple workaday cheese to works of gustatory art, again depending on the ingredients and the cheese maker.

After the first three weeks or so, most of the bacteria have died, having consumed the nutrients that they can use. But the enzymes they produced continue to break down the fat and protein into fatty acids, peptides, and some amino acids. It is this process from which the flavor develops.

Snook makes 130 pounds of cheese a day, four days a week. Beecher's sells about 80 pounds a month. Most of the rest of their cheese is sold through their farm store, though at Christmas their cheese goes worldwide. This in spite of their not advertising at all. There is no Pleasant Valley Web site. But the *New York Times* food editor has visited the farm a couple of times. With such occasional coverage and word of mouth, the only business problem Pleasant Valley seems to have is not being able to produce enough cheese to keep the aging room full.

Later, in the house, we taste Snook's cheeses chronologically. Two months. Nice flavor, mild, creamy. Six months. Umm. Getting interesting, a little sharpness developing.

And a year. Yes. This is what getting older is really all about.

The Time Is Ripe

The dairy industry has just gone through a century of consolidation, said Marc Bates. As an industry matures, it consolidates. The result is the identical-looking and -tasting cheddars and jacks that filled grocery store coolers not too long ago.

But that was then. Fortunately, we live on the downside of that cycle. Lack of diversity can last only so long. Those industrial cheeses are still clogging up the coolers, but joining them are fine, deeply luxurious farmstead cheeses from around the country. The bottom end of the market, said Bates, is opening up again.

Industry preference for consistency and shelf life over flavor and variety has provided opportunity.

"We also have organic and sustainable ag movements encouraging small manufacturers," said Bates. "Everything is ripe for this to happen."

We may not have reached cheese heaven quite yet. But we're well past the purgatory of cheese sameness. There is a lot more cheese to go with our wine than there was a few years ago. Besides the cheese course alumni mentioned earlier, Pierre Louis Monteillet, who attended this year's cheese making class, is making a fine goat cheese in Dayton. The already legendary Sally Jackson in Omak produces eccentric cow, goat, and sheep cheeses that hold their own with the finest cheese in the world. Appel Farms in Lynden, Estrella Family Creamery in Montesano, Grace Harbor Farms in Blaine, Port Madison Farm on Bainbridge

Island, and White Oak Farmstead in Battle Ground are all building Washington's new cheese culture.

And of course, all along we've had Cougar Gold, rich, tangy, with that smooth creamy finish. We live in a wonderful time.

An Exquisite Scar

Tim Steury

Palouse Falls

The trail down into the canyon below Palouse Falls is loose talus, poison oak, stinging nettles, and rattlesnakes. But mostly, it's steep, dropping quickly through a notch in the otherwise sheer basalt walls of the canyon. Still, WSU geologist Gary Webster, at 70 the oldest in our party, is the first to the bottom. In fact, he's already fishing before the next one of us arrives.

Webster is the picture of contentment, not only because of the anticipated bass eyeing his fly. He is deep within his element. Although we've dropped barely 400 feet in elevation from the canyon's edge, we've descended 12 million years in time.

The Palouse River at this point is about 60 feet across. The far bank is thick with willow. Above it is a shelf of prairie sage and arrowleaf balsamroot.

Upstream is a cloud of mist from the falls. The falls itself is still hidden around a bend, but the roar of the river falling 180 feet fills the canyon.

The falls has diminished somewhat from the earlier spring runoff. But even then, when it channels the melting snow and rain of the late-winter Palouse, the falls is an insignificant drip compared with the cataclysmic flow that created it, a mere 15,000 years ago.

In order to comprehend that extraordinary force, first consider the basalt.

Above the shelf of sage and balsamroot are the upper flows of the Columbia River basalts, the dense, black volcanic rock that underlies much of southeastern Washington. About 18 million years ago, said Webster between casts, the earth cracked, and great flows of lava erupted, spreading from vents in eastern Washington, northeastern Oregon, and Idaho across what is now the Columbia Plateau. (One of those vents is exposed below the dorms on the south end of the Pullman campus of Washington State University and can be traced all the way to

Davenport.) A succession of seven flows continued over the next many million years. Some of these flows reached as far as the Pacific Ocean. In fact, the basalt bluffs of the Oregon coast originated from vents near Lewiston, Idaho. In some places, the basalt underlying the region is 5,000 feet thick.

Much of what we now understand about the region's basalt is the work of geochemist Peter Hooper, who recently retired from WSU. He and Don Swanson, a former student who graduated in 1960 and moved on to the U.S. Geological Survey, mapped the basalts.

Webster's expertise is the Cenozoic, that relatively brief geologic period that, beginning about 65 million years ago, overlaps with the existence of mammals and seed-bearing plants on Earth. Webster, with colleagues from Yakima, Eastern Washington University, and University of Washington, mapped the interstitial deposits, the gravels and soils, that cover the basalt of the Columbia Plateau. He drove virtually every road in this area, he said.

As fundamental and permanent as the basalt would now seem, Webster points out the cracks in the opposite canyon walls, the very existence of the canyon itself. We are deep within otherwise solid rock. What possibly could have carved this canyon?

It's only recently that geologists broke out of the intellectual prison of uniformitarianism, the notion that geologic phenomena can always be explained by gradual, calmly fathomable events.

J Harlen Bretz started out within that camp. But years of contemplating the Channeled Scablands transformed him and Cenozoic geology.

A University of Chicago geologist who had become fascinated with Pacific Northwest geology as a high school biology teacher in Seattle, Bretz finally understood that the only thing that could have created the scablands was an unimaginably massive flood.

But the idea of a flood so cataclysmic that it ripped a scar down eastern Washington, scouring out the Grand Coulee, ripping through solid basalt to create the Palouse River canyon, was simply unfathomable to anyone who had not contemplated the scablands as Bretz had, particularly anyone comfortably ensconced in the sureness of uniformitarianism.

Webster recounted the story told him by former geology chair Charles Campbell, who was at the American Association for the Advancement of Science meeting in 1940 that was the turning point in the debate over the scablands' origin. Sure as he was about the giant ripple marks and clearly defined channels, Bretz was plagued by a lingering question: What was the source of the water?

Then Joseph Pardee got up to talk about giant ripple marks in the bed of Glacial Lake Missoula—which could only have been created by a sudden outrush of water.

As soon as Pardee finished, Bretz leaped up. "There's my water!" he said.

No one knows, said Webster, why Bretz had not yet connected his theory to Pardee's work. Pardee had first published his observations more than 20 years earlier. Regardless, Bretz finally had his water, and the reluctant uniformitarians gradually gave in.

What Bretz had understood about the strange and beautiful scablands is what we now understand. Fifteen thousand years ago, chunks of glacial ice had formed a dam above Clark Fork, Idaho, backing up a 180-mile-long lake that contained as much water as today's lakes Erie and Ontario combined.

When the dam collapsed, the water rushed westward at 45 miles per hour, scouring the landscape down to basalt, a flood so powerful it chewed into the volcanic basalt, following existing drainages as it could, then creating its own drainages when it overwhelmed them. One flow swept westward from Spokane, then down through the Quincy Basin, another down the Crab Creek drainage near Odessa. A third swept down through present-day Cheney, through Washtucna and Pasco. Near Pasco, the flows recombined at Wallula Gap, along the present-day course of the Columbia. Formed by bluffs only a mile apart, the Wallula Gap constricted the flow, forcing the water to back up behind it.

From there, it surged down the Columbia, still powerful enough when it reached the coast that it deposited huge granite boulders in the Willamette Valley it had carried, probably in chunks of ice, all the way from Idaho.

But this happened not just once, said Webster. It may have happened as many as 105 times.

A European Landscape

The last person to reach the bottom of the canyon is Rich Old, a 1977 and 1981 alumnus, distracted often on the way down by plants in general, weeds in particular.

He seems disturbed by the fact that a plant that he had hoped to find today, *Phacelia ramosissima*, is not yet in flower. But he's dazzled by the *Thelypodium*, lovely long-stemmed flower stalks growing out of the sheer cliffs. "It's incredible," he said, "not only that they're established there, but the seed rain it takes to get them there." The only way the seeds could have landed in the cracks of the basalt would be to have been carried by the fierce winds that sweep through the canyon.

Old, who is probably the leading expert on the plant life of the scablands, is also the creator of the most comprehensive weed identification guide ever written.

"The reason I'm into weeds," he said, "is I hate what they do to our native [plants]."

Old has been my guide through the scablands over the last couple of years. With him, I have tasted red ants (sour from formic acid) and dog lichen (tastes like bubblegum). I have learned that the flower stalk of mullein was burned by the local Indians to treat hemorrhoids and respiratory problems. Old's knowledge of the area's plants and ecology is encyclopedic. He seems to thrive on sharing his knowledge and excitement. He has taught survival classes for Army ROTC and poisonous plant identification to WSU veterinary students. He's a born teacher, though a little too straightforward and independent for academe. Though not didactic, he is demanding. Once he identifies something for you, he expects you to remember, no matter how many syllables.

Lomatium, Antennaria, Erodium. Camas, miner's lettuce, baby blue-lips.

Bromus tectorum. That's one I can remember. Cheatgrass: scourge and transformer of the arid West. But here's another one, even worse. *Taeniatherum caput-medusae*—Medusa head. Not many plant names send shivers up the spine. But this plant is truly diabolical in its survival strategy and persistence.

"See how it falls down and forms a thick litter layer," said Old. "It doesn't biodegrade." In fact, it builds up year after year, choking out everything else. But here's the truly ingenious adaptation. The seeds extend their radical down through the litter into the ground. Nothing else can do that, said Old.

And then there's fire. Fire was part of the scablands ecology, said Old. But the fires did not burn very hot. Natives such as bluebunch wheatgrass would come right back. But Medusa head, with its litter build-up, burns explosively, killing off everything else. Except for its own seeds.

Like Webster, though obviously within a different time frame, Old tends to look at things in terms of the past. "When we're talking about vegetation in eastern Washington," he said, "we're talking about history, about the way things used to be."

Pristine scabland looks bare, said Old. "If you were here a hundred years ago, it would look like a bunch and a bunch and bare ground," he said, referring to the native bunchgrass. "But it's not bare at all. It's got a solid skin of mosses and lichens. That's what held this together."

That fragile skin was largely destroyed by the trampling of cattle, as well as by pocket gophers, driven down into the scabland from the more hospitable loess by tillage. Gophers churn the ground up, again destroying the crust. And once that thin but protective skin is gone, the "original scabland" is history. As John Thompson, formerly of botany and zoology, and Dick Mack, botany, have argued, the ground of eastern Washington is so fragile because it was never grazed by large ungulates. Native plants had never adapted to such treatment, and exotics, some carried intentionally, some not, by European settlers, rushed in to take the natives' place.

"You could take a piece of ground and write out your species composition," said Old of the scablands today, "and you could be standing in southern Europe."

Hidden from View

That the scablands is a different world is illustrated by the tiny *Lomatium gormanii*. Old follows a ritual of venturing out on New Year's Day to find the first spring flower. *Lomatium gormanii* grows in exposed basalt faces, which absorb the heat even of the late-December sun. Last year Old found the first bloom on December 20.

That Old found the scabland flower in Pullman makes no difference. Although the great floods did not sweep over Pullman, the scabland species find their way out of the coulees and canyons of the scabland proper.

The effects of the great floods reach from the mouth of the Clark Fork River in Idaho to the Pacific Ocean. But because the corridor between Cheney and Pasco had no high hills or bluffs to contain the water, it spread over 2,500 square miles.

Much of that area is private land. The advantage of trekking with Old is he's fifth-generation to the area. He knows who owns what, who to ask. And so one day last spring we tramped through an area of the scablands that few people ever get to see, the canyon where Rock Creek flows into Rock Lake. Bounded by the lake and a series of waterfalls, it is a magical place, despite Old's regret.

"When I was first taking botany," said Old, "I found *Blepharipappus* here. I've been back yearly, but haven't seen it since."

Equally magical—and open to the public—is the Escure Ranch. Downstream from Rock Lake on Rock Creek, and purchased by the Bureau of Land Management in 1999, the Escure Ranch is classic scabland. An easy hike takes the visitor into one of the loveliest waterfalls in the Northwest. A large lake is another couple miles in. Although the plant life suffers badly from overgrazing, some natives persist.

Old leads us up a mesa, identifying plants as we go and decrying the invasion of pocket gophers from the wheatfields above us. The arrowleaf balsamroots have withered slightly from a late harsh frost the night before. North of us is another, much larger mesa that was formed by the floods, which scoured the sides and top of the basalt outcrop. Except for meadowlarks, the occasional raven flying over the valley, and our Latin-laden conversation, there is absolute quiet.

Like many of the flood's hidden channels, the 13,000-acre ranch is a harsh Eden within the monotony of the wheatfields, an exquisite scar through what Zane Grey called the desert of wheat, refuge to mule deer and badger, cliff swallows and ferruginous hawks, sage, bunchgrass, Jacob's ladder, and blue-eyed Mary. In spite of the European invasives, the ancient catastrophic beauty of the area prevails. In spite of the loss that he sees, Old is smiling the whole time.

Forgotten Fruit

Tim Steury

Dave Benscoter's obsession began innocently—as a favor to a neighbor, Eleanor, a retired missionary. Resettled near Chattaroy, and now beset with complications from childhood polio, she asked Benscoter, a 1978 WSU graduate, to harvest some apples for her from the old orchard above her house.

"Every apple was too high for me to pick," he said of his initial effort.

"One of the trees was 40 to 50 feet high. The trunk was split, and I couldn't get my arms around either trunk."

Determined to deliver Eleanor's apples at some point, he started pruning to encourage new growth lower down. Meanwhile, the old orchard had infected Benscoter with that most persistent of apple bugs—the need to know the names of apple varieties. And who planted them.

Fortunately, Benscoter had the chops to crack the mystery. Following a career with the FBI and the IRS Criminal Division, those mystery apples whetted his investigative skills.

He started modestly, with a Google search. Wwhat first popped up was Arcadia Orchard, the "largest orchard in the world," located in nearby Deer Park.

Arcadia founders bought thousands of acres of land in the early 1900s and marketed orchard plots nationwide. Promotional materials claimed that by 1916, 7,000 acres were planted to orchard.

Arcadia was only part of the area's orchards. In his 1905 Washington Agricultural Experiment Station Bulletin, "The Wormy Apple," A. L. Melander introduces his strategy against the codling moth with his observation on the regional industry: "It is asserted that 1,500 carloads of apples, valued at $600,000, were carried last year from the Inland Empire."

Historian John Fahey writes that by 1914, Whitman County had nearly 240,000 apple trees. Spokane and Stevens counties had nearly a million. Whitman County had three commercial nurseries.

Benscoter was rediscovering what has been repeatedly forgotten—that before it finally coalesced around Wenatchee and Yakima, the apple industry farther east was enormous and diverse.

Both orchards and nurseries were charmed by the apple's diversity. The Hanford Nursery in Oakesdale listed 64 varieties on its advertising flyer. The Inland Empire was a true garden of apple diversity and bounty.

But soon, it all started to disappear. Ultimately, the Inland Empire could not compete with the irrigated orchards to the west.

Although the large orchards are long gone, remnants, and scores of homestead orchards, are scattered throughout the area.

Early in his investigation, Benscoter made some key discoveries. One was that every year the *Colfax Gazette* would publish a list of the prizewinning apples at the county fair. From 1900 to 1910, over 110 varieties were entered. Though many of the names are familiar, others had disappeared, and Benscoter was determined to find them.

Benscoter tapped the efforts of other apple detectives across the country. He studied Lee Calhoun's *Old Southern Apples*, a large part of which is devoted to forgotten apples.

Benscoter combed Calhoun's descriptions and noted a number of "extinct" apples that appeared in the *Gazette*. He narrowed his investigation: Arkansas Beauty, Babbitt, Cornel's Fancy, Dickinson, Isham Sweet, Lankford, Nero, Pyles Red Winter, Scarlett Cranberry, Walbridge, and Whitman.

On an August morning, Benscoter and I plod down a long draw on Steptoe Butte through dry grass and wild roses toward a dense grove that someone told him was an orchard.

Fruit is sparse this year, following last year's bumper crop, frosts, and intense heat early in the summer. Even so, fruit speckles many of the trees, beckoning explorers in search of lost tastes.

Indeed, when we reach the grove, it is filled with apple trees, maybe 200 of several, as yet unidentified, varieties.

But why seek out these forgotten apples?

Some of it is simply wonder at the diversity of apples. Apple detective Dan Bussey estimates 17,000 named varieties in the United States since Europeans first arrived.

Rediscovered apples could also produce benefits such as genes for disease resistance or flavor. Indeed, Amit Dhingra's WSU genome lab is intrigued by Benscoter's efforts and is nurturing tissue culture of one of his "extinct" discoveries, the Nero.

One might hope to restore diversity to a market defined first by the Red Delicious and now by the Honeycrisp-type apple, all mouth-feel and initial burst of sweet-tart, delightful indeed, but with none of many older apples' subtlety and sophisticated complexity.

But none of this seems to be Benscoter's primary motivation, which has more to do with his professional drive to identify all the elements of an investigation, to find what was lost.

It is the satisfaction of matching unidentified apples to the USDA's stunning collection of apple watercolors, of interpreting plat maps, connecting family histories, and recovering human drama—of Robert and "Mecie" Burns, for example, who planted exuberantly on Steptoe, but misjudged their apples' marketability, thus losing their farm in 1899.

"I got to…walk in the orchard," said Benscoter, "and see and taste the fruit of the trees Robert Burns planted."

Finding Chief Kamiakin

Tim Steury

In July 1853, U.S. Army Captain James McClellan and a column of 61 men and 161 horses and mules headed east out of Fort Vancouver with instructions from territorial Governor Isaac Stevens to survey the middle Columbia region and Cascades passes. When they reached the Simcoe Valley in mid-August, they were greeted by Fathers Pandosy and D'Herbomez of the St. Joseph Mission. They introduced McClellan and George Gibbs, an ethnographer and geologist with the expedition, to "Kamiakin, the principal chief of the country."

The son of a Yakama mother and a Palouse father, Kamiakin grew up among the Yakamas, but as an adolescent also spent time among his father's people. Following the seasons, with their cyclical succession of plants and salmon, the family camped throughout eastern Washington. Kamiakin was about five years old when his people started hearing rumors of strangely dressed white men, the Lewis and Clark expedition, traveling through the region.

As he grew up, Kamiakin learned the horsemanship of his father and steadily built his wealth on horses. As early as 1840, he was recognized by a majority of Yakamas as their headman and was becoming increasingly prominent among other Sahaptin and Salish tribes.

Kamiakin and his brothers traveled widely, perhaps as far as California, bringing longhorn cattle and milk cows back with them to the Yakima Valley. They also introduced potatoes, peas, and other crops. In fact, note Richard Scheuerman and Michael Finley in their recently published *Finding Chief Kamiakin*, it is curious that Captain McClellan failed to acknowledge Kamiakin's gardens and grainfields as he assured Kamiakin that Americans would not settle in the interior. As Gibbs observed, "it is difficult to imagine" that the area would ever serve any "useful purpose."

Given Kamiakin's lingering presence across the state, his name having been attached to both high schools and buttes, it is also curious that it has taken so long for a biography to appear. The only previous book-length treatment was *Ka-Mi-Akin: The Last Hero of the Yakimas*, by A. J. Splawn in 1917. However, it focused primarily on Kamiakin's role in the 1855–1858 Yakima War.

Scheuerman and Finley's book, on the other hand, draws on much new material—including genealogical information and oral history—not only to correct what they consider misconceptions about how heavily Kamiakin influenced that war, but also to elucidate his earlier life and, significantly, his later life and his large family.

Through his friendship with Father Pandosy, Kamiakin accepted much of Catholic teachings and had his children baptized. But he would not accept Pandosy's insistence that a Christian be monogamous. Kamiakin had five wives. How could he give up any of them, he asked Pandosy, when he loved them all? The resulting progeny are many, produced over a long life. Kamiakin's lineage in the Northwest is complex and intricate.

Richard Scheuerman, a 1972 WSU alumnus, grew up near Endicott. "Growing up there, in the shadow of Kamiak Butte, Steptoe Butte, you can't help but wonder about those things." Those things being Kamiakin, of course, and his band, who camped at Kamiakin Crossing on the Palouse River just north of Endicott. After his defeat in the 1858 War and his subsequent exile in Montana, Kamiakin eventually ended up back in Washington, at Rock Lake, where he died in 1877.

The coauthor with Clifford Trafzer of *Renegade Tribe* (WSU Press 1993), the most complete treatment of the Palouse tribe, its role in the war, and Kamiakin to this point, Scheuerman has also written about his Russian ancestors who settled in eastern Washington.

"Even in high school, I knew our community was a little different from others, the nature of the families, relationships, all this talk about Russia. I decided I would track down everybody living in the community who was born in the old country. I don't think I got everyone, but I got most. I still have the notes.

"Several commented about life on the Palouse River when they first came from Russia and the relationships they had with the Native peoples when they'd come through every fall and every spring, trading their salmon for the fruits and vegetables.

"It sparked my interest, who are they and why they aren't here now."

Michael Finley's thesis advisor at Eastern Washington University told him that if he wanted to be an authority in Native history of the Inland Northwest, he had to know who the authorities were. "He probably meant pick up their books," said Finley. Which he did. But he also took his advisor literally, personally contacting Trafzer, Scheuerman, and Robert H. Ruby, another prolific scholar of Northwest Indians.

After finishing his thesis, on the three chiefs of the Colvilles, Skolaskin, Moses, and Joseph, Finley went to work for the Colville tribe in the history and archaeology division.

"I had some extra time on my hands outside of work. Coupled with that, I did a lot of research in my work. I'd come across references to Kamiakin," which he started e-mailing to Scheuerman.

Finley also had access to genealogy records, which interested Scheuerman very much.

Scheuerman wrote back, "I haven't seen that before." He said this is wonderful stuff, said Finley. What should we do with it?

Finley is currently vice chairman of the Colville Business Council for the Colville Confederated Tribes. He is a descendent of Jaco Finley, the explorer David Thompson's French-Indian guide. His wife Jackie is, through her father, a direct descendent of Kamiakin. Even though Kamiakin and his wives and younger children settled at Rock Lake, his adult children all moved to the Colville Reservation.

"I thought, what better tribute for my children than to work on their family history."

Kamiakin had watched cautiously as White people started moving into the region. He welcomed them, if a little nervously. Nevertheless, in 1848 he had invited the Catholic fathers to open the St. Joseph mission and assured them he would take full responsibility.

But Kamiakin's patience and goodwill had limits. Sometime around 1853, he contacted military authorities at Fort Dalles and asked them to remove a settler who had established a claim on Indian land about 20 miles north of the Columbia River. Not wanting to provoke an incident, they complied.

But Isaac Stevens was not so compliant. Stevens was not only governor of Washington Territory, but also the territory's superintendent of Indian affairs and the supervisor of the Northern Pacific Railroad Survey. In light of this last job, in particular, he thought it essential to extinguish Indian title to what federal officials considered public domain.

Stevens's belief in Manifest Destiny was resolute. "The great end to be looked to," he wrote, "is the gradual civilization of the Indians, and their ultimate incorporation with the people of the territory."

"The rapid dispossession of Puget Sound tribal domains," write Scheuerman and Finley, "confirmed Kamiakin's suspicion that the polite rhetoric of White officials concealed other motives."

His friend Father Pandosy was unable to encourage him. "It is as I feared," he told Kamiakin, "the Whites will take your country as they have taken other countries from the Indians... . You may fight and delay for a time this invasion, but you cannot avert it."

Angus McDonald, another friend of Kamiakin's with the Hudson Bay Company, affirmed Pandosy's warning. Killing a white settler was like killing an ant, he told Kamiakin. There would be hundreds more pouring from the nest.

Indeed, their warnings were prescient.

Increasing pressure from Stevens and deliberation among Indian leaders moved them all toward the 1855 Walla Walla Treaty Council. Piupiu Maksmaks, the Walla Walla chief, and Kamiakin had hoped that the assembled tribal leaders would present a united front against Stevens. But the Nez Perces, who had long been friendly to the White people, refused to join. In late May, hundreds of people—Yakama, Nez Perce, Palouse, Walla Walla, Cayuse—met with Stevens and other territorial representatives.

Stevens later observed of Kamiakin, "He is a peculiar man, reminding me of the panther and the grizzly bear. His countenance has an extraordinary play, one moment in frowns, the next in smiles, flashing with light and black as Erebus the same instant."

Another observer noted that Kamiakin was the "great impediment in the way of cession of Indian lands."

For over a week, Stevens presented federal Indian policy, pushing his proposals about reservation boundaries and fishing rights.

But Kamiakin was unmoved. "I am afraid that the White men are not speaking straight," he told Stevens.

Regardless, at one point, Stevens offered Kamiakin an annual salary of $500 to "perform many services of a public character." But Kamiakin refused, as he did all offers and gifts, believing that to accept anything from the White people would compromise him and imply he had sold the Indians' land.

When Kamiakin finally told Stevens he was leaving, that he was "tired of talking," Stevens pushed harder and, according to an interpreter's account years later, resorted to threat: "If you do not accept the terms offered and sign this paper…you will walk in blood knee deep."

Whether it was that threat or the combined advocacy of the other leaders, muse Scheuerman and Finley, Kamiakin finally signed with an X. According to one of the priests present, he was in such a rage that he bit his lip until it bled.

Under the terms of the Yakima Treaty of 1855, the 14 tribes of the confederated "Yakima Nation" ceded to the United States approximately 17,000 square miles in exchange for the exclusive use of 2,000 square miles of reservation land, two schools, and fishing and gathering rights at "all usual and accustomed places."

The Nez Perce and Walla Walla-Cayuse treaties were also drawn up.

Within weeks of the signings, however, the treaties, not yet even ratified, were broken. Gold was discovered on Indian land north of the Spokane River, and White people rushed to the new diggings. And where miners rushed in, other settlers would soon follow.

Kamiakin convened a conclave a month after the treaty signing, meeting with Teias and Owhi of the Yakamas as well as representatives of the Columbias and Wamapum.

Kamiakin asked them, "What of us then?" Shall we become "degraded people? Let us stop their coming, even if we must fight."

In spite of his despair, Kamiakin still sought reconciliation: "Let us send men to the mountain passes to warn the White men to go back." But "if they persist… we will fight."

As worthless as historical speculation might be, one cannot help but wonder what the former Washington Territory might be like had the moderating efforts of Kamiakin, the Catholic priests, and the U.S. Army prevailed over the volunteer militias, the ranting newspaper editors in Seattle and Portland, and the relentless momentum of impatient settlers.

But of course there was no stopping that momentum.

In July 1856, the Washington Volunteers attacked an encampment of 300 Cayuse, Walla Wallas, and Umatillas, and claimed they'd killed many Yakama warriors under Kamiakin in the process. They destroyed the camp's stores of dried beef, tents, and flour and took about 200 horses, many of which they shot.

According to Colonel George Wright, the new commander of the recently formed Ninth Infantry, the attack was on "women, old men and children, with a few of the young men." Kamiakin was not present. He was likely camped among the Okanogans with his brothers and the Yakama chief Owhi and Columbia chief Quiltenenock.

"As word spread," write Scheuerman and Finley, "Army officials railed again against Stevens and the volunteers' methods, which were 'to provoke a continuance of the war and to plunder the Indians of their horses and cattle.'"

A second Walla Walla Council in 1856 deteriorated under Stevens's inflexibility, alienating even the Nez Perce. Escalation of violence seemed inevitable.

Amidst the recorded vitriol and impatience of the Whites and the running battles between Indians and Whites, one factor is only slowly being recollected, and that is the impact of introduced disease on the fate of the Native peoples of the interior.

"I've often said," said Scheuerman, "before the war started in 1855, it was already finished." Some historians estimate that as much as 60 to 70 percent of the Native population was decimated by smallpox and measles in the preceding decades.

"There were villages on the lower Snake River that were totally uninhabited," he said. "Someone told the story of going upstream on the Palouse River and finding a village with one small child crying, the only one left."

If the physical decimation weren't enough, the psychic toll must have been profound. "On a grand scale," write Scheuerman and Finley, "epidemics demoralized and decreased Native populations, adversely affecting their overall social organization and strength."

Whatever their disadvantage, however, the growing tension led to a major victory.

Lt. Col. Edward Steptoe left Fort Walla Walla in May 1858 with a contingent of approximately 160 men, headed for Fort Colville in a show of strength. North of Rosalia, they met a large gathering of Indians.

Having crossed the Palouse River the night before, Steptoe had received intelligence of belligerent Palouses and Spokanes ahead, but sent a scout back to Fort Walla Walla with the message that he intended to "give them a good drubbing."

But the gathering was far larger than he had imagined, his men were under-armed, and the Indians were angry at the blatant incursion on their territory. Chief Vincent of the Coeur d'Alenes ordered him to turn around, and Father Joset of Sacred Heart mission desperately attempted to negotiate.

But as more and more Indians gathered, they finally attacked under no threat of a drubbing.

Fierce fighting continued throughout the day. Seven soldiers were killed and thirteen wounded, but finally they were able to slip away under darkness.

Such an embarrassment to the Army could of course not go unanswered. On July 4, 1858, General Newman Clarke, commander of the Army of the Pacific, issued orders to Colonel Wright for a "complete submission" of the warring tribes.

Wright marched 1,000 men across the Columbia Plateau. Kamiakin and other chiefs massed their people in Spokane and Palouse country to meet the advancing troops.

Wright's troops and the gathered tribes finally met in early September in the Battle of Four Lakes, about five miles north of present-day Cheney. The Indians were unprepared for the improved weaponry of the Army troops, and the warriors fell back under heavy fire in spite of Qualchan and Kamiakin's appeals to stand their ground. The companies that had been part of the Steptoe rout were "burning for revenge" and swept into the Indians. Warriors were overrun, shot down, or clubbed, leaving confusion and death across the plains.

After retreating, Kamiakin and other leaders tended their wounded and waited for Wright's next move. By September 5, they had regrouped several miles north of Four Lakes to meet the soldiers again in the Battle of Spokane Plains. "This proved to be the decisive action of the campaign and a defining moment in the region's primal clash of cultures," the authors write.

"Again Kamiakin and Qualchan led the Palouses and Yakamas at the Indians' center left and right, respectively. Stellam's Coeur d'Alenes took the right flank and Spokanes under Garry and Sgalgalt formed on the left. As rifles barked and the howitzer began thundering, Indians from the north dashed 'down a hill five hundred feet high and with a slope of forty-five degrees, at the most headlong speed,' in 'feats of horsemanship…never seen equaled.' They rushed forward to join other warriors attempting to contain the soldiers' horseshoe formation."

But horsemanship and valor were in the end no match for Wright's superior firepower.

Wright's strategy had relied on overwhelming force and a "focused assault on Tribal leadership," write Scheuerman and Finley. Wright, who earlier had pursued a diplomatic path, had now assumed a ruthless and uncompromising policy. When Qualchan rode into Wright's camp with his wife to speak of peace, Wright had him summarily hung along with some Palouses he had rounded up. The stream where Wright was camped was named Hangman Creek.

Wright demanded unconditional surrender and had his troops destroy camps, herds, and food caches. Three days after the battle, Wright had ordered his troops east through the Spokane Valley, overtaking a herd of a thousand Indian horses, which they shot.

The war of 1858 was over.

Kamiakin and his band fled eastward into the Bitterroots.

So why did it take so long for a biography of Kamiakin to materialize? Scheuerman and Finley gave slightly different answers.

Part of it is the nature of the Kamiakin family, Scheuerman ventured. Perhaps they feel a continuation of what Kamiakin himself felt, hurting from the divisions among the tribes, during and after the war. Kamiakin goes to live at the obscure Rock Lake and then drifts off himself into obscurity, the real story of his role and greatness remaining only within the family.

Perhaps more significant, even though it occurred over 130 years ago, the family is still enraged over the desecration of Kamiakin's grave. Soon after he died and was buried in a small family plot on the shore of Rock Lake, fossil hunter Charles Sternberg learned about the chief's grave from a local rancher. Another local resident encountered Sternberg and his brother leading packhorses. Sternberg mentioned casually that "Wouldn't the old chief's head look good on the shelves of the Smithsonian Institution."

When family members visited the gravesite and found Kamiakin's grave dug up and his head gone, they were devastated. They had a holy man supervise the moving of the cemetery to the other side of the lake. All swore never to reveal its new location.

Many attempts have been made to locate Kamiakin's skull, to no avail. Scheuerman himself has tried his best to track it down. He finally gave up.

Some of the reason for the biography's slow coming is simply a matter of privacy, said Finley. But there is also an unease with written history: "What you put in writing can be used against you down the road." Written accounts, both accurate and inaccurate, have been used in deciding treaty disputes.

"On the other hand," he said, "if you don't put anything out, you have nothing to stand on. It's important that you put stuff in writing. It's also important that you're very careful what you say and how you say it."

Scheuerman and Finley plan to donate royalties from their book to a memorial at the site of the Kamiakin camp at Rock Lake, if the family concurs. If not, they will go toward a scholarship in Chief Kamiakin's name.

Where Have All the Frogs Gone?

Rebecca Phillips

It happened again that morning. During their rounds, zookeepers found another tank of dead blue poison dart frogs. The tiny azure amphibians, native to South American rainforests, had been enjoying a successful breeding program at the Smithsonian National Zoo. Now, inexplicably, they were dying from a mysterious skin disease, and the cause remained elusive.

The year was 1996 and Allan Pessier had just begun a pathology residency at the National Zoo. As a lifelong amphibiophile, he was more than a little intrigued when the deceased dart frogs began arriving in his laboratory.

Together with senior pathologist Don Nichols, Pessier, who earned his DVM from WSU in 1996, used an electron microscope to search for the likely culprit. It wasn't long before they zeroed in on what appeared to be an unusual fungus called *Chytridiomycetes* or "chytrid" that typically grows on decaying vegetation.

Seeking verification, Pessier used their pre-Google web browser to locate one of the world's few experts on chytrids, a mycologist named Joyce Longcore. Longcore agreed their specimen seemed to be a chytrid but was unlike anything she'd ever seen before. Eventually, she identified it as an entirely new species and the first chytrid fungus known to infect vertebrates like frogs. They named it *Batrachochytrium dendrobatidis* or Bd.

Around the same time, researchers in Australia and Central America announced the discovery of a protozoan they believed was causing the ominous global decline in wild frogs that had been occurring since the 1970s. Incidents of these massive die-offs had risen sharply in the 1980s but no one could pinpoint exactly why.

When Pessier's team saw photos of the suspect microbe in the *New York Times*, they immediately knew the organism was not a protozoan, but was instead Bd, the chytrid fungus they had just identified. With a dawning awareness, they recognized their discovery could have enormous implications.

"We thought we'd discovered a cool thing in zoo frogs," said Pessier. "But, there was this window of time when we realized we may be the ones who knew exactly what was causing these enigmatic global die-offs. That's pretty exciting, especially when you're just a year out of veterinary school."

In time, their theory was validated and Pessier began providing diagnostic help to investigators in Central America. Since Bd thrives in a cool moist climate, frogs living in mountainous cloud forests suffered the most, particularly those in Panama like the iconic golden frog now thought to be extinct in the wild.

"It didn't hit me how devastating it really was until I went out into the Panama rainforest in 2006," Pessier said. Before the chytrid fungus went through, the forest was deafening with frog calls and they covered the ground everywhere you stepped. But after the chytrid fungus, it was completely silent and you had to search for 45 minutes to find a single frog.

"Bd has truly earned its name as the most deadly pathogen ever recorded," he said, speaking of the worldwide analysis published last March in the journal *Science*. The report concluded that Bd, unrivaled in its ability to kill untold hundreds of millions of frogs, was responsible for the decline of more than 500 species with at least 90 forced into extinction. Deadlier than the 1918 influenza pandemic or medieval bubonic plague, Bd is the worst infectious disease known to science.

In 2017, Pessier, Nichols, Longcore, and colleague Elaine Lamirande were honored with the Golden Goose Award from the American Association for the Advancement of Science. The award is given to groups of researchers whose seemingly obscure, federally-funded research has led to major breakthroughs in medicine, science, technology, the environment, and more.

Today, in an office adorned with frog paintings and posters, Pessier has returned to Washington State University as a pathologist in the Washington Animal Disease Diagnostic Laboratory (WADDL) and clinical associate professor in the College of Veterinary Medicine. With 20 years' experience in aquatic pathology, Pessier is the "go to guy" when zoos and other organizations have tough questions about amphibian disease. Each year, WADDL receives hundreds of samples from people across the world seeking Pessier's expert knowledge and diagnostic skills.

But Pessier is just one of several WSU scientists taking amphibian research to the global level. Caren Goldberg in the School of the Environment is a pioneer in the development of environmental DNA (eDNA) techniques that simplify the ability to screen for pathogens like Bd that can be spread through the international pet trade.

Other researchers in the School of Biological Sciences are investigating physiological and environmental stress factors that could help trigger mass amphibian die-offs. Their findings have applications for many other species as well.

Together, this diverse group of scientists has created a synergy that puts WSU in the national spotlight as an emerging center for amphibian research. They share a critical goal: To prevent the occurrence of a second fungal pandemic—an explosive threat looming just over the horizon.

Rain clouds are gathering but, for the moment, it's a sunny April afternoon as I follow a muddy path around the little pond at Virgil Phillips Farm Park just outside Moscow, Idaho.

Making my way through trees and cattails, I join assistant professor Goldberg, who is busy assembling her eDNA collection system. Dressed in jeans and tall rubber boots, she kneels in faded grass near the edge of the water where two male Columbia spotted frogs have staked out territories.

Goldberg quietly lowers a plastic tube into the pond and uses a hand pump to draw water up through a filter and into a flask. With tweezers, she carefully removes the wafer-like filter and stuffs it into a test tube.

Back in her laboratory, she will extract DNA from the skin cells, feces, urine, and other bits of material left behind by aquatic inhabitants. The DNA is then run through assays to identify target species of fish, amphibians, snails, turtles, and other creatures. With that one sample, Goldberg can also detect rare and invasive species as well as disease-causing organisms like Bd and ranavirus.

As one of the world's leading amphibian eDNA researchers, Goldberg analyzes more than a thousand samples each year from all over the world, including endangered frogs from the Panama forests visited by Pessier. She and her team have developed nearly 50 assays, each uniquely designed for a particular species.

Not only does eDNA improve and simplify the process of monitoring aquatic species, it's also safer, more efficient, and minimally invasive. Now, instead of tromping through fragile wetlands—turning over rocks and kicking up mud, which can harm the animals living there—scientists can get answers with only a few water samples.

When Goldberg first learned of the concept as a graduate student in 2008, it transformed her world.

"As an ecologist, I spend a lot of time looking for rare species out in the field and not always finding them even though we know they are probably there," she said. "When I heard about eDNA that detected amphibians in water, I was so excited. I knew it could have huge implications for managing and conserving rare species."

By 2011, Goldberg had a contract with the Department of Defense to bring eDNA surveillance into the real world as a practical tool for wildlife conservation. Joined by fellow researchers Katherine Strickler and Alex Fremier in the School of the Environment, they set out to develop reliable techniques that would enable them to detect rare amphibians and fish on military bases across the United States.

"Our military bases are some of the last preserved parts of ecosystems that have otherwise been developed or plowed under," Goldberg said. "They contain a lot of the nation's endangered species. If you think about it, even a bombing range, for example, is much less disturbance to a salamander than is a shopping mall."

She began the project by adapting protocols for working with poor-quality DNA that she'd learned as a doctoral student at the University of Idaho. In 2015, she joined WSU and designed her lab to use these new methods for processing eDNA samples.

Recently, Goldberg, Strickler, and wildlife biologist Jeff Manning in the School of the Environment were awarded another $1.4 million DoD contract to continue improving eDNA detection especially for species that are very rare and present in low numbers. They want to increase test sensitivity to handle some of nature's most challenging conditions such as highly acidic water or very large ponds.

The biggest challenge for eDNA surveillance, however, may lie in the frontline battle to prevent a deadly salamander fungus from entering the United States and other vulnerable parts of the world.

In 2013, scientists were alarmed to discover massive salamander die-offs occurring throughout Europe from a new strain of chytrid fungus similar to Bd. Known as *Batrachochytrium salamandrivorans*, Bsal, or salamander chytrid, the disease is especially threatening to the United States, a global hotspot for salamander biodiversity.

Thanks to lessons learned during the frog Bd pandemic, the new infection was quickly identified and international barriers were established to prevent spread of the pathogen. By 2016, the U.S. Fish and Wildlife Service had banned imports of 201 salamander species.

Jesse Brunner, associate professor in the School of Biological Sciences, is on the National Bsal Task Force and said the fungus has not yet been detected in North America.

"That's really a good thing," he said. "Allan Pessier, Caren Goldberg, and I are working on developing better approaches to screen animals and try to prevent it getting here. Millions of amphibians are imported into the U.S. every year, mostly through the pet trade.

"It's very unregulated—we know Bd is found in some of these animals," Brunner said. "We want to use eDNA testing to screen a whole shipment at a time rather than test each animal individually. The idea is that we can collect a handful of samples from the water and have a high probability of ensuring there isn't infection in that group of animals."

Worldwide surveys indicate these infectious fungi likely emerged from Asia where over millions of years, the local amphibian species developed a resistance to it.

"The exact origin may be uncertain but what is clear is that the movement of animals for the pet trade is moving pathogens like Bd and Bsal around the world," said Brunner. "So, we can expect to see more emerging dangerous pathogens in the future rather than fewer."

And while Asian frogs and salamanders seem to have a natural immunity, the fungus can wreak havoc when moved to a new location or into a novel species, he said. "That's when you often see some of the worst outcomes."

The Bd fungus is a devastating example. Brunner said frogs rely on their skin for breathing as well as electrolyte balance. When Bd invades skin cells, it disturbs the frog's ability to regulate water and electrolytes, which leads to changes in the blood that essentially cause a heart attack.

"It's sort of like whole-body athlete's foot that ends up killing them," he said.

Though most salamanders breathe using both lungs and skin, it's a similar story when they're infected with Bsal—within days the fungus causes ulcers and sloughing tissue that lead to apathy, loss of appetite, and death. As one researcher put it, "It's death by a thousand holes."

Besides the fungus, Brunner is also concerned about one more "cold-blooded killer" called ranavirus that can cross-infect fish, reptiles, and amphibians.

"Ranavirus has a global distribution now," he said. "It can be a really nasty infection—the virus gets into every bit of tissue they have, every cell, where it causes massive damage and organ failure. Thankfully, it doesn't replicate at warm-blooded temperatures."

The curious question is how some animals manage to control these viral and fungal infections so they don't cause severe illness or death. Part of Brunner's research is aimed at determining the factors that lead to this resistance and why catastrophic losses occur in some places and not others. He and his fellow scientists are following several clues.

Erica Crespi, a physiologist and associate professor in the School of Biological Sciences, studies the way stress affects an amphibian's early development. Frogs and salamanders are very sensitive to environmental changes which can trigger spikes in their stress hormone corticosterone.

"Just as in pregnant mammals where elevated stress hormones can cause premature birth, high corticosterone can shorten an amphibian's development time and affect how the brain and lungs develop and cause other lifelong impacts," she said.

Brunner said the idea that long-term chronic stress can suppress the immune system and make it harder for an animal to fight off infections has been studied by biologists for decades.

"In its simple form, the hypothesis says that anywhere we see human activities or other stressors, we should see big outbreaks of disease, but it's not that simple. Stress doesn't always translate into outbreaks."

He and Crespi are trying to determine how individual animals respond to environmental stressors such as increased salinity or water temperature, and how that scales up to negative population outcomes like a pond full of floating frogs.

"The underlying stress mechanisms we're studying apply to all sorts of animals like elk, fish, or any other species—and disease outbreaks in general," said Brunner.

The investigation continues at WSU Vancouver, where Jonah Piovia-Scott, assistant professor in the School of Biological Sciences and a member of the National Bsal Task Force, is exploring the effects of climate change on chytrid fungal diseases.

"Neither Bd nor Bsal tend to do well when it's hot," he said. "So, some aspects of climate change may actually help amphibians with these pathogens. But other aspects may make them more susceptible. For example, if ponds dry up earlier in the season, it will decrease the amount of time amphibians have to develop. The stress will force them to develop faster, which may make them more susceptible to disease later in life."

Piovia-Scott is often asked why we should care about amphibians, and his answer is unequivocal.

"These amazing, beautiful, and wonderful organisms have intrinsic value, and are a part of our world we're losing quite rapidly," he said. "They are also integral components of the ecosystem—an important food source for some animals and they themselves eat insects, worms, and snails. Like salmon who are eaten by bears and fertilize the forest, amphibians are also an important link between aquatic and terrestrial systems."

Indeed, isolated and far away, every frog and salamander die-off creates a domino effect that ultimately impacts the planet. Streams that were once crystal clear turn green without tadpoles to eat the algae. Human infections like malaria and dysentery spread more rapidly without amphibians to eat mosquitos and flies.

"It's a very good example of how small the world has gotten," said Pessier, who also specializes in biosecurity and reintroduction programs for endangered species.

"Diseases like Bd and Bsal are moved around by people. Domestic cows don't move from Asia to the U.S. without a huge number of diagnostic tests. But for frogs, you just need the right permits, and you can move them all over the world without concerns about disease.

"Once Bd has moved through an area, the amphibian biodiversity drops to virtually nothing and there is no way to mitigate the fungus in the wild," he said. "So, the last resort strategy is to develop survival assurance populations (SAP). We capture threatened species to preserve their genetic diversity and then try to breed and maintain a colony in captivity until they can be reintroduced to the wild, once we have a way to deal with the fungus."

Pessier works with SAP in Madagascar, Ecuador, Panama, and many other areas around the world to diagnose disease issues such as vitamin A deficiency in captive Panamanian golden frogs.

Closer to home, he is joining Crespi and Goldberg to protect Washington's last surviving remnant of northern leopard frogs in the Columbia Basin. Working with the Washington Department of Fish and Wildlife, they hope to reintroduce and expand populations within the state.

Their intentions clearly reach beyond academia to a deeper love of the Pacific Northwest and our amphibian wildlife. Drafted in the spirit of Teddy Roosevelt, their proposal reads, "Do what you can, with what you have, where you are."

It's a philosophy all five faculty members stand behind. Their shared interests and mutual support have multiplied efforts to protect frogs and salamanders throughout the world.

"Conservation is an interdisciplinary science," Crespi said. "Having Jesse, Caren, Allan, and Jonah here allows me to do projects I could never do in isolation."

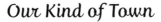

Our Kind of Town

Tim Steury

Coming Home

Nancy and John Janzen grew up in Spokane. They went to high school together, then on to Washington State University. Nancy earned a degree in education in 1989, John in electrical engineering in 1991. Following graduation, they married and, like many of their fellow Cougars, moved to Seattle.

John traveled around the country as a software consultant. Nancy concentrated on raising their two daughters, now 12 and 11, while maintaining ties to her profession. Their family had started just a little earlier than they had planned. But still, things looked good.

And then they decided to come home.

They knew that building a software company was not going to be as easy as it would be in Portland or Seattle. But their family was here. Spokane was home- and a very attractive place to live.

Their bet on Spokane paid off. Their business is booming. Maplewood Software specializes in customized databases and Web-based applications. A new spin-off company develops healthcare scheduling software.

And the Janzens, with the help of the Spokane Regional Chamber of Commerce, would like to encourage a trend.

The Janzens are ambassadors for the new Homecoming campaign established by the chamber in collaboration with the city's Economic Development Council, Washington State, Eastern Washington, and Gonzaga Universities, and Whitworth College. The goal of the campaign is simple, to draw people who grew up in the area, or who went to school there, home. Not only the people, of course, but also their talents, ideas, and businesses.

"It's really an economic development tool," said Nicole Stewart, who coordinates the program.

Although the program has been in place only since last February, it has already enjoyed some successes. It's unlikely, however, that such a program could be successful were it not for the fact that the future looks very bright for Spokane, an outlook that people are just getting used to.

Knowledge as a Product

Not so long ago, Spokane was stymied by one of the few easily defined realities of regional economics. The base of its economy, natural-resource extraction and processing, was shrinking. The area is always going to have agriculture and natural-resource-based industry, said Tom Reese, economic development advisor for the Spokane mayor's office. "But it's not going to be the driver it was.

"In the 1980s," said Reese, "civic leaders recognized that they needed to identify some real strategic activities that were going to be catalysts" for economic development.

Higher education was one of the top three priorities.

"That really was the genesis of Riverpoint being here," he said.

Riverpoint is the campus shared by WSU and Eastern Washington University on the south banks of the Spokane River just east of Division and downtown Spokane.

Although WSU has had an academic presence in Spokane since 1919, the development of the Riverpoint campus provided a physical and visual focus for WSU's participation in Spokane's renaissance. Obviously, WSU has benefited from and contributed to the rise of Spokane's version of the so-called knowledge economy.

As oft repeated as terms such as "knowledge economy" or "information economy" are, the concept can be hard to grasp. However, in the case of the role knowledge and higher education play in Spokane's renaissance, the various pieces fit together in a coherent and tangible picture. "It's a real synergy," said Reese.

The first thing to consider is the contribution of research to the healthcare industry in Spokane. Spokane has long been the center of healthcare in the Inland Northwest. WSU's College of Nursing has fed the need for nurses, and research efforts such as the Health Research and Education Center have contributed both to healthcare capabilities and to the economy by drawing private investment, federal grants, and talented researchers. As is the case with 1984 WSU graduate Lisa Shaffer, whose laboratory specializes in the analysis of chromosomal abnormalities, these researchers also bring with them their own companies, employees, and further economic stimulation. Shaffer and research partner Bassem Bejjani, also a geneticist, both hold clinical appointments at Sacred Heart Medical Center.

"Knowledge is about innovation," said Reese.

Plans for the Riverpoint campus include a new building for the College of Nursing, which, along with a proposed university district, will more closely link the campus with the hospital district, which is steadily advancing north.

Designing a place to live and learn

The Interdisciplinary Design Institute at WSU Spokane has been a major player as Spokane redefines itself. One of the most forward-looking and deliberate concepts within this redefinition is the university district. The notion of a university district gained momentum about six years ago, said Reese, when the idea was presented through articles by then-WSU Spokane campus dean Bill Gray, Gonzaga University president Father Robert Spitzer, and state senator Jim West, who is now mayor of Spokane. The idea was temporarily shifted to a back burner, but then resurrected when a group of design institute students met with the East Sprague Business Association to conceive of developing the area on the south side of the railroad corridor that runs between the Riverpoint campus and Sprague Avenue, the main east-west street in Spokane. Driving the concept was the burgeoning need for student housing. WSU Spokane expects to enroll over 2,000 within the next decade. The move of over 450 nursing students to the Riverpoint campus upon the completion of their new building will jump-start this growth.

"They quickly began to realize that this idea had a lot more legs to it as an overall district," said Reese.

Presented with an opportunity, design institute students put together a proposal to present in Washington, D.C., the result of which was not only an overall concept encompassing the Gonzaga area north of the river, the Riverpoint campus, and East Sprague Avenue, but also $1 million in funding through Senator Patty Murray, a 1972 WSU alumna, for transportation planning by the City of Spokane.

Long a mosaic of rail yards, industry, used car lots, and other businesses spanning a spectrum from stolid to seedy, the area encompassed by the proposed university district seems, in spite of the aptly named Division Street, a natural expansion of the revitalized downtown.

Everyone's Going Downtown

"Downtown Spokane has had a very strong run since 1999," said Mike Edwards, director of the Downtown Spokane Partnership (DSP). He cites five major building or renovation projects that have inspired the city's renaissance: the Davenport Hotel, Riverpark Square, the Museum of Arts and Culture, the Convention Center, the Big Easy, and the WSU library and administration building now under construction at Riverpoint.

The combined effect of these projects has reestablished downtown Spokane as the core of the region, said Edwards, one project spurring the next, inspiring new business, sparking the imagination. "It's inconceivable," he said, with a gesture that takes in the busy shop where we've met, "that this coffee shop would be here without the Davenport."

Edwards is in charge of the awards committee for the International Downtown Association's 50th anniversary meeting this fall. One of its achievement awards will go to Jane Jacobs, the urban prophet and author of *The Death and Life of Great American Cities*. Edwards smiles with satisfaction as he describes Spokane as returning to her prescription of "a natural ballet of people living over their storefronts."

One of the measures of Edwards's industry is the number of hours each day that people use a downtown.

"Six years ago, it was eight hours," he said. "Now we're a 12-hour downtown. What it's leading to is the restoration of downtown as a viable neighborhood, where you can live, work, and play."

Indeed, Spokane residents are moving back downtown to live.

Developer, historic preservationist, and urban planner Jim Kolva lives in a stunning art-filled loft eight blocks west of the downtown core. He and his wife sold their South Hill home and, just a year ago, their car, to make the urban plunge. "I love living downtown," he said.

Kolva, a 1968 WSU graduate, is also developing two commercial gallery spaces and a street-level apartment in the same building as his loft, a former automobile dealership.

A recent housing study by Downtown Spokane Ventures, a subsidiary of the DSP, revealed a demand for 300 living units a year for the next five years in the downtown area. "Anecdotally, a lot of people are looking for downtown loft space," said Kolva. "There are no vacancies downtown right now."

In the same building, 1971 WSU alumnus Steve Thosath and Susie Luby developed the Blue Chip lofts, 11 condos, all of which were pre-sold. Matt Melcher, an interior design professor at the design institute, and his wife and business partner, 1993 WSU graduate Juliet Sinisterra, designed a number of the lofts, which range in size from 650 to 1,350 square feet.

The project became part of three classes that Melcher teaches. "A student here for more than a year," he said, "could follow the design process, see the construction, how it was put together."

Interestingly, said Melcher, all the loft buyers were local, a mix of young professionals, retirees, someone in the military, people looking to downsize.

Near Nature

The Spokane city park system was designed by the Olmstead landscape architectural firm, sons of the great Frederick Olmstead, who envisioned New York's Central Park and other classic landscapes. But part of the Olmsteads' vision has not yet been realized, the Great Gorge Park. Proposed in 1908, the Great Gorge remains merely on paper. But if planners such as Mike Terrell can persist, the Olmsteads' great vision may be fulfilled.

The Great Gorge Park encompasses the area surrounding the Spokane River, from the Monroe Street bridge downriver.

Again, students with the design institute have participated in the fulfillment of the Olmstead vision, working with the Friends of the Falls to develop concepts for the gorge area in one of their annual community design and construction charrettes. Edwards, who is also active with Friends of the Falls, credits the students' work with helping land a $250,000 legislative appropriation for the project. He can't say enough about the value of putting a "design face" on great ideas, from the river gorge to downtown housing, to get buy-in and build momentum for critical projects.

Whether it is ever realized or not, the Great Gorge is simply a part of the final synthesizing factor that has made possible the renaissance of Spokane-place.

What drew Nancy and John Janzen home was not job opportunity, but family and place. Increasingly, said economic developer Tom Reese, knowledge workers can locate where they want. Rather than migrate to where the jobs are, they can choose place first.

That's what the chamber's homecoming strategy is all about, said Reese.

"But," he wonders, "what if they never left? What if we attracted them here as students, and they were so compelled to be here, that they were compelled to stay here as businesspeople?

"You look at cities we compete with around the world, and they all are about that, all recognizing that what sets them apart, incentives aside, tax breaks aside, availability of infrastructure aside-what sets them apart is place."

The numbers

As nice as the place is, though, as nice as the knowledge economy sounds for both the city and universities, as nice as the 12-hour downtown feels, it takes more than attitude to drive an economy.

Don Epley, an urban economist and professor of real estate studies at WSU Spokane, conducts an ongoing analysis of the Spokane-area economy. Basically, he tries to approximate the local version of the gross national product and tracks about 20 economic indicators.

In his latest report, released in August 2004, every one of those indicators was positive.

"That's remarkable," he said, "because they never are that way. There's always something negative."

Epley explained the indicator numbers in terms of economic growth. And he is confident where the credit lies.

"We've got a large educational complex here and a large medical complex here, and you look at the numbers, the medical complex and educational complex are driving the economy."

With such clearly defined economic forces and his analysis, Epley the academic is as excited as Reese, the Janzens, and other players in the economic surge.

"The future," said Epley, "looks good.".

Where Water Meets Desert

Eric Apalategui

The Columbia Basin Project transformed a vast area of Washington from shrub-steppe to some of the most fertile farmland anywhere. It also created extraordinary habitat for birds and wildlife.

Headlights slice the darkness and fall on a coyote loping across the gravel road. The coyote turns for a moment, and its carnivore eyes flash in the beams before vanishing—swallowed in sagebrush that quilts an aromatic blanket over the gentle hills.

From here, the dark land seems arid, stark, endless.

But when the car shudders over the next washboard rise, the silent air explodes with a cacophony of ducks. The eastern horizon lights up, and layers of flame and slate fall upon calm water, backlighting the grassy hummocks that stretch as far as the first glow of dawn. As the landscape awakens, a squadron of American white pelicans sweeps across the sky, Caspian terns begin diving for small fish, and great blue herons and egrets settle into their hunting haunts along the shore. On the horizon, coyotes yip at the fading moon.

Such bold contradictions clash daily where water meets desert in Washington's Columbia Basin.

A Sage in the Brush

The clerk at our motel, who moved to Moses Lake from a mountainous Oregon hamlet, calls her adopted region "ugly."

Among locals, you occasionally hear the word "wasteland" used to describe sagebrush-studded lands that biologists prefer to call native shrub steppe.

It's impossible to take such a harsh view when Robert Kent is your guide to the Columbia Basin Wildlife Areas.

The preserved habitats are a vast collection of some 200,000 state-managed acres collected into more than a dozen wildlife areas on federal and state lands within the basin. The complex of wildlife areas is the largest in the state, a full 130 miles from north to south and 500 miles around the edges.

Combining those wildlife areas with more than three times as much irrigated farmland and tracts of high desert, the entire Columbia Basin is a tapestry of colorful crops, diverse desert, teeming wetlands, soaring cliffs, and deep coulees stretching eastward from the Columbia River's big bend in central Washington.

Kent, who graduated with a wildlife management degree from WSU in 1975, retired last February after a 27-year career with the Washington Department of Fish and Wildlife. He arrived in the Columbia Basin in 1981 and was promoted to manager of the wildlife areas a few years later.

"I spent the rest of my career here," said Kent, who grew up on a farm 70 miles to the east, survived war in Vietnam, and married his high school sweetheart. "It was a good place to be for me."

Compactly fit at 56, Kent loses neither footing nor enthusiasm as he hikes through a steep area of shrub steppe overlooking Lind Coulee. Along the way, he points out various species of native sagebrush, rabbitbrush, and wheatgrass that dominate the land on about half the wildlife areas he managed.

Compared to the dramatic cliffs of the Quincy Unit to the west, the flocks of sandhill cranes that make raucous stopovers, or the walleye that bite in Potholes Reservoir, this inconspicuous hillside is no tourist attraction. The path we follow through the sage is far more familiar to cottontail rabbits and mule deer than humans.

Yet this spot illustrates, better than most, what much of the basin looked like before ranchers and farmers arrived in numbers a century ago—and especially before one of the nation's largest federal irrigation projects transformed a grayish brown land into the vibrant greens and yellows that now color some of the world's best farmland.

When ranchers ruled, livestock grazed across this hill, mowing the tender grasses while leaving the woody sagebrush in their wake. As a result, even 50-plus years later the long-lived sagebrush covers most of the ground, with sprigs of grass coming up on perhaps a third. The ratio should be reversed, with sagebrush growing on just 30 percent of the land and grasses carpeting the rest, said Kent, citing the research of late WSU botany professor Rexford Daubenmire.

"We still have a very disturbed site, even though it's good for the Columbia Basin," said Kent, who spent much of his career trying to preserve the very types of extremely wet or especially arid lands that others consider worthless.

"The shrub steppe habitat wasn't really recognized as important by our agency leaders until after I had recognized it here," said Kent, who grew up in similar country. "Shrub steppe is kind of like old-growth forest. It's something you can lose and not get back."

He kneels beside a big sage with branches that are beginning to buckle and decay. As the bushes age and crowd one another, some will die. It could take decades more, but gaps will form between the sage, grasses will fill those spaces, and the shrub steppe will be restored.

"Daubenmire will be correct," Kent said. He rises to his feet and scans out across the sagebrush.

"People who are interested in commercial [uses] might call this wasteland," he said, turning back toward the car, "but wildlife like it."

Water, water everywhere

When most homesteaders settled the Columbia Basin in the early 1900s, it was a hardscrabble land where fewer than 10 inches of rain fell each year.

The soil was rich and the growing season long, but the country was so parched, farmers had to leave their fields fallow every other year to save up enough moisture for a single wheat crop.

"There was hardly any agriculture, really," said John Kugler, a WSU Extension educator for Grant and Adams counties. "There were wheat growers, but that was about it."

Ranchers grazed cattle and sheep, but there was so little forage, it took huge holdings to turn a profit. After spring green-up, ranchers needed hay to get their livestock through the year.

Then along came the U.S. Bureau of Reclamation's Columbia Basin Project.

The agency, then the fledgling Reclamation Service, set its sights on the basin a hundred years ago, at about the same time dry-land farming grabbed hold. However, it took half a century to work through the political process, the acquisition of private lands, the engineering challenges, the multimillion-dollar costs, and the difficult construction of Grand Coulee Dam. World War II elevated the nation's need for inexpensive electricity, and Grand Coulee would soon become the largest federal hydroelectric plant.

In 1952, a decade after the major construction of Grand Coulee Dam was complete and a year after installation of the last electricity generators and power pumps, the first irrigation water diverted from the dam to Banks Lake started flowing southward. That year, the water reached about 66,000 acres of farmland in the basin.

Today, the project delivers water to ten times that much acreage—671,000 acres—the rough equivalent of irrigating half the state of Delaware. At the early summer peak of irrigation season, canals deliver about 9,000 cubic feet of water every second to fields in the basin. That's enough water to fill a million-gallon Olympic pool within 15 seconds, but it's still only a fraction of the Columbia River's natural flow.

The ingenious system employs 300 miles of large canals, 2,000 miles of smaller "laterals," 3,500 miles of drains and wasteways, a handful of large reservoirs, and natural features such as depressions, coulees, and underground passages to move and hold water. The system delivers, recollects, and redelivers irrigation water down a hundred-mile corridor from Coulee City to Tri-Cities.

The federal government still owns tens of thousands of acres in the Columbia Basin used to operate the system or that remain unsuited for agriculture. The agency contracts with the state to manage about 160,000 of those acres for wildlife habitat and recreation. The wildlife areas contain another 40,000 acres of state lands.

Originally, during the Great Depression, the federal government allotted $63 million to build the project under the National Industrial Recovery Act. Now, in an average year, the project's value is about $20 million in prevented flood damage, $50 million in recreational opportunity, $500 million in power generation-and a whopping $700 million-plus at the farm gate for agricultural products.

"That wouldn't be there if it weren't for the project's development and the acquisition of lands," said Bill Gray, the Bureau of Reclamation's deputy area manager. "The area would have ended up in large sheep and cattle ranches."

Gray, a 1974 WSU alumnus, oversees the Columbia Basin Project and 15 other federal irrigation projects in northwestern states from his Ephrata office in the heart of the basin. Without the irrigation water, he figures, the basin would have few jobs, a tiny tax base, and scant recreation.

In other words, said Extension's Kugler, "The place would dry up."

Outstanding in the Field

For the past 50 years, the Columbia Basin has helped drive Washington's large agricultural economy. In fact, the basin is one of the world's best places to grow potatoes, carrots, onions, beans, mint, hay, vegetable seeds, and dozens of other vegetables, fruits, and grains, as well as dairy and beef cattle.

Many of the region's new farmers were World War II veterans, allowed to enter a drawing to buy a share of those lands the federal government reverted back to private ownership in the newly irrigated basin. They repaid government loans with the fruits of their toil.

Lee Williams's farm and other holdings along Lind Coulee originally were sold to those veterans. Williams calls his farm the Trail's End Ranch, partly because he never plans to leave this patch of sandy soil south of Moses Lake.

By the basin's big standards, Williams, a 1964 WSU alumnus, is a small-time farmer, growing five acres of chestnuts and leasing the rest of his property to another farmer, who rotates crops such as potatoes with the dark green alfalfa growing there now. Williams also is a full-time field veterinarian for the state Department of Agriculture.

Williams takes us to a ridge on the far side of his property, where his circle irrigation system passes across an eye-shaped patch of brush as it slowly pivots across the alfalfa. The water creates lush places for wildlife to feed and hide. Across the alfalfa, he's planted a few acres of millet, which brings cover and food for songbirds and ringneck pheasants. A nearby pile of woody debris, he said with a chuckle, is "rabbitat."

Williams is among the farmers who worked out a trade with Robert Kent and the Washington Department of Fish and Wildlife. In exchange for dedicating some of his own acreage and water rights to improve wildlife habitat, Williams farms nearly 20 acres of wildlife-area land that falls under the sweep of his irrigator.

"I've tried to work with the neighbors as much as possible," Kent said. "We almost always get more [from the trade than is required]. People like to do things for wildlife, in general."

Williams agrees: "You've got to give back a little bit sometimes."

Suddenly, something catches the farmer's eye. He points toward the water at the bottom of Lind Coulee, to a four-point buck swimming toward the sagebrush hill where Kent stood the morning before.

"He's a big son of a gun."

A Cast of Thousands

This clear October day is rare for Bob Peterson.

Peterson didn't fool a single walleye before pulling his boat from a ramp where Lind Coulee forms an arm of Potholes Reservoir, a giant storage facility that gathers up irrigation water from the northern end of the Columbia Basin to reroute it to farms in the south.

Peterson is far from alone among outdoor lovers, who make well over a million stops in the Columbia Basin each year. Grant County, once almost pure desert, today is the state's top freshwater-fishing destination and a magnet for waterfowl hunters.

While fishing and hunting reign, "non-consumptive" recreation such as bird watching, hiking, wildlife photography, mountain biking, and canoeing are increasingly popular.

All of that, said the Bureau of Reclamation's Gray, exists in "a county where there was virtually no water" before the project.

"I didn't manage just for hunters, just for fishermen, or just for birdwatchers. I managed for everyone," said Kent.

Trouble in Paradise

On the Desert Wildlife Area, southwest of Potholes Reservoir, Kent points out a weedy pond that provides ideal feeding and nesting habitat for dabbling ducks.

If it weren't for Kent's staff, the pond would be a mud hole, full of common carp and little else. The carp, a non-native fish in the goldfish family, have a habit of taking over small waterways and consuming every morsel of food.

"They're so good at it that everything else loses," Kent said. "If you have carp in the water, they're going to win."

But wildlife officials won by building a dike to wall off access to the pond. They then killed off the carp and restocked the pond with fish that will leave enough food for ducks.

"That has been a very important waterfowl habitat improvement strategy here in the Columbia Basin," Kent said.

Inarguably, the Columbia Basin Project was a godsend for agriculture, a windfall for many species of native wildlife, and a perfect home for some introduced species that sportsmen love, including pheasants and walleye.

But it hasn't come without a price.

"The water has brought in a lot of invaders," said Kent, who over the years battled the unwanted animals and plants. From bullfrogs that eat native fish and turtles to Russian olive trees that shade out natural wetlands, invasive species are barging across the basin.

On the same dike that guards against carp, for example, a grassy invader called phragmites is pushing its feathery seed heads toward the sky. In many places, the invasive grass is overwhelming the basin's wetlands more than the infamous purple loosestrife. Kent helped get control of the latter with help from WSU entomologist Gary Piper and some insects imported from the purple loosestrife's native range.

Just down the road, Kent employed another non-native species—the cow— to salvage prime waterfowl habitat known as Birders Corner. Wildlife purists don't often consider livestock to be compatible with wildlife habitat. But in this instance, shoreline plants were wiping out open mudflats that wading and dabbling birds prefer-until Kent signed a contract allowing a farmer to graze his livestock across the area while the birds are gone.

"We use the cattle for mowing machines, basically," he said. "We don't have people to do it, and we don't have equipment to do it. We got cattle to do it, and [farmers] pay us."

It's that kind of simple, effective approach that wins Kent praise for his work.

"He has just done an incredible job protecting and managing the wildlife resources in the basin for future generations to enjoy," Gray said.

"You have to keep your eye on the goal," Kent said. "We want to have as many kinds of wildlife habitat as we can support out here."

The Atomic Landscape

Tim Steury

Seven decades later, we consider our plutonium legacy

Works considered in this article:

Plume
Kathleen Flenniken
University of Washington Press 2012

Made in Hanford: The Bomb that Changed the World
Hill Williams
Washington State University Press 2011

Making Plutonium, Re-Making Richland: Atomic Heritage and Community Identity, Richland, Washington, 1943-1963
Lee Ann Powell
Thesis, Department of History, Washington State University 2007

When President Franklin D. Roosevelt gave the go-ahead for the Manhattan Project, he set in motion an extraordinary collaboration amongst scientists and the military to develop an atomic bomb, driven by fears of Hitler's creating one first. Whether or not the eventual dropping of the bombs on Japan was necessary to end the war in the Pacific will probably never be resolved. But the bomb undoubtedly changed the world, as well as the cultural, historical, and physical landscape of southeastern Washington.

On the afternoon of February 26, 1943, Lt. Col. Franklin Matthias appeared in the office of the *Pasco Herald* and asked to talk with the editor. The editor, Hill Williams, invited him in.

After asking that the door be closed for privacy, "Matthias told him a secret project of utmost importance to the war effort would be built nearby," writes Williams's son Hill in *Made in Hanford*. "He gave no hint as to the nature of the project but said it would be huge and stressed again its importance to the war effort and the necessary secrecy."

Having undoubtedly commanded Williams's full attention, Matthias then made his request, that Williams not publish anything about the top-secret project.

Twenty years later, a young Kathleen (Dillon) Flenniken sits on her father's shoulders as they watch President Kennedy dedicate a ninth production reactor at Hanford, as Flenniken, a 1983 WSU alumna, now recalls in her volume of poetry *Plume*:

> Somewhere in that sea of crisp white shirts
> I'm sitting on my father's shoulders
> as you dedicate our new reactor and praise us
> for shaping history. The helicopter that set you down
> in our proudest moment
> waits camera right, ready to whisk you away.
> A half century later, I click play again and again
> for proof you approve—
> but the nuclear age is complicated.

> —Excerpt from "My Earliest Memory Preserved on Film"

Because Hanford is so complicated, poetry might be an apt way to contemplate it.

"I wrote the book so I could figure out what I thought," said Flenniken.

For anyone interested in understanding the atomic legacy of both Washington and the nation—which I would urge you to do, not out of moral obligation or such, but simply because it is so fascinating—an excellent way to start would be to combine Flenniken's work with Williams's book and other notable texts.

Although Hanford might be a classic example of how history gets made and remade, as WSU Tri-Cities historian Robert Bauman puts it, the area has yet to produce a big, definitive book about itself. Michele Stenehjem Gerber's excellent history of the area's toxic legacy, *On the Homefront* (University of Nebraska, 2002), follows a timeline from the creation of the B Reactor—the reactor that produced the plutonium for Fat Man, the bomb that was dropped on Nagasaki in 1945—through the development of and resulting waste of an additional eight reactors during the Cold War. But it does not attempt to encompass the complexity of identity and emotion that the Hanford phenomenon has produced.

Other works, including the fine oral history, *Making the Bomb* (S. L. Sanger, Portland State University Continuing Education Press, 1995), present a fascinating and sweeping account of the era. But to get a sense of the time, from the urgency of the scientists rushing to head off Hitler's presumed nuclear progress to the revolutionary science involved, to the toxic hangover of a landscape dedicated to producing bombs with insufficient caution and foresight, these three slim and very approachable works lend concise history and insight to our understanding.

True to his newspaper sensibility, Hill Williams, who was science writer for the *Seattle Times* for 35 years, has produced a volume about as succinct as can possibly be, considering the scope of his work runs from Leo Szilard's realization in 1933 of how a nuclear chain reaction might be feasible to the author's visit as a journalist to Runit Island in the Bikini Atoll in 1964.

The original plan for the Manhattan Project was for the plutonium to be produced in Tennessee. But given the risk and uncertainty of the endeavor, the idea was abandoned, as Knoxville was a mere 15 miles from the proposed plant.

So the planners set their sights west. The frontier. Wide open spaces with few people. Southeast Washington's apparent desolation, the Columbia, for cooling water, and the Grand Coulee project, for the huge amounts of electricity required, coalesced to produce plutonium.

> …Our families all came from elsewhere,
> and regarded the desert as empty,
> and ugly, which gave us permission
> to savage the land. …

> —Excerpt from "Rattlesnake Mountain"

What Williams recounted as a journalist, Flenniken tries to make sense of.

Flenniken's *Plume* is a remarkable volume of poetry that presents a vivid and gripping blend of documentary and her emotional history of Cold War Hanford. Flenniken's father, a doctoral chemist, started working at the "area" in 1951. As with many of Richland's scientists and engineers, the actual nature of R. L. Dillon's job was shielded from his children by Cold War secrecy. Although she found a few references to her father's work in technical papers, all she originally knew about it, primarily in the site's 100 Area, was his description of himself as a "manager."

> You're eighteen. It's August brim to brim
> and your father is at the wheel. He points proudly
> at distant reactors and spires, sun-baked highway
> and barbed wire, and offers them to you.
> You've waited all your life.

A gate patrolman waves you across the threshold
into the Cold War world. …

—Excerpt from "Self-Portrait with Father as Tour Guide"

Flenniken's parents would tell the story that sometimes in the middle of the night, her father would get a phone call from a security guard, who had found a filing cabinet open. He would drive the 50 miles to his office to lock the cabinet, then drive back.

After graduating in civil engineering from WSU in 1982, Flenniken herself took a job, in hydrology, in the 200 Area, rising each morning at 5:30 to catch a bus for the 45-minute ride to her laboratory.

Perhaps the key to understanding the cultural history of Richland is its intense pride over its accomplishments in both WWII and the Cold War. But Flenniken suggests the emotional part of Hanford is as complicated as the science behind fission.

As Richland native Lee Ann (Hall) Powell recounted in her thesis, Hanford workers were considered war heroes:

"Almost immediately after the Americans dropped the atomic bombs on Japan, the national spotlight focused on Hanford, its people, and its secret wartime mission. The government and the nation recognized HEW [Hanford Engineering Works] workers as war heroes…by helping to make the bomb they had won the peace. General Groves reinforced this identity when in October 1945 he visited the Village to congratulate HEW workers and present all of them with the Army-Navy 'E' award, the highest civilian production commendation of World War II."

Powell discusses three eras of Richland history: "the Indian history, the pioneer history or pre-atomic era, and the history that begins with the Manhattan Project. Synthesizing these parts is difficult." The combined histories of the region are "wonderfully rich but fragmented."

Throughout the Cold War, residents transformed that sense of historic accomplishment to a patriotic certitude. Part of the area's creation myth, as historians refer to it, involved a distinct separation. A souvenir program from the 1948 Atomic Frontier Days noted that "the old farming center of Richland was evacuated and transformed into a modern community."

Indeed, the transformation accompanying that accomplishment was so dramatic, it required a disassociation with the region's past.

"The impact of the Hanford project on a relatively undeveloped central Washington, even while land was still being acquired," writes Williams, "seemed astounding to those whose memories of the Great Depression were vivid." The

Hanford landscape changed almost literally overnight. In April 1943 work began on facilities for an estimated 25,000 workers. By July 1944, some 1,200 buildings had been erected and nearly 51,000 people were living in the construction camp. At its peak, the construction camp was the third most populous town in Washington state, and Hanford operated a fleet of more than 900 buses, bigger than Chicago's.

Hardly anyone knew what was being produced at Hanford except that it was part of the war effort. Since DuPont was the civilian contractor, some guessed that nylon stockings would be one eventual product.

Regardless, because the project progressed so unbelievably quickly, the secrecy was also short-lived. The elder Hill Williams was at the press conference hurriedly organized on August 6, 1945, by Colonel Matthias following the startling announcement by President Truman that an American plane had dropped a bomb on Hiroshima with "more power than 20,000 tons of TNT…an atomic bomb…a harnessing of the power of the universe."

The next issue of the *Pasco Herald* headlined the biggest type that Williams owned: IT'S ATOMIC BOMBS!

On August 9, the bomb containing plutonium produced at Hanford was dropped on Nagasaki. Shortly after, but before Japan surrendered, the "Smyth Report" was released. Written by physicist Henry D. Smyth, the report had been commissioned by the director of the Manhattan Project, Major General Leslie Groves, to explain to the public the general science involved in the bomb. Williams believes it is the first time the word "plutonium" was used publicly.

That sense of purpose and pride in its role toward winning the war and changing the world became as integral to the cultural landscape as Rattlesnake Mountain is to the geographic landscape:

> On the morning I got plucked out of third grade
> by Principal Wellman because I'd written on command
> an impassioned letter for the life of our nuclear plants
> that the government threatened to shut down
> and I put on my rabbit-trimmed green plaid coat
> because it was cold and I'd be on the televised news
> overseeing delivery of several hundred pounds of mail
> onto an airplane bound for Washington DC addressed
> to President Nixon who obviously didn't care about your job
>
> —Excerpt from "To Carolyn's Father"

But that cultural pride also included a set of blinders.

Prior to the dropping of the Nagasaki bomb, which finally revealed to all what was actually going on at Hanford, most who worked there had no understanding whatsoever about what they were building. But in the Cold War years, with the destructive power of the area's plutonium now a matter of history, residents faced another part of the site's dark side.

"When I was growing up, people just didn't talk about that part of it," said Flenniken. "It was never about the actual bombs and what happened. It was more about the race to create it and the amazing feat that people could do under these circumstances, these hardships, come up with this amazing new technology, human miracle.

> "The story just ends right there."
> I remember the red phone, and missile codes,
> how every movie hinged
> on a clock ticking down.
> We call it the arms race
> and there were two sides.
> It was simple.

—Excerpt from "The Cold War"

Although the selection of Hanford to produce plutonium was not a foregone conclusion, it ultimately met the criteria determined essential by Leslie Groves.

B Reactor went critical September 20, 1944. Its criticality began not only a new era and new potential for destruction, but also an entirely new form of pollution.

The B Reactor produced plutonium for the Trinity test in New Mexico and for Fat Man, the bomb that was dropped on Nagasaki in 1945 and, with its predecessor the uranium-fueled Little Boy, which was dropped on Hiroshima, hastened Japan's surrender.

The B Reactor is an engineering marvel. Built in only 13 months, it was completed less than two years after President Franklin Roosevelt approved the Manhattan Project. Enrico Fermi managed the first sustained nuclear chain reaction at the University of Chicago in 1942, then supervised the design of the B Reactor. On February 3, 1945, B Reactor plutonium was delivered to Los Alamos, New Mexico.

According to the Department of Energy's history division, the reactor core is a 1,200-ton, 28 by 36-foot graphite cylinder, penetrated horizontally by 2,004 aluminum tubes. Two hundred tons of uranium slugs, the size of rolls of quarters, were inserted into the tubes. Cooling the reactor core required water pumped from the Columbia at the rate of 75,000 gallons per minute.

As Williams writes, when that water was first pumped through the reactor core to cool it, it marked the first time large quantities of radioactive material were deliberately released into environment.

The most worrisome byproduct of plutonium production at Hanford was the highly radioactive waste deposited, temporarily, in underground tanks. According to Williams, each ton of uranium slugs produced 10,000 gallons of liquid waste containing, among other products, fission products.

If you visit Richland's Columbia River Exhibition of History, Science, and Technology (formerly the Hanford Science Museum) and examine the replica cross-section of the storage tanks, your worries about that waste might be temporarily assuaged. Thick concrete is faced with thick plate steel in the single wall tanks. The double wall tanks, with room for inspection, would reassure even the most skeptical—unless of course, as Williams suggests, one thinks too much about the definition of "temporary":

But military demands for plutonium during the Cold War…took precedence over finding a permanent solution. Hanford ended up with a much greater volume of waste than anyone anticipated in 1945 and temporary storage turned into semi-permanent. Twenty or so years after the end of the war, tank waste was leaking into Hanford's dry soil and drifting toward the river, causing problems we still face today.

If production had ended with the dropping of Fat Man, the waste would likely still be problematic. But, Williams pointed out, that initial waste was dwarfed by the combined production of eight reactors during the Cold War years. A plume of radioactive waste moves inexorably toward the Columbia, underlying a stark and transformed terrain with a legacy against which we seem powerless. And a grand plan for turning Hanford's tank wastes into stable glass has so far been stymied by the complexity of the problem and process, an unfortunate mirror to the fascinating complexity of the area's landscape.

Inside Outside

Rebecca Phillips

Listen. There's something padding down the wooded trails, bubbling over waterfalls, and rustling in the pines. No, not your meditation app. It's an international movement called biophilia and you can hear it blooming in the voice of a busy little girl at the Into the Forest Outdoor Learning Center and Preschool in Spokane Valley.

"I'm making peanut butter," she said as she wields a spatula in the aptly-named mud kitchen. A small boy beside her fills muffin cups with dirt while another adds water to the "batter."

The three are playing in a big fenced yard, complete with vegetable garden, where a dozen or so other children scamper on tree stumps, roll tiny pumpkins, and scavenger hunt for colors. There's not a cry or whimper among them.

"I've worked at a lot of daycares and I feel like kids are significantly calmer here and overall better behaved," said preschool teacher Jordan Hinegardner. "I feel that's because they get so much outside time—at least two hours in the morning and afternoon."

Co-owners Megan Benedict and Chelsey Converse opened the center—Spokane's first outdoor preschool—in August 2017 and within a year, classes were full with a waiting list. A second preschool will open this March.

Similar stories are unfolding all over the world, as children leave desks behind to spend days outdoors interacting with nature, running, playing, and studying science in the wild.

Biophilia, our innate affinity for and connection to nature, is not only for children—parents, too, are taking time from hectic schedules to unwind with meditative forest bathing, and many doctors now prescribe visits to the park instead of pills.

Much of the credit goes to Richard Louv, whose 2005 breakout book, *Last Child In The Woods: Saving Our Children from Nature-Deficit Disorder*, detailed the costs of alienating ourselves from the natural world, especially with today's pervasive use of technology.

Though nature deficit disorder is not a true medical diagnosis, restoring our connection to a living green biosphere has been shown to enhance health, well-being, mental acuity, and creativity, while also reducing stress, depression, and obesity.

"Nature is often overlooked as a healing balm for the emotional hardships in a child's life," Louv writes. "You'll likely never see a slick commercial for nature therapy as you do for the latest antidepressant pharmaceuticals. But parents, educators, and health workers need to know what a useful antidote to emotional and physical stress nature can be."

It's an idea that Washington State University 4-H adventure education director Scott VanderWey has embraced for years as part of his mission "to get as many kids outside as possible." Stationed at the Puyallup Research and Extension Center, VanderWey helps county 4-H leaders develop ropes courses as well as programs in rock climbing, boating, skiing, and rite of passage wilderness training.

He said it was Louv's work that led to the 2008 creation of Washington state's pioneering No Child Left Inside (NCLI) grant program, which is managed by the state recreation and conservation office.

As one of the founding NCLI board members, VanderWey reported that the program has already provided $5 million in funds to get kids outside for unstructured play. Organizations in every part of the state have benefitted from the grants including the Tiny Trees Preschool in Seattle, Waskowitz Environmental Leadership Service in Burien, and the Spokane Parks Rx Outdoor Adventure Camp.

VanderWey said NCLI has also inspired a tremendous growth in outdoor schools with at least half of Washington counties now offering some form of outdoor preschool.

Getting kids outside is nothing new to Jeff Sanders, WSU associate professor and environmental historian. He said the idea of a nature deficit goes back at least 150 years to the Industrial Revolution, when many Americans left rural areas for work in Chicago or New York along with a large influx of immigrants. If the children weren't helping in factories, they were often left to fend for themselves on the streets.

Fearing for the youth's health as well as the future of our nation, social reformers advocated for changes that led to the playground movement of the late 1800s. Around the same time, summer camps reached their heyday, and the Boy Scouts of America was established. The first "streetcar suburbs" also took root, where people with means could escape grimy cities for more leafy areas like Brookline, Massachusetts.

Sanders said people today are still trying to escape cities for an idyllic respite in nature. "But, if we always focus on nature as being someplace else, we'll keep befouling the places we live in," he said. "Many historians are looking at it more like a garden—we should be tending to the places we actually live in, our backyard, cities, and streets—that's all a part of nature."

The contented little fellow playing in the vegetable garden at Into the Forest Preschool would certainly agree. Though a single frost-blackened sunflower now remains, the children had grown and eaten potatoes, carrots, tomatoes, and squash throughout the summer. For them, nature has become an integral part of their daily lives whether they're digging in the sand box or rolling a big wooden spool under the open sky.

Unfortunately for many children, carefree days playing outside are a thing of the past, said WSU clinical assistant professor of human development Robby Cooper. Today, a child seen walking to the park alone might well trigger a call to police and a warning to parents.

Cooper said Richard Louv blames this phenomenon on an increasingly fear-based society. Although statistics show crimes against children have dropped to their lowest rates ever, social media and 24-hour news cycles can make it feel like every abduction is happening in our backyards.

So now, instead of exploring, making up games, or riding bikes to local parks, kids spend much of their freetime indoors using tech devices and staring at screens.

Cooper said all this screen time may affect attention span and leaves little room for imagination and creativity, things research suggests are important for brain development and learning.

"As a teacher, it's a challenge now to get people to slow down and notice things," he said. "To be ok with uncertainty and flexible in their thinking."

Getting them outdoors is a good place to start. "Studies show that just being out in nature can provide benefits for ADD, mood, and well-being," Cooper said. "I've taken college students on backpacking trips where, without access to phones or internet, they can be mindful and less distracted. You see barriers break down more quickly and social connections happen faster."
He also notices the effect on his toddler who, said "Ohhhh!" when he goes outside and sees the moon or rustling leaves. "He doesn't do that with the TV," said Cooper. "I don't see that wonder in his face when he looks at a screen."

Today, children worldwide are more likely to experience that sense of wonder as urban planners bring natural elements and green spaces into modern designs for cities, schools, and playgrounds. The biophilic spaces they create provide access to nature through green streets, wildlife refuges, parks, trails, bike paths, and more. Some architects take playground design a step further by incorporating hills, valleys, mountains, and hideouts.

"Once kids get outside, there's a way in which nature calms the body," said VanderWey, who struggled with dyslexia in high school. It was through a WSU-sponsored challenge course that he developed self-confidence and found his professional calling. Now, his efforts with 4-H and No Child Left Inside enrich the lives of thousands of other Washington children, many of whom are low income and would never otherwise experience outdoor adventure.

VanderWey also credited Washington governor Jay Inslee, who said, "Getting kids outdoors can nourish the mind, body, and soul. I've fought hard for budgets that have increased funding for state parks, outdoor recreation, conservation, and earth science education."

VanderWey said Inslee's strong commitment to NCLI not only makes Washington a national trailblazer, but ensures that our young stewards of the future will continue to enjoy Northwest deserts, ancient forests, and the salty spray of the Sound.

SR 26 Revealed

Andrea Vogt

"The task is not so much to see what no one yet has seen, but to think what nobody yet has thought about that which everybody sees."

—Arthur Schopenhauer

There are landscapes that move us and landscapes through which we simply move.

State Route 26 has always been considered one of the latter: a notoriously dull 133 miles between Vantage and Colfax that has for decades been the main transportation link between the West Side and Washington State University.

It's the asphalt welcome mat for more than 10,000 WSU students who travel this highway between their homes in western Washington and WSU, along with thousands of parents, alumni, and employees. They speed. They scan radio stations past ballgames, Mexican folk music, talk shows—anything to stay alert.

A few may chuckle at the folksy coincidence of a sign for a place called "Hay" followed by a sign for a place called "Dusty," but for many the effect is lost amid the vast rural tedium.

Two years ago, WSU architecture professor Paul Hirzel and 13 of his students set out to improve the reputation of this much-maligned stretch of road. They researched and produced The SR 26 Gift Collection that included a guidebook, scenic postcards, posters, and a two-hour CD matching music to the scenery.

Since publication, the hardcover guidebook, *Motion Pictures: A Portrait of an American Highway*, has sold approximately 1,000 copies, and one Seattle bookstore can hardly keep the funky eastern Washington postcards stocked. Spokane's Northwest Museum of Arts and Culture (formerly the Cheney Cowles Museum) recently asked the WSU School of Architecture to exhibit its perspectives of the Washington roadway in a January 2003 show.

The highway project began as an assignment to help budding architects recognize subtle beauty. Hirzel had wearied of hearing about Mount Rainier and Puget Sound while students complained there's "nothing worth seeing" on the East Side. Most could name only two SR 26 landmarks, the Othello Rest Stop and the Pepto Pig, a smiling pink pig fashioned by a farmer out of a steel barrel. So Hirzel gave this assignment: "Upgrade a landscape viewed as ordinary to extraordinary stature by revealing its attributes in more creative venues."

The students, many of whom bemoaned the boring highway, were skeptical at first.

"When we all started out we thought, 'What are we going to find?' By the time we got done, we were talking mile markers," said Diana Wicklund, of Redmond, who worked on the project while a WSU student.

The result was *Motion Pictures: A Portrait of an American Highway*. It includes unusual stories, photos, statistics, geography, and a local and global history of roads. One master's degree student went on to envision a motel for Dusty that featured projected Palouse-themed images on the side of the town's massive grain elevators.

So just what does SR 26 have to offer? Maps show just a thin red stripe through vast white space, with tiny dots marking the handful of towns: Colfax, LaCrosse, Dusty, Washtucna, Othello, and Royal City, home of Washington's largest golf ball.

But there's much more, insisted Hirzel and his students: two major north-south railways, the Palouse and Columbia Rivers, the Saddleback Mountains, and a landscape formed by the cataclysmic Missoula Flood, for starters.

"You go from desert to scabland to ranching to wheat, and that's just the tip of it," said Wicklund. There are abandoned barns, dueling windmills, poplar trees that grow 15 feet a year. The smell of wheat, onions, mint. Love proclamations scrawled on roadcuts despite futile "Do Not Paint Rocks" signs. One WSU alum made an even grander gesture on a large spud shack east of Othello.

Farmer Orman Johnson is the third of four generations in his family to have attended WSU. Johnson spent $5,000 to have special crimson siding cut to spell "Go Cougs" in letters so large the message can be seen for miles.

SR 26 also has its share of nostalgic Americana: funky fruit stands, Sara's Country Store in Hooper, blast-from-the-past smalltown diners like the Dusty Cafe. A recent addition is "The Waving Lady" at Becky's Burger's in Colfax, a towering wooden cutout woman in a blue blouse and pink skirt. One arm cradles a basket of burgers while the other waves tirelessly to passersby, thanks to a motorized mechanism designed locally by a retired NASA engineer.

"We have college kids who come by here to have their pictures taken and guys who stop to see how her arm works," said owner Becky Hovey. "She seems to be quite a hit."

Whether she's waving hello or goodbye depends on which direction you're headed, since this is where SR 26 both begins and ends. Either way, she's now part of what Hirzel called "a 133-mile-long museum."

"There is an appeal to this road that goes beyond the local people who are forced to drive it," said Hirzel. "People like it when an underdog wins, it's part of an American myth: You take something underappreciated, recognize it, and then celebrate it."

A Fine Thin Skin—Wind, Water, Volcanoes, and Ice

Tim Steury

"To be a successful farmer, one must first know the nature of the soil."

—Xenophon, Oeconomicus (The Economist), 400 B.C.

Sometimes in late spring and late summer, when the fields of eastern Washington have been tilled for spring planting or recently harvested, a wind will build out of the west, gathering the loose loess soil of the dry fields, lifting thousands of tons of it into an ominous cloud that shrouds the region in a murk. The dust that grates in the eyes and leaves a dirty skiff on everything is a lesson in both geology and agronomy.

The Big Picture

The soils of eastern and western Washington, different as they seem and are, have one thing in common, as do most. They come, either by water or wind, primarily from elsewhere.

Within the geologic timescale, most soils are very young. Within a human timescale, they are ancient. They also form a minute part of the earth in general, a fine thin skin.

University of Washington geologist David Montgomery, in his recent book *Dirt: The Erosion of Civilizations*, describes soil as the "frontier between geology and biology." Stressing how thin that frontier is, he compares it to human skin. Whereas human skin, at less than a tenth of an inch thick, represents a little less than a thousandth of the height of a person, soil accounts for barely one ten-millionth of Earth's 6,380 kilometer radius.

East of the Cascades, the loess soils of the Columbia Plateau and the Palouse, some of the deepest soils of Washington, are the result of the return of windblown silts, said Bruce Frazier, recounting the major geological events that created Washington's diverse soils. Frazier, a soil scientist, recently retired from WSU where he spent much of his career mapping Washington soils.

Southwest Washington is quite different, Frazier continues. Sedimentary materials interspersed with old basalt flows support mountain forests. Chehalis has a coal mine, he noted, highlighting the region's much different geology.

Much of the northeast soil is volcanic, the ash blown, again by prevailing winds, from the volcanoes of the Cascades, St. Helens, Baker, Glacier Peak.

Northwestern Washington is dominated by glaciation. The urban corridor strung together today by I-5 is primarily glacial till, materials scoured and absorbed by glaciers, then deposited at the end of their travels when they melted.

Craig Cogger, a soil scientist at Puyallup, continues the west side narrative. Glaciers extended as far south as the middle of Thurston County, he said. When they retreated, they left behind a variety of soils. The glacial till soils are okay for agriculture, he said. But they have limitations. Their texture is coarse, so they won't hold water.

Whereas glaciers played a dominant role in the nature of Puget Sound area soils, there is also a marvelous diversity. Past eruptions of Mount St. Helens and Mount Rainier loosed huge mudflows, said Cogger, resulting in heavy wet soils interspersed with rocks—not suitable for row crops, but great for pasture and dairy. To the north, in Whatcom County, windblown silts, similar to the eastern loess, create fertile farmland. To the south of Olympia are older clay soils.

The best agricultural soils of the Puget Sound region are in the alluvial river valleys, which collect the sediments from the erosion of the surrounding landscape and the Cascades. "When you combine the soil with the climate," said Cogger, "you have some of the best farmland in the world.

"The problem," he continued, "is we've paved it over."

In geologic terms, those soils have been around for barely a whisper. The soils in the glaciated area are barely 15,000 years old. The soils of the alluvial valleys are just a few thousand.

Considering that European settlement came a mere geological yesterday, we've taken only brief agricultural advantage of this resource. Skagit Valley is an exception. Much rich farmland remains, and farmers seem determined to keep it. After it lost the Kent valley to development, said Cogger, King County "got fairly aggressive about farmland preservation. So Snoqualmie Valley farmland seems to be fairly well protected. It floods every winter, so that keeps development out."

Pierce County, unfortunately, has made little attempt to preserve its soil and farmland, said Cogger. "In the 27 years I've been here, I have seen the valley paved over. There's no will to preserve farmland."

Terroir: Not Just for Wine

Alan Busacca gave up his academic career as a soil scientist several years ago to help people grow wine grapes, one of the latest and most lucrative manifestations of Washington's agricultural geography.

Within the soil cognoscenti, Busacca is perhaps best known for continuing J Harlen Bretz's solution to the channeled scablands puzzle. It was Bretz who first understood that the strange eastern Washington landscape known as the scablands was the result of an unfathomably enormous flood, or series of floods, toward the end of the last ice age. Building on the work of Bretz and others, Busacca gradually established that the upper layer of loess that forms the Palouse hills is the indirect result of those floods. After the floods scoured the existing loess that once layered the scablands, the silt settled out to the south, then was blown back up by the prevailing winds. And beneath that surface layer? More loess, more ancient soil ("paleosols" in the nomenclature), the results of two million years of prevailing winds.

Busacca started out in geology, giving him a very fundamental understanding of soil formation, which comes from a combination of five rudimentary factors: parent material, climate, topography, time, and microorganisms.

Parent material, the beginning of soil, is created from organic material or from bedrock through weathering, which happens through various physical and chemical reactions. The rate of soil formation over time is determined by climate.

Busacca started working with grape growers in the mid-1990s, drawing on his understanding of soil formation and climate, which together determine what is understood as a site's terroir, the personality of the site, if you will, the effect on the grapes determined by the same factors as soil formation: parent material, climate, time, topography, and microorganisms.

Since leaving WSU to devote himself full-time to consulting and viticulture, Busacca has taken his fascination with terroir to its conclusion. He and winemaker Robert Smasne, a 1999 WSU grad, have developed a label of "terroir expressive" wine, Alma Terra. Using identical technique, they use syrah grapes from three very different vineyards to make three wines that express the terroir of their respective sites.

The soils of the Minick Vineyard in the Rattlesnake Hills north of Prosser comprise a little loess over shattered basalt. The resulting wine yields red fruit flavors, a little cedar and spice.

The soils of Coyote Canyon in the Horse Heaven Hills are 4–5 feet of loess over hardpan and basalt. Syrah from this site yields a blueberrry flavor with a medium body.

The soil of the Ciel du Cheval vineyard on Red Mountain is windblown sand. Combined with its heat, wind, and drought stress, the site yields tiny berries with thick skins, an inky black juice with pleasing tannins and a blackberry taste.

Terroir might not be as pronounced in wheat or peas as it is in wine grapes, but geography and the resulting soil types work together to give Washington an extraordinarily diverse agriculture and landscape.

For Busacca, soil geography determines a region's story of settlement and agricultural development. Washington, its agricultural diversity second only to the much larger California, is still discovering the potential and beauty of its geographic diversity, not only for wine grapes, but for the more than 200 other crops it grows.

The sandy plateau of Horse Heaven Hills grows some of the best wine grapes in the country, but also carrots and a wide variety of other crops. The alluvial soils and silts of the Wenatchee Valley and Yakima Valley have established Washington as the apple capital of the world. Cherries, pears, and other tree fruits love those same soils.

West of the Cascades, the rich alluvial soils that Cogger celebrates have established the region not only for its berries and vegetable crops, but also for its huge seed industry.

And then there's the rich loess, blown in from elsewhere and just as apt to blow away.

Good Dirt
Karl Hipple, who was formerly Washington's state soil scientist, is cataloging Washington's soils in an online atlas, an ambitious task that one might not ordinarily associate with retirement.

Classification and description of soil seems fascinatingly arcane to a novitiate. Even the general soils map of Washington, compiled by Frazier and Busacca, with its psychedelic mix of colors, only suggests the complexity that lies beneath.

For example, Hipple describes the Palouse soil series, which are mollisols, as fine-silty, mixed, superactive, mesic, Pachic Ultic Haploxerolls.

In spite of the dazzling array of soils, however, there is a logic. Perhaps the most useful approach to order is the soil taxonomy used in the United States and some other countries that was developed by the USDA.

Soil taxonomy recognizes 12 orders, explained WSU soil scientist John Reganold in his chapter, "The Nature of Soils," in *Natural Resource Conservation: Management for a Sustainable Future*. "Most soil orders," he writes, "are defined on the basis of having diagnostic horizons, that result from distinctive soil-forming processes and have specific physical and chemical properties."

The orders reflect geography, climate and, to some extent, their use.

Mollisols, for example, are generally associated with prairie and are some of the most productive silts in the world. Approximately 7 percent of the world's soils are mollisols, said Reganold. But nearly 23 percent of U.S. soils are mollisols, reflecting the agricultural advantage the United States enjoys.

"It's not even fair," he said.

Whereas the orders reflect soil quality to an extent—aridisols, for example, form in hot desert areas—the matter of soil health is not that simple.

A good definition of "soil quality" or "soil health" is tough to pin down. But all definitions include certain things, said USDA soil microbiologist Ann Kennedy: pH, soil structure, permeability, all the nutrients, all the chemicals, cation exchange capacity, and then all the things growing in it, the microbes, springtails, and nematodes.

Even with awareness of the wild diversity of soils, however, one might understandably assume soils on a small scale would generally be homogeneous.

Rather, said soil scientist Doug Collins, they are variable.

Geography dictates variability even within a particular field.

Not only does the definition of "healthy soil" shift from, say, vineyard to wheat field, conditions can be variable across that vineyard or wheat field.

Increasingly, soil scientists and farmers are focusing in more specifically to determine proper agronomic practices that might vary over a field or farm.

Whereas Collins, who is an extension educator for the WSU Small Farms Program, is encouraging small farmers to pay closer attention to their farms' variability, some larger farmers are doing so already with technology.

For example, said Benton and Franklin County extension educator Tim Waters, the agronomist for Mercer Canyons in Horse Heaven Hills pulls a machine across the fields that measures electrical conductivity of the soil. From this, he develops a map relating conductivity to soil fertility, allowing them to apply fertilizer with a variable rate spreader according to need.

All about Humus

It is late April and unseasonably cold. We sit on metal chairs in a farm shop west of Dusty, a propane heater roaring in the background, as Michael Stubbs recounted his conversion as a farmer.

"We're direct seeders," he begins.

Still in a distinct minority, direct seeders minimize soil disturbance by planting directly in the ground without tilling.

Although the pulling equipment has evolved dramatically, from mule to steam engine to crawler to 500-horsepower behemoths with 12 tires that can work a 60-foot swath, conventional tillage is much the same as it was when farmers first worked the prairie and shrub-steppe of eastern Washington in the late 19th century.

Tillage is a hard habit to break. Any farmer will tell you, whether you're trailing a mule team or riding in a climate-controlled cab, there's a great satisfaction in looking behind you and seeing the furrowed soil you've just turned over. And the smell of the freshly tilled field is heavenly. There's also a definite aesthetic appeal and matter of pride attached to a cleanly tilled field.

"I can't talk negatively about someone who likes to look behind and see a plowed field," said Stubbs. "But if you consider all factors of tillage—time, fuel, manpower—those things all have to be taken into account when you feel the need to plow. To get a cleanly tilled field requires many hours, much fuel, equipment."

On the other hand, tillage solves a lot of problems, which vary from site to site.

Weeds are just one of those. The easiest way to get rid of a weed problem, at least temporarily, is to plow it under. Another advantage of tillage is it warms the soil more quickly, assuring earlier seed germination and growth.

Soil scientists and direct-seeder farmers alike are frustrated with the slow acceptance region-wide of direct seeding. But all will admit it's not an easy process. The long-established approach to tillage remains the norm for a reason.

But tillage also destroys the soil structure that attuned farmers and other soil aficionados extol like a wine connoisseur talks about a wine's body and structure.

"Not to cast aspersion," said Stubbs, "but the more tillage you perform, the more you break down that microbial community."

More dramatically, once disrupted, the soil more easily washes or blows away.

In a paper titled "Erosion Impacts on the Palouse Misunderstood," the late University of Idaho soil scientist Roger Veseth reported that since the Palouse was first cultivated in the late 1800s, all of the topsoil has been lost from about

10 percent of the cropland. Another one-quarter to one-third of the topsoil has been lost from another 60 percent of the cropland. Erosion rates of up to 200 tons per acre, or more than an inch of topsoil, have been measured on steep slopes, with a total of up to three feet of topsoil gone from hilltops and ridges.

"When you get rain on the Palouse and you see the Palouse River," said Stubbs, "you see how brown it is, you question sustainability…that soil we'll never get back. It's a very precious resource."

Ann Kennedy has been thinking for much of her career about soil microorganisms, about the extraordinary diversity of microscopic critters that make up a soil ecosystem. But lately, her thoughts have turned more to humus, to carbon, to organic matter.

"We're not seeing the microbes," said Kennedy. "We're not seeing the nutrients stuck on the carbon chains to support plant growth."

And so she has reached a conclusion. No organic matter, no microbes. No microbes? Well, without microbes, it's not soil. It's just a growth medium, something to hold the plants up as they feed on outside inputs.

So suppose you want soil? How do you create more organic matter?

"On the west side, organic matter is not as much of an issue," said Kennedy. "There's more rain, more plant matter produced."

But east of the mountains, where annual precipitation can dip down toward 10-11 inches, it's extremely difficult to produce much organic matter under conventional tillage. Soil science still has plenty of unanswered questions to address. But one answer is obvious, said Kennedy. "The way to increase organic matter: Don't till, produce high-residue crops, leave soil as intact as possible so the roots can act as a slow-release fertilizer."

Or, to put it another way: "No-till is a great way to build organic matter."

On no-till research plots at the Palouse Conservation Field Station, soil organic matter increased from 1.9 percent to 3.6 percent over 20 years. On drier plots near Ritzville, organic matter surpassed native levels, increasing from 0.9 to 2.5 percent. These increases are significant both for demonstrating how slowly soil builds even under optimal treatment and also for no-till's soil-building superiority over conventional methods.

No-till, low-till, direct-seeding are all similar approaches within the broader practice of conservation tillage. No matter what the term or the degree, however, their aim is to keep the soil as intact as possible and build organic matter.

Unfortunately, it isn't easy.

Even after 15 years of direct-seeding, Stubbs continues to "refine, build, change on that system. The learning curve is pretty steep. Especially under such dry conditions." Stubbs's land gets about 15 inches of rain a year.

"Most years it's closer to 13 or 14 than a low 16. That extra one or two inches makes a tremendous difference."

"With this limited moisture, it is a bumpy ride," he continued. "But we're able to see changes in soil structure, to see porosity increase, the ability of water to infiltrate soil at a given rate, rotation cropping, seeding the fall canola, the tap root that goes down to break up soil, the ability to get soil structure, the top six inches to have it regain what was lost during the tillage period—that's very rewarding."

It's Complicated

You don't have to get very far into farming in its broadest sense to start noticing some contradictions. A particularly interesting one is the organic contradiction.

There's a lot to like about raising food organically, no synthetic fertilizers and pesticides, generally a friendlier approach to the soil. Some of the most interesting research, including that by John Reganold and Preston Andrews in horticulture, is showing high nutrient values in organic crops and in some cases yields equivalent to conventional methods.

But attractive as it is, one of organic ag's unfortunate little secrets is that it requires a lot of tillage, at least in field crops. Unless you've sired a dozen kids who love to spend their time pulling weeds, it's hard to control weeds without herbicides or tillage.

On the other hand, no-till or direct seeding requires a good amount of herbicides to control weeds. Even if the herbicides were completely benign, still, any farmer would just as soon give up the expense of applying what often are very expensive chemicals.

Combining no-till and organic right now might be one of the holy grails of production ag.

And it will remain an elusive holy grail for a while longer, because that is a very difficult thing to do. But it doesn't stop Puyallup soil scientists Craig Cogger and Doug Collins from trying. They are working on using cover crops to out-compete the weeds. The basic idea is to direct-seed cover crops to grow over the winter. Then, at an appropriate time, you terminate them without chemicals, either by mowing or otherwise mechanically stopping their growth so they do not compete with the main crop.

The Nematodes Know

Nematodes are the most abundant multicellular animal on the planet, said Collins.

Unless it has been fumigated or otherwise sterilized, all soil will contain nematodes. And they are amazingly diverse, said Collins. And because of their diverse roles in soil, they are excellent indicators of what's going on in the soil environment.

"The other beautiful thing about nematodes," said Collins, "you can look at them under a microscope and tell what they do by the shape of their face." For example, pathogens have a proboscis that they inject in the root or the epidermal cells of the plant.

One-third of a cup of soil will contain between 2,000 and 12,000 nematodes. Some nematodes are bacteria feeders, some are fungal feeders, some are predators. Some nematodes eat other nematodes or protozoa, some are omnivores, and some are pathogenic.

"If you have all bacteria-feeding nematodes," said Collins, "it tells you there's been a recent disturbance or a lot of fertility."

C. elegans, a bacterial feeder, can go from egg to egg-laying female in four days.

The presence of predator nematodes, on the other hand, will indicate a more stable soil, as they take 14 months to go from egg to egg laying. Larger bodied nematodes, which correlate with earthworms, also reflect the degree of disturbance, as it takes a long time for them to complete their life cycle.

A disturbed system can still be fertile, said Collins. "From a farmer's point of view…, ultimately it's the soil's function that is important, not necessarily diversity."

As diverse as they are, nematodes make up only a fraction of the microbial life of a healthy soil. In a fascinating paper in *Annals of Arid Zone*, Ann Kennedy and Tami Stubbs (who is married to direct-seeder Michael Stubbs) review what is known and unknown about soil ecology.

"The functions of these diverse communities range from nutrient cycling and residue decomposition, to soil structural component, to plant growth effects," they write. "Soil crusts [created by microorganisms] provide a source of added carbon and nutrients in arid soils as well as protecting the soil from wind and water erosion."

Much of this diverse realm, however, is still beyond our comprehension, simply because of the vast numbers. Kennedy and Stubbs cite one analysis of soil bacterial DNA that indicated the presence of 4,000 genomic types—reflecting a possible 40,000 species.

Soil and Civilization

Nematodes and bacteria, of course, are not the only indicators of soil health. The ultimate expression of soil health is our survival. From ancient Greece to Easter Island, as the soil goes, so goes the civilization.

Washington's inordinate share of rich soil and land area, combined with its rich agricultural diversiy and favorable climate, offer a relative guarantee of survival. However, the continuing erosion of the rich loess of eastern Washington and the locking away of equally rich alluvial soils of the west side beneath an impermeable shell should stir unease in anyone interested in the future of eating. Also, a growing dependence by the rest of the world on those relatively few rich agricultural pockets around the world and factors such as political upheaval and climate change preclude complacency.

With Washington's diverse geography, matched by awareness, appropriate agricultural research by a responsive university, and innovative agricultural practices, we can look forward not only to survival, but to continuing to eat and live very well indeed.

Golden Light Palouse
Photo Chip Phillips

References

The stories presented in this anthology originally appeared in the following *Washington State Magazine* issues:

Apalategui, Eric. "Bob Gaston and Journalism's Grandest Prize." *Washington State Magazine* 5, no. 3 (Summer 2006).

Apalategui, Eric. "Lonely, beautiful, and threatened—Willapa Bay." *Washington State Magazine* 3, no. 3 (Summer 2004).

Apalategui, Eric. "Where water meets desert." *Washington State Magazine* 4, no. 2 (Spring 2005).

Caraher, Pat. "Bulbs and Blooms." *Washington State Magazine* 1, no. 4 (Fall 2002).

Caraher, Pat. "Friendly People: Bill Hewitt built Tillicum Village on NW traditions." *Washington State Magazine* 2, no. 1 (Winter 2002).

Caraher, Pat. "Washington's marine highway." *Washington State Magazine* 3, no. 1 (Winter 2003).

Clark, Brian Charles. "A point of reference." *Washington State Magazine* 18, no. 3 (Summer 2019).

Clark, Brian Charles. "A river rolls on." *Washington State Magazine* 17, no. 4 (Fall 2018).

Clark, Brian Charles. "Wood takes wing." *Washington State Magazine* 16, no. 1 (Winter 2016).

Janovich, Adriana. "Cosmic Crisp®, WA 2, and what's next." *Washington State Magazine* 20, no. 1 (Winter 2020).

Janovich, Adriana. "Faces of small farmers." *Washington State Magazine* 19, no. 4 (Fall 2020).

Janovich, Adriana. "New stars on the market." *Washington State Magazine* 20, no. 1 (Winter 2020).

Janovich, Adriana. "Rainier cherries." *Washington State Magazine* 18, no. 4 (Fall 2019).

Janovich, Adriana. "Remains of the day." *Washington State Magazine* 19, no. 3 (Summer 2020).

Janovich, Adriana. "Significantly Washington." *Washington State Magazine* 20, no. 3 (Summer 2021).

Phillips, Rebecca. "Inside outside." *Washington State Magazine* 18, no. 2 (Spring 2019).

Phillips, Rebecca. "Streaming solutions." *Washington State Magazine* 16, no. 4 (Fall 2017).

Phillips, Rebecca. "Where have all the frogs gone?" *Washington State Magazine* 18, no. 4 (Fall 2019).

Sorensen, Eric. "A new land." *Washington State Magazine* 10, no. 1 (Winter 2010).

Sorensen, Eric. "What's the catch?" *Washington State Magazine* 10, no. 3 (Summer 2011).

Steury, Tim. "A fine thin skin—wind, water, volcanoes, and ice." *Washington State Magazine* 10, no. 4 (Fall 2011).

Steury, Tim. "A place at the table." *Washington State Magazine* 2, no. 4 (Fall 2003).

Steury, Tim. "An exquisite scar." *Washington State Magazine* 3, no. 4 (Fall 2004).

Steury, Tim. "Eating well to save the Sound." *Washington State Magazine* 5, no. 3 (Summer 2006).

Steury, Tim. "Finding Chief Kamiakin." *Washington State Magazine* 8, no. 4 (Fall 2009).

Steury, Tim. "Forgotten fruit." *Washington State Magazine* 15, no. 1 (Winter 2015).

Steury, Tim. "How Cougar Gold Made the World a Better Place." *Washington State Magazine* 4, no. 1 (Winter 2004).

Steury, Tim. "It happened at the World's Fair." *Washington State Magazine* 6, no. 4 (Fall 2007).

Steury, Tim. "Ozette Art and the Makah Canoe." *Washington State Magazine* 7, no. 2 (Spring 2008).

Steury, Tim. "Our kind of town." *Washington State Magazine* 4, no. 1 (Winter 2004).

Steury, Tim. "The atomic landscape." *Washington State Magazine* 11, no. 3 (Summer 2012).

Steury, Tim. "Water to the promised land." *Washington State Magazine* 12, no. 4 (Fall 2013).

Sudermann, Hannelore. "A Feast of good things." *Washington State Magazine* 11, no. 2 (Spring 2012).

Sudermann, Hannelore. "Back to the city." *Washington State Magazine* 9, no. 3 (Summer 2010).

Sudermann, Hannelore. "Master Gardeners." *Washington State Magazine* 8, no. 4 (Fall 2009).

Sudermann, Hannelore. "On the waterfront." *Washington State Magazine* 8, no. 3 (Summer 2009).

Sudermann, Hannelore. "Outside In—Architecture of the Pacific Northwest." *Washington State Magazine* 10, no. 2 (Spring 2011).

Sudermann, Hannelore. "Something Old, Something New—A History of Hospitality." *Washington State Magazine* 12, no. 3 (Summer 2013).

Sudermann, Hannelore. "The making of mountaineers." *Washington State Magazine* 5, no. 3 (Summer 2006).

Sudermann, Hannelore. "Vancouver Lake: A search for solutions great and small." *Washington State Magazine* 9, no. 2 (Spring 2010).

Sudermann, Hannelore. "Washington's wine crush." *Washington State Magazine* 5, no. 1 (Winter 2005).

Vogt, Andrea. "The man who gave away mountains." *Washington State Magazine* 5, no. 4 (Fall 2006).

Vogt, Andrea. "SR 26 Revealed." *Washington State Magazine* 1, no. 1 (Winter 2001).

Wasson, David. "Call It the Urban Extension." *Washington State Magazine* 16, no. 1 (Winter 2016).

Contributors

Eric Apalategui founded—and serves as owner and editor of — BestFishingInAmerica.com, a website for recreational anglers.

Pat Caraher served as editor of Washington State University's *HillTopics* magazine for more than 30 years and was a founding editor of *Washington State Magazine*.

Brian Charles Clark is a former *Washington State Magazine* staff writer.

Larry Clark is the editor of *Washington State Magazine*.

Adriana Janovich is the associate editor of *Washington State Magazine*.

Rebecca Phillips, a former *Washington State Magazine* staff and science writer, is now retired.

Eric Sorensen, now retired, was a science writer for *Washington State Magazine* and research news coordinator for Washington State University.

Tim Steury, now retired, was a founding editor of *Washington State Magazine*.

Hannelore Sudermann is a former *Washington State Magazine* associate editor and staff writer.

Andrea Vogt is an independent filmmaker and journalist.

David Wasson is the director of news and media relations at Washington State University and former associate editor of *Washington State Magazine*.

Index

More exceptional stories from across

Washington State are available at:

magazine.wsu.edu